FEMINIST MOTHERING

SUNY SERIES IN FEMINIST CRITICISM AND THEORY

———————————

Michelle A. Masse, editor

FEMINIST
MOTHERING

Edited by
ANDREA O'REILLY

STATE UNIVERSITY OF NEW YORK PRESS

Published by
STATE UNIVERSITY OF NEW YORK PRESS
ALBANY

© 2008 State University of New York

For information, contact
State University of New York Press, Albany, NY
www.sunypress.edu

Production, Laurie Searl
Marketing, Fran Keneston

Library of Congress Cataloging in Publication Data

Feminist mothering / edited by Andrea O'Reilly.
    p. cm. — (SUNY series in feminist criticism and theory)
Includes bibliographical references.
ISBN 978-0-7914-7557-7 (hardcover : alk. paper) 1. Motherhood. 2. Feminism.
3. Parenting. I. O'Reilly, Andrea, 1961–

HQ759.F367 2008
306.874'301—dc22

                                                2008003112

                    10 9 8 7 6 5 4 3 2 1

Contents

Acknowledgments

ANDREA O'REILLY

I WOULD LIKE TO EXPRESS my deepest thanks to the following people who helped bring this book to life. Special thanks are due to my research assistants Roni Hoffman and Sarah Trimble and to my proofreader Randy Chase. I am grateful to Larin McLaughlin for her continued faith in this manuscript and to Laurie Searl for her skill in turning it into a book. Thank you also to the members of the *Association for Research on Mothering*: my thinking on mothering, as always, was enriched and sustained by this splendid community of scholars. My deepest gratitude goes to the contributors of this volume who sustained and inspired me in their commitment to and belief in the possibility and power of feminist mothering. Special thanks to Renée Knapp, my closest friend and colleague at *ARM* who commiserates and comforts when I need it the most. Finally, my deepest appreciation and love to Jesse, Erin, and Casey: thank you for becoming the feminist children I had longed for and dreamed of.

Introduction

ANDREA O'REILLY

A REVIEW OF recent publications on motherhood in the mainstream media would suggest that the selfless and doting mother of yesteryear has, like the eighteen-hour bra, fallen out of fashion. These authors, particularly those who write in the self-help genre, call for a new style of mothering, one that advocates balance and admonishes guilt. Bria Simpson, for example, asserts in *The Balanced Mom: Raising Your Kids Without Losing Your Self* (2006): "We need to continue, rather than deny, the development of ourselves to be fulfilled" (2). She goes on to write: "As you try so fervently to help your children develop into their best selves, I encourage you to refocus some of that energy into living *your* best life" (3, emphasis in original). Likewise, Amy Tiemann, in her recent book *Mojo Mom: Nurturing Your Self While Raising a Family* (2006), claims that "all women need to continue to grow as individuals, not just as Moms" (xvi). Overcoming the guilt of motherhood is the focus of many recent books, as with the best-selling, appropriately titled *Mommy Guilt: Learn to Worry Less, Focus on What Matters Most, and Raise Happier Kids* (Bort, Pflock, Renner, 2005). Other writers challenge the excessive child-centeredness of contemporary parenting practices and call for a more "children should be seen and not heard" philosophy of childrearing. Christie Mellor in *The Three-Martini Playdate: A Practical Guide to Happy Parenting* (2004), for example, asserts:

> You were here first. You are sharing your house with them, your food, your time, your books. Somewhere, in fairly recent memory, we have lost sight of that fact. Somehow a pint-sized velvet revolution was waged right under our very noses, and the grown-ups quietly handed over the reins. We have made concession after concession, until it appears that well-educated, otherwise intelligent adults have abdicated their rightful place in the world, and the littlest inmates have taken over the asylum. (12)

1

She goes on to say that "it is time to exert a little autonomy and encourage some in your child" (13). Other writers advocate shared parenting. In *How to Avoid the Mommy Trap: A Roadmap for Sharing Parenting and Making It Work* (2002), Julie Shields argues that *"the best alternative to parenting by mother is parenting by father"* (17, emphasis in original). She goes on to explain, "Since fathers can parent, too, we should not start from the assumption that mothers, and mothers alone, must choose whether to work, cut back, or hire a replacement caregiver. Instead, we can change our approach to seeking ways to provide babies the best start in life, at the same time, giving mothers *and* fathers the best opportunity for happiness, individually and together" (19).

Whether the emphasis is maternal autonomy or shared parenting, less guilt and more balance, these writers challenge traditional (or, in academic parlance, patriarchal) motherhood practices. Similar to Betty Friedan, who exposed "the problem that has no name" more than forty years ago, these writers insist that women must achieve and sustain a selfhood outside of and beyond motherhood. And similar to Adrienne Rich, who attributed mothers' exhaustion and guilt to the isolation of patriarchal motherhood and its impossible standards of perfection, these writers likewise recognize that mothers require more support and less judgment if they are to obtain satisfaction in motherhood.

However, while these authors certainly challenge patriarchal motherhood, they do not use the word *feminist* in this critique, nor do they call their new mother-positive mode of mothering a feminist practice. Given this, can these new models of mothering be called feminist mothering? Does the mother have to identify as a feminist for her mothering to qualify as a feminist practice? Or, more pointedly, can we have a practice of feminist mothering without a politic of feminism? And who decides and determines this?

I open with these questions to underscore a central concern of this introduction; namely, the difficulty of defining a feminist practice and theory of mothering. Although a challenge to patriarchal motherhood has been a central concern of feminist scholarship since at least Rich's classic book *Of Woman Born*, in 1976, there has been very little academic discourse on the subject of feminist mothering. As a result, there has been little sociology and no theory of feminist mothering in feminist scholarship. Likewise, while examples of empowered mothering are found in popular fiction, there is no theory of feminist mothering developed in this discourse. And, as noted above, the term *feminist mothering* is seldom used in popular writings on motherhood. The aim of this collection is to investigate various practices of feminist mothering across a wide range of maternal experience in order to identify common themes, concerns, and issues of a feminist maternal practice. This, in turn, will enable us to develop a theory of feminist mothering.

Any discussion on feminist mothering must begin with the distinction Adrienne Rich made in *Of Woman Born* (1976) between two meanings of motherhood, one superimposed on the other: "the *potential* relationship of any woman to her powers of reproduction and to children"; and "the *institution*—which aims at ensuring that that potential—and all women—shall remain under male control" (13, emphasis in original). The term *motherhood* refers to the patriarchal institution of motherhood that is male-defined and controlled and is deeply oppressive to women, while the word *mothering* refers to women's experiences of mothering that are female-defined and centered and potentially empowering to women. The reality of patriarchal motherhood thus must be distinguished from the possibility or potentiality of gynocentric or feminist mothering. In other words, while motherhood, as an institution, is a male-defined site of oppression, women's own experiences of mothering can nonetheless be a source of power.

It has long been recognized among scholars of motherhood that Rich's distinction between mothering and motherhood was what enabled feminists to recognize that motherhood is not naturally, necessarily, or inevitably oppressive, a view held by some Second Wave feminists. Rather, mothering, freed from motherhood, could be experienced as a site of empowerment, a location of social change if, to use Rich's words, women became "outlaws from the institution of motherhood." However, as *Of Woman Born* interrupted the patriarchal narrative of motherhood and cleared a space for the development of counternarratives of mothering, it did not generate a discourse on feminist mothering. While much has been published on patriarchal motherhood since Rich's inaugural text—documenting why and how patriarchal motherhood is harmful, indeed unnatural, to mothers and children alike—little has been written on the possibility or potentiality of feminist mothering. "Still largely missing from the increasing dialogue and publication around motherhood," as Fiona Joy Green writes, "is a discussion of Rich's monumental contention that even when restrained by patriarchy, motherhood can be a site of empowerment and political activism" (31).

A review of motherhood literature reveals that only three books look specifically at the topic of feminist mothering: *Mother Journeys: Feminists Write About Mothering* (1994), *Feminist Mothers* (1990), and *Daughters of Feminists* (1993), books now fourteen plus years old.[1] More recently, the journals *off our backs* (2006) and *Journal of the Association for Research on Mothering* (2006) include articles on feminist mothering in their issues on "Mothering and Feminism." Likewise, two of my recent edited volumes *Mother Outlaws: Theories and Practices of Empowered Mothering* (2004a) and *From Motherhood to Mothering: The Legacy of Adrienne Rich's* Of Woman Born (2004b) incorporate sections on feminist mothering. However, even as these recent publications provide much needed insight and understanding into feminist mothering, the topic remains insufficiently developed, particularly compared to the scholarship on patriarchal motherhood. This dearth of research on motherhing is indeed perplexing and troubling. Feminist scholarship on motherhood is now an established field. So why is the topic of feminist mothering not explored in scholarship that is explicitly about both feminism and motherhood? Feminist mothering is also an evident example of empowered mothering and so provides a promising alternative to the oppressive institution of patriarchal motherhood, first theorized by Rich and critiqued by subsequent motherhood scholars. In other words, feminist mothering bridges motherhood and feminism, makes motherhood doable for feminism, and feminism possible for motherhood.

This volume will look specifically at the topic of feminist mothering. In so doing, it is the first scholarly collection on this subject matter. The volume will identify the salient themes of this maternal practice and seek to develop a theory of feminist mothering. However, since the chapters illustrate various characteristics and concerns of feminist mothering to fashion a theory of it, the volume will work from a very open-ended definition of what it means to practice feminist mothering. There are several reasons for this and they will be discussed in some detail below. For the purpose of this volume, I use the term *feminist mothering* to refer to an oppositional discourse of motherhood, one that is constructed as a *negation* of patriarchal motherhood. A feminist practice/theory of mothering, therefore, functions as a counternarrative of motherhood: it seeks to interrupt the master narrative of motherhood to imagine and implement a view of mothering that is *empowering* to women. Feminist mothering is thus determined more by what it is not (i.e., patriarchal motherhood) rather than by what it is. Feminist mothering may refer to any practice of mothering that seeks to challenge and change various aspects of patriarchal motherhood that cause mothering to be limiting or oppressive to women. Rich uses the word *courageous* to define a nonpatriarchal practice of mothering, while Baba Cooper calls such a practice *radical mothering*. Susan Douglas and Meredith Michaels, more recently in *The Mommy Myth*, use the word *rebellious* to describe outlaw mothering. *Hip* is Ariel Gore's term for transgressive mothering. For this volume, the term *feminist* is used— though with a proviso as explained below—to signify maternal practices that resist and refuse patriarchal motherhood to create a mode of mothering that is empowering to women. Or, to use Rich's terminology, a feminist maternal practice marks a movement from motherhood to mothering, and makes possible a mothering against motherhood.

DEFINING FEMINIST MOTHERING

In her book *Feminist Mothers*, the first and still only book-length study of the subject matter, Tuula Gordon in her concluding chapter "What Is a Feminist Mother?" observes, "[I]t seems impossible to conclude by explaining what a feminist mother is, or to answer the underlying question of how people conduct their lives according to alternative ideologies, in this case feminism" (148). However, Gordon does say that her study of feminist mothers reveals some "particular factors"; they are:

> The way in which [mothers] challenge and criticise myths of motherhood; the way in which they consider it their right to work; the anti-sexist (and anti-racist) way in which they try to bring up their children; the way in which they expect the fathers of the children to participate in joint everyday lives; and the way in which many of them are politically active. (149)

Gordon goes on to conclude:

> Feminism emphasizes that women are strong, that women have rights as women, and they can support each other as women. Thus 'feminist mothers' have been able to develop critical orientations towards societal structures and cultures, stereotypical expectations and myths of motherhood. They do that in the context of exploring how the personal is political, and with the support of the networks of women which place them beyond 'collective isolation.' (150)

Rose L. Glickman in her book *Daughters of Feminists* (1993) likewise emphasizes that feminist mothering must be understood as lived resistance to the normative—stereotypical—expectations of both motherhood and womanhood. She writes: "[For these feminist mothers] there is no 'apart from their feminism' and no matter how ordinary their lives seem from the outside to the casual observer, *their feminism was a profound defiance of convention*. . . . Flying in the face of tradition, feminist mothers expected their daughters to do the same" (22, emphasis added). "The mothers' struggle," Glickman continues, "to shake off the dust of tradition was the basic dynamic of the daughters' formative years" (21).

Whether it manifested itself in combining motherhood with paid employment, performing antisexist childrearing, insisting that partners be involved in childcare, engaging in activism, or creating a life outside of motherhood, these studies reveal that feminist mothering developed in response to the mother's dissatisfaction with, and dislike of, traditional motherhood. Gordon alerts us, as Erika Horwitz notes, to the possibility that "*the process of resistance entails making different choices about how one wants to practice mothering*" (2003: 58, emphasis added). Commenting on Gordon's study, Erika Horwitz emphasizes that "her findings suggest that mothers can hold beliefs that are not in agreement with those promoted by the dominant discourses on motherhood" (2004: 58). Fiona Joy Green, likewise, as discussed in her chapter in this volume, emphasizes that central to feminist mothering is a "critique [of] the mythical standards of motherhood and the social neglect of the real isolation many mothers experience" (163). Moreover, as Green, continues, "for these women, feminist mothering is an essential strategy for contributing to positive political social change" (166).

Gordon, Green, and Glickman look specifically at mothers who identify as feminists, while Horwitz is interested in "the experiences of women who believe they were resisting the dominant discourse of mothering . . . [but] who may or may not see themselves as feminist" (2004: 44, 45). This volume likewise considers various nonpatriarchal modes of mothering and does not limit their meaning or practice exclusively to mothers who identify as feminist. Nonetheless, there are crucial differences between feminist mothering and empowered mothering that need to be identified to better understand the various ways nonpatriarchal mothering functions as a counterdiscourse. To this discussion I now turn.

In her chapter, "Resistance as a Site of Empowerment," Erika Horwitz argues that while resistant, empowered mothering is characterized by many themes, they all center on a challenge to patriarchal motherhood. These themes include: the importance of mothers meeting their own needs; being a mother does not fulfill all of women's needs; involving others in their children's upbringing; actively questioning the expectations that are placed on mothers by society; challenging mainstream parenting practices; not believing that mothers are solely responsible for how children turn out; and challenging the idea that the only emotion mothers ever feel toward their children is love. In an earlier collection *Mother Outlaws* (2004a), I explored how empowered mothering begins with the recognition that both mothers and children benefit when the mother lives her life and practices mothering from a position of agency, authority, authenticity, and autonomy. This perspective, in emphasizing maternal authority and ascribing agency to mothers and value to motherwork, defines motherhood as a political site wherein mothers can affect social change through the socialization of children and the world at large through political-social activism. Empowered mothering thus calls into question the dictates of patriarchal motherhood. Empowered mothers do not regard childcare as the sole responsibility of the biological mother nor do they regard 24/7 mothering as necessary for children. They look to friends, family, and their partners to assist with childcare and often raise their children with an involved community of what may be termed *co-mothers* or *othermothers*. In most instances, these mothers combine mothering with paid employment or activism, and so the full-time intensive mothering demanded in patriarchal motherhood is not practiced by these mothers. In addition, many of these mothers call into question the belief that mothering requires excessive time, money, and energy, and thus they practice a mode of mothering that is more compatible with paid employment. Also, they see the development of a mother's selfhood as beneficial to mothering and not antithetical to it as assumed in patriarchal motherhood. Consequently, empowered mothers do not always put their children's needs before their own nor do they only look to motherhood to define and realize their identity. Rather, their selfhood is fulfilled and expressed in various ways: work, activism, friendships, relationships, hobbies, and motherhood. These mothers insist on their own authority as mothers and refuse the relinquishment of their power as mandated in the patriarchal institution of motherhood. Finally, as noted earlier, empowered mothers regard motherhood as a site of power wherein mothers can affect social change, both in the home through feminist childrearing and outside the home through maternal activism. Motherhood, in the dominant patriarchal ideology, is seen simply as a private, and, more specifically, an apolitical enterprise. In contrast, mothering for feminist mothers is understood to have cultural significance and political purpose. Building on the work of Sara Ruddick, these mothers redefine motherwork as a socially engaged enterprise that seeks to effect cultural change through new feminist modes of gender socialization and interactions with daughters and sons.

Feminist mothering differs from empowered mothering insofar as the mother identifies as a feminist and practices mothering from a feminist perspective or consciousness. A feminist mother, in other words, is a woman whose mothering, in theory and practice, is shaped and influenced by feminism. Thus, while there is much overlap between empowered and feminist mothering, the latter is informed by a particular philosophy and politic, namely, feminism. The women's demands that their husbands be more

involved or that they need time off from motherhood in the Horwitz study
did not derive from a larger challenge to gender inequity. For example, one
woman in the study remarked that "if I was going to love that baby, have any
quality of time with that baby, I had to get away from that baby. I had to meet
my own needs" (2004: 48); and another mother "chose to paint her nails while
her baby cried in her crib because 'she has needs and wants'" (2004: 47). These
women resisted patriarchal motherhood, in one woman's words, "to have a
higher quality of life," or in the words of another, "to make me a better mother
for my children" (2004: 52). The reasons for their resistance are more personal
than political and as a consequence are not developed from an awareness of
how motherhood functions as a cultural/ideological institution to oppress
women in patriarchal society. These mothers resist patriarchal motherhood
simply to make the experience of mothering more rewarding for themselves
and their children. Insofar as this aim challenges the patriarchal mandate of
maternal selflessness, sacrifice, and martyrdom, these mothers are resistant in
their insistence on more time for themselves and support from others. However, these demands do not originate from a feminist desire to dismantle a
patriarchal institution. In contrast, feminist mothers resist because they recognize that gender inequity, in particular male privilege and power, is produced,
maintained, and perpetuated (i.e., though sexist childrearing) in patriarchal
motherhood. As feminists, feminist mothers reject an institution founded on
gender inequity, and, as mothers, they refuse to raise children in such a sexist
environment. Thus, while in practice the two seem similar—demanding more
involvement from fathers, insisting on a life outside of motherhood—only
with feminist mothering does this involve a larger awareness of, and challenge
to, the gender (among other) inequities of patriarchal culture.

   While this discussion helps to distinguish between empowered and feminist mothering, it begs the larger question of how to define feminism itself.
Feminism, as scholars of women's studies are well aware, is composed of many
perspectives and positions: socialist, liberal, radical, womanist, third wave, to
name but a few. For the purpose of this collection, I rely on a very open-
ended definition of feminism: the recognition that most (all?) cultures are
patriarchal and that such cultures give prominence, power, and privilege to
men and the masculine and depend on the oppression, if not disparagement,
of women and the feminine. Feminists are committed to challenging and
transforming this gender inequity in all of its manifestations: cultural, economic, political, philosophical, social, ideological, sexual, and so forth. Also,
most feminisms (including my own) seek to dismantle other hiearchical
binary systems such as race (racism), sexuality (heterosexism), economics
(classism), and ability (ableism). A feminist mother, therefore, in the context

of this definition of feminism, challenges male privilege and power in her own life and that of her children. In her own life, this would mean the mother insisting on gender equality in the home and a life and identity outside of motherhood. It would also mean that the important work of mothering would be culturally valued and supported and that mothers, likewise, would perform this motherwork from a place of agency and authority. In the context of children, feminist mothering means dismantling traditional gender socialization practices that privilege boys as preferable and superior to girls and in which boys are socialized to be masculine and girls feminine. Feminist mothering thus seeks to transform both the patriarchal role of motherhood and that of childrearing.

However, the word *feminism* remains troubled. In her book on feminist daughters Glickman wrote: "I ruled out daughters whose mothers' lives can surely be described as feminist, but who reject the label. Once, in my search for Latina daughters, I spoke with the head of a Latino women's health collective. She said she couldn't help me because 'although we have the consciousness, in our culture we don't use the word'. The consciousness without the word is not what I'm looking for" (xv–xvi). However, in insisting on the word *feminist*, you will inevitably, as the previous incident demonstrates, exclude the mothering experiences of women of color. The term *feminism*, as African American scholars Patricia Hill Collins and bell hooks among others have argued, is understood to be a white term for many black women. As one daughter, a woman of color, in Glickman's study commented: "[Feminism] has overwhelmingly, statistically, benefited white women disproportionately to women of colour" (168). And another daughter remarked: "Here you are reading all these feminist writers who are telling you to bust out of the kitchen and get into the work force. What does that have to do with the majority of women of colour who have always been in the kitchen *and* the work force at the same time?" (169, emphasis in original). Indeed, as the mothers of color in Gordon's study emphasized, "black women are critical of feminism dominated by white women for ideological, political and strategic reasons" (140). The question thus remains: how do you develop a specific study of feminist mothering without excluding the many women—women of color and working-class women—who eschew or disavow the word *feminism*?

In this collection, I include chapters on mothers who may not call themselves feminist but who do, nonetheless, challenge patriarchal motherhood in their practice of empowered mothering. The aim of this volume is to examine feminist mothering across a wide range of perspectives, themes, and disciplines; to do so we need to begin with an inclusive definition of it. Only then are we able to develop a comprehensive theory of feminist mothering.

TOWARD A THEORY OF FEMINIST MOTHERING

Feminist mothering functions as a counterpractice that seeks to challenge and change the many ways that patriarchal motherhood is oppressive to women. Numerous feminist scholars have detailed the various ways that patriarchal motherhood constrains, regulates, and dominates women and their mothering. In an earlier volume, *Mother Outlaws* (2004a), I organized these themes under eight interrelated 'rules' of 'good' motherhood as dictated by contemporary patriarchal ideology. They are: (1) children can only be properly cared for by the biological mother; (2) this mothering must be provided 24/7; (3) the mother must always put children's needs before her own; (4) mothers must turn to the experts for instruction; (5) the mother must be fully satisfied, fulfilled, completed, and composed in motherhood; (6) mothers must lavish excessive amounts of time, energy, and money in the rearing of their children; (7) the mother has full responsibility, but no power from which to mother; (8) motherwork, and childrearing more specifically, are regarded as personal, private undertakings with no political import. The patriarchal ideology of motherhood makes mothering deeply oppressive to women because it requires the repression or denial of the mother's own selfhood; it also assigns mothers all the responsibility for mothering, but gives them no real power from which to mother. Such "powerless responsibility," to use Rich's term, denies a mother the authority and agency to determine her own experiences of mothering. Moreover, in defining mothering as private and nonpolitical work, patriarchal motherhood restricts the way mothers can and do effect social change through feminist childrearing and maternal activism.

The dominant ideology also reserves the definition of good motherhood to a select group of women. I open my women's studies course on "Mothering–Motherhood" asking students to define a 'good' mother in contemporary culture: what does a good mother look like; who is she? Students commented that good mothers, as portrayed in the media or popular culture more generally, are white, heterosexual, middle-class, able-bodied, married, thirty-something, in a nuclear family with usually one to two children, and ideally are full-time mothers. Words such as *altruistic, patient, loving, selfless, devoted, nurturing, cheerful* were frequently mentioned to describe the personality of this ideal patriarchal mother. Mothers who, by choice or circumstance, do not fulfill the profile of the good mother—they are too young or old, or are poor or lesbian—are deemed 'bad' mothers. Likewise, women who do not follow the script of good mothering—they work outside the home or engage in maternal activism—are seen as 'fallen' mothers in need of societal regulation and correction.

Feminist mothering refuses this patriarchal profile and script of 'good' mothers and 'good' mothering. And, in so doing, it challenges and changes the various ways patriarchal motherhood becomes oppressive to women, as noted previously in the eight themes. Thus, while feminist mothering functions as an oppositional discourse and thus defies definition, it is characterized by several themes that coalesce to form a specific theory of feminist mothering. A theory of feminist mothering begins with the recognition that mothers *and children* benefit when the mother lives her life, and practices mothering, from a position of agency, authority, authenticity, and autonomy. Thus, a feminist standpoint on mothering affords a womam a life, a purpose and identity outside and beyond motherhood; it also does not limit childrearing to the biological mother. Likewise, from this standpoint, a woman's race, age, sexuality, or marital status do not determine her capicity to mother. A feminist theory on motherhood also foregrounds maternal power and confers value to mothering. Mothering, thus from a feminist perspective and practice, redefines motherwork as a social and political act. In contrast to patriarchal motherhood that limits mothering to privatized care undertaken in the domestic sphere, feminist mothering regards itself as explicitly and profoundly political and social.

The various features of feminist mothering noted here may be organized by way of four interrelated themes that I have termed: *motherhood, family, childrearing*, and *activism*. Central to each theme is a redefinition of motherhood from a feminist-maternal perspective. 'Good' mothers in patriarchal motherhood, for example, are defined as white, middle-class, married, stay-at-home moms; 'good' mothers from the feminist perspective are drawn from all maternal identities and include lesbian, poor, single, older, and 'working' mothers. Likewise, while patriarchal motherhood limits family to a patriarchal nuclear structure wherein the parents are married and are the biological parents of the children and the mother is the nurturer and the father is the provider, the formation of feminist families are many and varied to embrace single, blended, step, matrifocal, same-sex, and so forth. And as patriarchal motherhood characterizes childrearing as a private, nonpolitical undertaking, feminist mothers foreground the political-social dimension of motherwork. More specifically, they challenge traditional practices of gender socialization and perform antisexist childrearing practices so as to raise empowered daughters and empathetic sons. Finally, for many feminist mothers, their commitment to both feminism and to children becomes expressed as maternal activism. Mothers, by way of maternal activism, use their position as mothers to lobby for social and political change. Whether it is in the home or in the world at large, expressed as antisexist childrearing and maternal activism, motherwork, for feminist mothers, is redefined as a social and political act through which social change is made possible.

The chapters in this collection are organized by way of these four themes. Part one looks at how feminist mothering challenges patriarchal motherhood by redefining the identity and role of mothers. Older, feminist, and working mothers are examined in this opening part. Family is the theme of part two. Here, the focus is on how feminist mothers transform the meaning of family to include lesbian and dual-earner households and matrifocal, communal, and extended families. Part three looks at feminist childrearing, and the final part considers maternal activism. Evidently, there is much overlap between the parts: lesbian motherhood results in the redefinition of both family and the mother role. Likewise, being a feminist mother means a new mother role and gives rise to antisexist childrearing. However, to allow for clarity and to highlight the different elements of feminist mothering, this volume has been organized into these four parts.

MOTHERHOOD

Michele Y. Pridmore-Brown, in the opening chapter "Professional Women, Timing, and Reproductive Strategies," explores how older motherhood challenges notions of passive self-sacrifice and thus of traditional gender roles in several ways. As writer and older mother Mona Simpson has put it, for the older woman, the choice to mother involves an extension of the self rather than its contraction. Increasingly, older women have children to realize themselves in an existential sense after having achieved professional goals. They create a child and subsequently mother that child from a position of privilege: one of power rather than of dependency—as embodied strategic actors who have actively chosen motherhood (often via technology and often via the purchase of gametes) rather than simply "letting nature takes its course." The chapter explores how being an older mother affects strategies of mothering; it also examines how older motherhood affects the emotional bond between mother and child. To this end, the chapter examines how a group of older/single women define the politics of their mothering strategies; how they negotiate the divide between their expectations and the realities of an actual child; and how, as women who have themselves overturned traditional roles, not to mention the traditional life-course, they address their child's future as a gendered individual in a still sexist society.

The following chapter "No, I'm Not Catholic, and Yes, They're All Mine" by Kecia Driver McBride examines the author's experience of being a feminist mother of four children, about to come up for tenure at a state university. Her central argument is that the real challenge of feminist mothering should not be about choosing toys and books that are nongender specific or talking to sons about the problematic representation of women on MTV, but about modeling a mothering style that is fully engaged and confident, both "at work" and "at home." We must, the author argues, reach beyond our own children. It is not enough to develop complicated personal solutions to problems like quality childcare, or to experience individually the rush and the fear when the boundaries between personal and professional work are blurred. Feminist mothering requires that we build stronger networks between ourselves as parents, in order to reeducate the communities in which we live, work, and raise our children.

Shelley Martin, in the chapter that concludes this part, "Feminism, Motherhood, and Possibilities in the Writing of Bronwen Wallace," argues that, for Wallace, writing about motherhood is a political statement because not only was she doing it while raising a son as a single mother, she was using it to convey the complex realities of women's maternal experiences—the conflicts and stresses as well as the pleasures. The honesty of her account, Martin argues, is a refusal of the idealized maternal portraits found in much traditional literature. The chapter explores the intersections of Wallace's expressed political beliefs, her writing, and her life, as they are represented in her writing. Wallace's goal in telling these stories, Martin emphasizes, is to effect political change by revising the social and cultural attitudes that devalue both the stories and the women who live them. In this, Wallace's writing gives rise to a redefinition of the maternal role.

FAMILY

In the opening chapter of this part, "Planned Parenthood: The Construction of Motherhood in Lesbian Mother Advice Books," Kristin G. Esterberg examines how lesbian advice books, published between 1981 and 2001, both challenge and conform to existing ideals for childcare. Unlike traditional advice books, lesbian mother advice books provide a critique of heterosexist models of parenting, encouraging an egalitarian model. Yet by focusing on issues of choice, this advice literature encourages women to see their mothering in terms of consumer choice. This model is only partly liberating, Esterberg argues. While lesbian mothers may offer a more egalitarian alternative, they may not consider how class and race inflect choices about parenting. Nor do they challenge a privatized and commercialized model of parenthood in which individual women (and occasionally men) are seen as responsible for children's care. In this regard, lesbian mothers are little different from other mothers. Because lesbians are seen as making an *individual* choice, they do not challenge the privatized arrangements by which parents are expected to care for 'their' children. At the same time, lesbian mothers are encouraged to detach maternity from biology and thus have the potential to challenge essentialist beliefs about the nature of the mother–child relationship.

Aimee E. Berger, in "The Voice of the Maternal in Louise Erdrich's Fiction and Memoirs," argues that the centrality of mother figures in works by Native American author Louise Erdrich has been noted in all her writing. However, Berger argues that *The Blue Jay's Dance: A Birth Year* (1995) is a watershed text that signals and perhaps even brings about a significant shift in Erdrich's fictional portrayal of maternal subjectivity and representations of mothers in her later novels. Through writing this memoir, Berger writes, Erdrich not only claims her own maternal subjectivity, but also comes to terms with a central paradox of mothering, power/powerlessness, which structured representations of maternal experience in her earlier texts and led to generally ambivalent portrayals. Addressing this paradox frees Erdrich's later writing from the discomforts of ambivalence and allows maternal experience to emerge as a central focus. Central to this mother-centered writing and explored in this chapter is Erdrich's emphasis on Ojibwe language and storytelling. Her stories become vessels for holding and transmitting cultural values. In this way, *Erdrich can be seen to mother the culture itself.* After *The Blue Jay's Dance*, Berger concludes, Erdrich's writing becomes, in multiple and distinct ways, an act of feminist mothering.

Shirley A. Hill's chapter, "African American Mothers: Victimized, Vilified, and Valorized," examines how African American scholars have broadened and enriched feminist debate on motherhood by showing how it is shaped by both race and class. The chapter begins with an overview of the historic construction of motherhood and family and how it differed for African American and white women. In agricultural America, black and white women were expected to produce as many children as possible; neither had much control over their sexuality or reproductive activities, but enslaved black women were especially victimized because they gave birth to 'property' owned by white slaveholders. With modernization, images of mothers diverged sharply, Hill argues, with white women seen as angelic, self-sacrificing mothers and black women vilified as reckless breeders and welfare mothers. The civil rights era, however, ushered in a spate of revisionist research that rejected narrow, ethnocentric, and class-biased notions of families that,

Hill emphasizes, revalued the survival of black families in a harshly racist environment. It redefined African American families as functional units, but also valorized motherhood. The chapter analyzes the consequences of this image in the context of postindustrialized America, and looks at new possibilities of supporting today's mothers and their families.

In the final chapter, "Mothering as Relational Consciousness," Amber E. Kinser explores some of the irresolvable "messiness" of feminist living and advances an understanding of mothering as relational consciousness. In an effort to pay more pointed attention to what mothering is like from the mother's point of view, she examines some of the ways that its work is informed and complicated by the blurred boundaries delineating one's multiple selves and relationships. Drawing from her own childrearing experiences, she first examines how her mothering practices "rub against" her relationship with her own mother, as well as her relationships with her partners. Second, she examines the erotic dimensions of motherhood by confirming its location on a sexuality continuum. She discusses the necessity and messy complexities of a maternal erotic and evokes the intense and sometimes "grim" connection between mothers and their children. Kinser argues that a view of mothering as relational consciousness requires a recognition of the emergent tensions not as oppositional and in need of resolution, but as interdependent parts of a larger whole and mutually necessary.

CHILDREARING

This part opens with Colleen Mack-Canty and Sue Marie Wright's chapter "Feminist Family Values: Parenting in Third Wave Feminism and Empowering All Family Members." The chapter explores how Second Wave feminism enabled people to become more aware of, and to act on, gender-constructed inequality. Today, as a result, some parents, including some men, work especially hard to ensure gender equality within their families, for both parents and children. In the meantime, feminism generally has become increasingly concerned with the intersectionality of various "isms," such as racism, classism, heterosexism with sexism, and works against the notion of hierarchy itself Many feminists view this broadened emphasis in feminism as a Third Wave of feminism. This chapter explores the effects of these changes through the perspectives of feminist parents and their children. These families all challenge some hierarchal systems, such as sexism, racism, heterosexism, unnecessary adult authority, and universal family form. The parents, in their study, consciously practice nonsexist parenting. They also parent in ways that seem to enable their children to become conscious of and to challenge oppression generally. They suggest that these practices are empowering to all members of these families and coincide with Third Wave feminism.

The following chapter, "Feminist Motherline: Embodied Knowledge/s of Feminist Mothering" by Fiona Joy Green, attempts to enrich and enhance our understanding of feminism and feminist mothering by investigating the ways in which feminism is central to the personal identity and mothering strategies of ten self-identified feminist mothers living in Winnipeg, Canada, in 2005. Drawing on a decade-long study into the realities of conscious feminist parenting, she reveals some of the challenges these women face, aspects of their feminist mothering they view as successful, and elements of their mothering they may have done differently. Green concludes with a call for more research into feminist mothering that attends to a feminist motherline that carries the many embodied experience/s and knowledge/s of feminist mothering. Such a feminist motherline may be useful in assisting mothers in re/claiming their feminist mothering authority and providing a foundation for their ongoing political activism as feminist mothers.

"(Un)usual Suspects: Mothers, Masculinities, Monstrosities," the next chapter by Sarah Trimble, employs a spatialized theoretical framework to explore possibilities for transformative encounters between feminist mothering practices and masculinities. Invoking Adrienne Rich's notion of the mother outlaw, Trimble suggests that feminist mothers raise their sons on the frontiers of patriarchal cultures—and that the overlapping marginalities of mother and son have the potential to productively destabilize the son's masculinity via his alliance with his mother and her community. Through a reading of John Irving's *The World According to Garp*, the chapter argues that Garp is able to (re)imagine himself as an outlaw from hegemonic masculinity only when he abandons his illusions of self-sufficiency and begins to participate in the healing practices associated with his mother's maternal activism. Trimble's chapter infuses contemporary theorizations of feminist mothering with concepts articulated by Giorgio Agamben, Gilles Deleuze, and Félix Guattari to draw out the implications of the outlaw, the spaces she or he moves through, and the disruptive becomings in which the outlaw engages.

In my chapter that concludes the part, "'That Is What Feminism Is— The Acting and Living And Not Just the Told': Modeling and Mentoring Feminism," I argue that feminist mothering must first and primarily be concerned with the empowerment of mothers. In contrast, much of current literature on feminist mothering involves antisexist childrearing, or, more

specifically, raising empowered daughters and relational sons with little attention paid to the mother herself or the conditions under which she mothers. A
challenge to traditional gender socialization is, of course, integral to any
theory and practice of feminist mothering. However, I argue that the empowerment of mothers must be the primary aim of feminist mothering if it is to
function as a truly transformative theory and practice. To fully and completely
liberate children from traditional childrearing, mothers must first seek to liberate themselves from traditional motherhood; they must, to use Rich's terminology, mother against motherhood. By way of a conversation with my two
daughters—Erin (eighteen) and Casey (sixteen)—this chapter will explore
the interface between the empowerment of mothers and antisexist childrearing and the argument that the latter depends on the former. More specifically,
I will argue that, for mothers to mentor feminism for their daughters, they
must model it in themselves.

ACTIVISM

The opening chapter of the final part, Judith Stadtman Tucker's "Rocking the
Boat: Feminism and the Ideological Grounding of the Twenty-First Century
Mothers' Movement," considers what has been termed the "motherhood
problem"—the combination of cultural factors, social trends, and policy
shortfalls that make mothers and other caregivers disproportionately vulnerable to financial insecurity and the daily work of mothering harder than it has
to be. The chapter examines how the growing cultural awareness of this problem presents an important opportunity for organizations and grassroots
activists intent on mobilizing mothers for social change. However, there is no
clear consensus among leaders of the emerging mothers' movement about the
best way to describe mothers' contributions to society or how to define and
defend their rights. According to Stadtman Tucker, there is a shared conviction among movement activists that the present generation of mothers is
indifferent or antagonistic to traditional feminist analyses of gender, power,
and systems of oppression. In public statements, mothers' advocates blend
and weave compatible and incompatible political theories and ideological
frameworks to validate their agenda for change, with liberal feminism, maternalism, and feminist care theory among the predominant influences. The
results of this exercise are often inconsistent and unpersuasive, and this strategy, she argues, may ultimately impede the movements' growth and visibility.
The chapter discusses some of the underlying challenges to articulating a

coherent politics of motherhood in today's cultural context and suggests that the future success of the mothers' movement will depend on leaders' ability to develop and communicate an effective change narrative.

In the following chapter, "Women Staging Coups through Mothering: Depictions in Hispanic Contemporary Literature," Gisela Norat argues that in the Hispanic world we find a variety of ways in which women stage coups (in the sense of brave and unexpected or uncommon acts that effect changes) against patriarchal systems that oppress them. While most female rebellions go unnoticed and undocumented because they lack political impact, the ones orchestrated by the Mothers of the Plaza de Mayo in then-dictatorial Argentina of the 1970s and 1980s, Norat argues, made news around the world, politicized the institution of motherhood, and challenged a repressive military regime. Their story sets the parameters for Norat's analysis of other manifestations of feminist mothering recorded in contemporary Latina and Latin American literature. The chapter looks at several mother-centered "coup" narratives by Hispanic women, including the Chilean Isabel Allende who writes as a mother grieving her dying daughter, and Mexican American Cherri Moraga who writes as a lesbian mother; it also examines various daughter-centered fiction by Latina writers who, as daughters, turn the tables on tradition by socializing their mothers in feminist ways.

Janice Nathanson, in "Maternal Activism: How Feminist Is It?" argues that a growing number of feminists and activists are seeing motherhood as a starting point for social change as women increasingly join forces, as mothers, to address the issues that affect their families most: health, education, crime, housing, safety, drunk driving, and drugs, to name a few. While maternal activism is not new, it now has a feminist focus. Paradoxically, feminism is rarely its motivation. This chapter explores whether maternal activism, in fact, promotes a feminist agenda and argues that it does so on three counts. It exemplifies the very core of feminist ideology—that the personal is political. It helps negate essentialist notions of motherhood by transforming views of it from a private experience to a catalyst for visible and widespread change. And it enables women (often unintentionally) to upset gender roles and power relations simply by virtue of their activism. Not surprisingly, feminists fall on both sides of the debate. Some decry maternal activism as an essentializing force that returns women to the destiny of anatomy. Others believe it reframes motherhood in terms of its power and breadth. Wherever one falls on the continuum, this chapter aims to stimulate dialogue and advance thinking around a growing phenomenon.

In "Balancing Act: Discourses of Feminism, Motherhood, and Activism," the final chapter, Pegeen Reichert Powell looks at how, in the popular media, the dominant metaphor employed to describe the experience of working mothers is "balance." Balancing work and family is the elusive goal of motherhood that dominates advice columns, news reports about businesses' attempts to help women achieve it, and scathing articles about the negative effects on children when we fail to do so. Balance, however, Powell argues, is a static condition; one has achieved balance when one is not being pulled, or pushing oneself, in one direction over another. Indeed, one of the markers of balance, women are told, is enough time for rest. In this chapter, the author develops a sociolinguistic analysis of the discourse of "balance" in popular media and then juxtaposes this to a study of an activist organization that works toward improved climate and policies (such as paid leave, flextime, etc.) for employees at a prominent university in the United States. The chapter concludes that feminist mothering should question and challenge the notion of *balance* and instead forward a more dynamic understanding of motherhood, an understanding focused on activist *movement*. But, as the study demonstrates, the discourse of balance and attempts at activism are not always mutually exclusive, and together they construct a complicated backdrop against which feminist mothers work.

CONCLUSION

I opened this introduction with the speculation that the dearth of popular literature and academic discourse on feminist mothering may be attributable to our inability to define what we mean or more specifically, what we want or expect to achieve from and in feminist mothering. The following chapters, while they do not lead to a definition of feminist mothering, do provide us with the stories and theories necessary to realize what Adrienne Rich defined as the potentiality of mothering and thus allow for a theory of feminist mothering. In each of its four themes, *motherhood, family, childrearing*, and *activism*, the practice of feminist mothering may be envisioned metaphorically as a cartwheel or somersault, insofaras its aim is to invert and subvert patriarchal motherhood: to turn patriarchal motherhood on its head. As patriarchal motherhood confines mothers to the home and limits childrearing to private care, feminist mothering positions mothers in the public realm by way of activism and views childrearing as a social-political act. Moreover, as patriarchal motherhood reduces a woman's purpose and identity to her maternal function, feminist mothering accords a woman a selfhood outside and beyond motherhood; it also expands childrearing beyond the care of the biological mother. Finally, as the dominant ideology of motherhood limits 'good' mothering to a patriarchal nuclear family, feminist mothering champions various and diverse family formations.

These themes of feminist mothering are found in the chapters that follow. However, not every feminist mother practices each theme of feminist mothering. The overall aim of feminist mothering is the redefinition of patriarchal motherhood to make mothering less oppressive and more empowering for mothers. Or, more specifically, feminist mothers seek to fashion a mode of mothering that affords and affirms maternal agency, authority, autonomy, and authenticity and confers and confirms power to and for mothers. However, such mothering, it must be emphasized, is practiced in a culture wherein patriarchal motherhood is the norm. In other words, feminist mothering, as it seeks to challenge patriarchal motherhood, remains defined by it. Consequently, while themes of feminist mothering, in theory, may be fully and clearly catalogued, feminist mothering, in practice, is far more contested and elusive, achieved and expressed in negotiation with the institution of patriarchal motherhood that it resists. Many of the chapters in the collection examine this theme of negotiation.

Feminist mothering, as it creates new nonpatriarchal families, challenges traditional gender socialization, critiques gender (and other) equities at home and in the world at large, champions motherwork, and calls for the empowerment of women through maternal activism and an identity outside of motherhood that enables, nay empowers, women to both live apart from and in resistance to patriarchy. Feminist mothering thus functions as both a sanctuary (however tenuous and fragile) from patriarchy *and* a stronghold against it. Or, put another way, feminist mothering both shelters us from patriarchy and makes possible our resistance to it. In this, feminist mothering does more than redefine patriarchal motherhood; it undermines and transforms the larger patriarchal culture in which we live. This is a cause for hope, and a place to begin.

NOTES

1. Several books have examined the relationship between feminism and motherhood, but very little has been published on feminist mothering. For two important works on feminism and motherhood, see Laura Umansky, *Motherhood Reconceived: Feminism and the Legacy of the Sixties* (New York: New York University Press, 1996) and Susan E. Chase and Mary F. Rogers, *Mothers & Children: Feminist Analysis and Personal Narratives* (New Brunswick, NJ: Rutgers University Press, 2001).

REFERENCES

Bort, Julie, Aviva Pflock, and Devra Renner. *Mommy Guilt: Learn to Worry Less, Focus on What Matters Most, and Raise Happier Kids.* New York: American Management Association, 2005.

Chase, Susan E., and Mary F. Rogers. *Mothers & Children: Feminist Analysis and Personal Narratives.* New Brunswick, NJ: Rutgers University Press, 2001.

Collins, Patricia Hill. *Black Feminist Thought,* 2nd ed. New York: Routledge Press, 2000.

Cooper, Baba. "The Radical Potential in Lesbian Mothering of Daughters." *Politics of the Heart: A Lesbian Parenting Anthology.* Eds. Sandra Pollack and Jeanne Vaughn. Ithaca, NY: Firebrand Books, 1987.

Douglas, Susan J., and Meredith Michaels. *The Mommy Myth: The Idealization of Motherhood and How It Has Undermined Women.* New York: Free Press, 2004.

Friedan, Betty. *The Feminine Mystique.* New York: Norton. 1963.

Glickman, Rose L. *Daughters of Feminists: Young Women with Feminist Mothers Talk about Their Lives.* New York: St. Martin's Press, 1993.

Gordon, Tuula. *Feminist Mothers.* New York: New York University Press, 1990.

Gore, Ariel, and Bee Lavender. *Breeder: Real Life Stories from the New Generation of Mothers.* Seattle: Seal Press, 2001.

Green, Fiona Joy. "Feminist Mothers: Successfully Negotiating the Tensions Between Motherhood and Mothering." *Mother Outlaws: Theories and Practices of Empowered Mothering.* Ed. Andrea O'Reilly. Toronto: Women's Press, 2004. 31–42.

hooks, bell. *Talking Feminist, Talking Black.* Boston: South Ends Press, 1989.

Horwitz, Erika. "Mothers' Resistance to the Western Dominant Discourse on Mothering." Ph.D. Thesis: Simon Fraser University, 2003.

———. "Resistance as a Site of Empowerment: The Journey Away from Maternal Sacrifice." *Mother Outlaws: Theories and Practices of Empowered Mothering.* Ed. Andrea O'Reilly. Toronto: Women's Press, 2004. 43–58.

Journal of the Association for Research on Mothering. "Mothering and Feminism" 8.1,2 (Winter/Summer 2006).

Mellor, Christie. *The Three-Martini Playdate: A Practical Guide to Happy Parenting.* San Francisco: Chronicle Books, 2004.

off our backs. "Feminism and Motherhood." 36.1. (2006).

O'Reilly, Andrea. *Mother Outlaws: Theories and Practices of Empowered Mothering.* Toronto: Women's Press, 2004a.

———. *From Motherhood to Mothering: The Legacy of Adrienne Rich's Of Woman Born.* Albany: SUNY Press, 2004b.

Reddy, Maureen, Martha Roth, Amy Sheldon, eds. *Mother Journeys: Feminists Write About Mothering*. Minneapolis: Spinsters Ink, 1994.

Rich, Adrienne. *Of Woman Born: Motherhood as Experience and Institution*. New York: Norton, 1986 (1976).

Ruddick, Sara. *Maternal Thinking: Toward a Politics of Peace*. Boston: Beacon Press, 2002 (1989).

Shields, Julie. *How to Avoid the Mommy Trap: A Roadmap for Sharing Parenting and Making It Work*. Sterling, VA: Capital Books, 2002.

Simpson, Bria. *The Balanced Mom: Raising Your Kids Without Losing Your Self*. Oakland, CA: New Harbinger, 2006.

Tiemann, Amy. *Mojo Mom: Nurturing Your Self While Raising a Family*. Chapel Hill, NC: Spark Press, 2006.

Umansky, Laura. *Motherhood Reconceived: Feminism and the Legacy of the Sixties*. New York: New York University Press, 1996.

PART ONE

Motherhood

CHAPTER ONE

Professional Women, Timing, and Reproductive Strategies

MICHELE PRIDMORE-BROWN

BACKGROUND: MOTHERING IN MANHATTAN

My son was born when I was thirty-six. And although my Manhattan obstetrician reassured me that I was one of the youngest expecting mothers in her practice, it was of course true that in another time or another place, or even in this time and place, but in a different culture, such as the one fifteen blocks north of me, on the other side of 125th Street, I could have just as easily been becoming a grandmother. (Simpson 242)

THE RATIONALE FOR MOTHERHOOD, like the rationale for marriage, has changed seismically, particularly in the last thirty years and particularly among members of the professional class. In her essay, writer Mona Simpson muses that it is a "strange moment in our culture" when we can speak of "*deciding*" to have a child. Having a child is no longer a matter of fate or of the natural order of things; it is not a matter of economic necessity as in agrarian times, and it is certainly not a social badge signaling full adulthood. Rather, the decision to mother is considered in privileged places like Manhattan to be optimally a matter of thought, of judicious timing under uncertainty. Increasingly, this decision involves weighing three variables: career momentum and the presence of a suitable partner against *time left*—until ovarian senescence, for instance, or some other less fuzzy deadline like a certain chronological age. Because upward mobility is in most cases predicated on delaying motherhood, it follows that, in Manhattan, first-time motherhood at thirty-six is routine, even "young," and since 1997 it has become "younger" still.

Economists are likely to explain later motherhood in strictly rational terms, as an epiphenomenon of our postindustrial economy. Well-documented evidence indicates that having children early in their professional career puts women forever behind their male colleagues.[1] But it was actually in the 1970s that Gary Becker, a University of Chicago economist, first made the then radical suggestion that "mother love" is not priceless; the earlier in her career a mother has children the greater the cost in terms of her lifetime earnings. He related the cost of a mother's time to her education level as a marker for the wages she forgoes. The effective price of children thus rises with a woman's education, which at least from the economist's point of view explains why, with prosperity, people have fewer children on average. Ridiculed for his work in the 1970s, Becker then received the Nobel Prize in the 1990s, and now the notion of the "opportunity cost" of a mother's time (her loss in earnings and presumably in related intangibles like fame, career momentum, writerly/scientific productivity, etc.) has become one of those seemingly self-evident truths that has infiltrated all aspects of the debate around women, careers, and mothering.

It is even embedded, albeit in different terms, in feminist discourse: in Adrienne Rich's early dictum that one *should* realize oneself before realizing another: as if self-birthing, whether via a career or some other means, were a kind of moral imperative before launching another self. Rich and others have deconstructed what past eras have troped as "the good mother," and as the domestic angel of the house. Indeed, from the vantage of feminist gains, the good mother has been read as an aborted or unrealized self: what Derrida calls the faceless enabling background for others; the one who creates a place and meaning for others through her own effacement (1982: 245). However effaced in actual life, we do well to remember that this "good mother" has been a powerful cultural icon—for several centuries the image of her selflessness symbolically guaranteeing the family, not to mention a moral universe. I will argue later that older motherhood destabilizes but also reinvents this icon from the position of power.

Not so long ago, the foil to the "good mother" was the so-called selfish-neglectful mother—whom Simpson paints from the vantage of feminist gains. Her own mother, fashionably clad, miniskirted, was, she writes, intent on forging her own life. Like Simpson's father, her mother was a "too-early" parent who happened, rather than decided, to have a child "on the way to something else" (245). Hence the implied insouciance of her parenting, which Simpson does not condemn (quite the contrary, insofar as she paints her childhood as an unsupervised Rousseauesque Eden), but also chooses not to repeat—indeed *cannot* repeat. The implication is that, at age thirty-six, Mona Simpson is not "on the way to something else." Rather, she has *arrived* at a place and time, a stage in life, that compels a radically different kind of mothering: neither effaced nor insouciant. Indeed, this is my point. I want to suggest that older mothers' narratives are worth examining because they herald new mothering strategies and new family constructs, an argument I will explore later.

First, however, it is worth asking why older women choose to have a child at all? Why opt for "the complete annihilation of life as you know it" (Simpson 244) when you are a successful professional? The writer Mary Gaitskill, for instance, acknowledges that, though many writers are mothers, she knows she could not have been a writer had she been a mother (256). In short, why opt at forty for sleepless nights, pay cuts, curtailed career options, and possibly fertility treatments—all of which are threats to self, health, relationships, and even longevity? In many ways, women appear to opt for a child as a bid for connection and some kind of permanence. Most women cite qua-existential imperatives: a child as the creation of meaning and the setting of a stake in the future. Many claim that the desire to have child at forty is about "authenticity," about a return in fact to "nature," the "real," to the imperatives of the flesh. While delay may be "rational" according to the economist's paradigm, the frequent use of the word *authenticity* suggests that older women see motherhood as transcending instrumental rationality: as a way not only of recouping meaning but, to cite Mona Simpson again, of causing ripples in another self, of having one's death signify, of having one's "daily kindnesses or meannesses, mean more because felt by [another] as determining, central" (Simpson 245). I am suggesting here that older motherhood, partly because it is a choice—rather than socially or, by fiat of nature, compulsory—can be viewed as a self-conscious relinquishing of egotism but also as an assertion of egotism.

Many older mothers emphasize especially their willingness to sacrifice to a degree that they would not have at an earlier age, a point that makes intuitive sense (one has only to think of Madonna as a twenty-year-old mother and as a forty-year-old new mother churning out children's books). Anthropologist Sarah Hrdy explains maternal self-sacrifice in strategic terms. In the primate world, writes Hrdy, an older mother will invest more in her baby than she would if she were young and knew she could always have more

(276f). Older mothers do not practice infanticide—there are no Medeas in the old new mother population. Maternal age, generalizes Hrdy further, is a far better predictor of how effective a mother will be than any specific personality traits. There is no reason to believe humans are different from their primate cousins in this regard. New mothers will invest more in their progeny when the arc of their own lives has plateaued: when motherhood is perceived as an opening rather than a closing of possibility, an extension of youth rather than its end, the *New Atlantis* rather than a straitjacket.

ACTUAL LIVES: INTERVIEWS WITH OLDER MOTHERS IN SILICON VALLEY

For a larger project, I interviewed about thirty older mothers in Silicon Valley (professionals ranging in age from thirty-eight to fifty-two at the birth of their first child, with one notable outlier who was fifty-nine at the birth of her son, sixty-two when I interviewed her, and "single by choice"). All had had their children, a singleton or twins, between 1992 and 2004. Silicon Valley is not representative of the country as a whole by any stretch, but I would argue its family configurations are worth studying because they are at the vanguard of postindustrial work/family transformations; in addition, Silicon Valley has one of the highest older mother populations,[2] and is a node of the booming fertility industry. I should mention that I am not myself an older mother, though I do happen to be the daughter of a mother who happened to have me in her mid-forties: a fact that actually led several older mothers to talk to me, even to seek me out, who might not have otherwise. With most of my interviewees I conducted two to three interviews separated by several months; I interviewed them with their child if that was agreeable—and on occasion I was able to interview their child's teacher. I focused on women who chose (a term I use loosely) to have children late rather than those who struggled ever since their twenties with decades of infertility before having a child thanks to innovations in reproductive technologies. For some of the women I interviewed, age forty presented a kind of magic age: a deadline in some instances. This was especially true for single women; at forty or so, they often reconciled themselves to not having a suitable partner and typically turned to sperm banks. Others, however, did not plan on having a child at all—but then met the "right" partner in their forties. All of the women were professionals, or retired professionals, but not all were necessarily well-off by the standards of the place in which they lived. For the purposes of this chapter, I will focus on only a handful of case histories that include heterosexual married women and single mothers (by choice); the latter, like lesbian and adoptive parents, for instance, are a significant and growing segment of the older mother population. Here, in the interest of space, I will focus not so much on the texture of their lives, but on how they framed their decisions and how they talked about shaping their progeny.

FORGING FAMILY: WHAT DOES FEMINISM HAVE TO DO WITH OLDER MOTHERHOOD?

The single mothers with whom I spoke insisted on the word *choice*. The very words *single mothers "by choice"* suggest an assertion of autonomy, and tacitly imply that the right to have a child is in some sense the flip side of the right not to have one. The absolute number of single older new mothers is still small, yet growing at a rate that suggests an emerging trend. A national group led by psychotherapist Jane Mattes in fact calls itself "Single Mothers By Choice," or "SMC"; its Web site (http://mattes.home.pipeline.com) advertises newsletters, a yearly conference, and advice. Its membership has grown from seven in 1981 to "several thousands" in 2007, according to Mattes; members are typically in their thirties to forties, college educated, well established in their careers, and living in metropolitan areas. The word *choice*, states the philosophy statement, means that "we have made a serious and thoughtful decision to take on the responsibility of raising a child by ourselves, and we have chosen not to be in a relationship rather than be in one that does not seem satisfactory."[3] The SMCs I interviewed were not members of Mattes's group, but their philosophy, at once conservative yet destabilizing to conventional norms, was much the same.

Helen,[4] the outlier who had her child at fifty-nine, was adamant in invoking the language of rights: she stated several times in the course of conversation that, if men could have children late, then why not women. As a retired schoolteacher taking classes in journalism, she was hoping to embark on a second career because she "wanted a change"; she said she always wanted to be in "a state of growing" and "learning new things"—and that by her fifties she felt life getting "stale," too easy, too humdrum (her house was paid off, her job was secure, etc.). She cites a 'superfit' eighty-two-year-old male role model whom she had met at 14,000 feet while hiking in her youth and with whom she had always identified. The new fertility technologies (egg and sperm donation) made motherhood possible for her. Though Stanford rejected her as a patient because of her age, another clinic accepted her after putting her through a battery of tests. Two embryos had been transferred in

1999 (her first try). Only one survived—which she reads as an act of divine intervention since, as she puts it, "multiples could have problems." Her son is hardly an easy child, according to his preschool teacher, whom I also interviewed. Helen, however, adamantly calls him "the best thing"; he keeps her young, "flexible," "on her toes"—whereas when she was younger she was "rigid" and "could not have had a child." Interestingly, though she had lived through all the changes wrought by Second Wave feminism and was clearly capitalizing on those changes, she would not call herself a "feminist" but an "individualist"; in other words, she rejected any kind of "group" mentality (indeed, did not want anything to do with the SMC group) and preferred to think of herself as a trailblazer; "people need to realize times are changing," she asserts somewhat defensively.

Though most of the single mothers did in fact call themselves feminists and in some cases had been and sometimes still were activists, another single mother, Debra—age forty-three when she had her daughter and fifty-five when I last interviewed her in 2004—did not particularly. She was a lawyer specializing in family law with a modest practice. Contrary to Helen (for whom relationships seemed to have played little or no part in her life), she would have preferred to have a male partner—but, as she put it, had always had trouble making relationships work long term. She was able to use her own egg and had selected a "dear friend" (with the active approval of the friend's wife) to be her sperm donor; she had her daughter on her third try in 1992. The child saw her biological father casually once or twice a year and knew him to be her father; Debra was adamant that he was "great"—if uninvolved as agreed via contract. She does not refer to her act as a feminist act, but as a "desperate act" (she wanted a child at all costs), though she loves the idea that she was a forerunner of a growing trend. Whereas Helen mentioned being isolated from former friends and other new mothers, Debra is anything but: a people person par excellence with a keen sense of humor, she actually has been seamlessly absorbed by married circles (largely composed of parents of her daughter's friends) while also maintaining friendships with what she calls "alternates": singles, gays, and so on. She muses that she did not feel "fully adult" as a lawyer until her forties, but more as if she were impersonating a professional; for someone like her, "young parenthood would be far more stressful" because "you would still be trying to find yourself professionally." Nonetheless, she acknowledges that, in her own life, financial difficulties ensure that stress is a constant and cheerfully pronounces her life chaotic. She mentions that her work (with divorce and custody cases) makes her realize, however, "how much less complicated" her life is than that of many of her clients—though she also muses that her daughter ends up missing out on the

experience "of watching two parents work things out." She had thought seriously of having a second child, but reconciled herself to the fact her life was
already "hectic enough."

Fiona, a self-described feminist who had always been "very ambitious,"
was an interesting case insofar as she did not stretch or reinvent traditional
gender roles, but rather reversed them in more ways than one. A former
dancer and current tenured professor of French language and culture, she had
a number of long-term relationships in her twenties and thirties with men in
academia that, she enigmatically says, were "unhealthy." The daughter of a
mother who gave birth to her at age forty-three, she actually had her baby
two years earlier at forty-one. She became pregnant the traditional way—
though "timing" was, she quips, of the essence. She had met the man who was
to become her son's father in Morocco (while doing research there); she
encountered him in what she calls "the last village before the desert," part of a
family that a decade or two ago had been nomadic. Ali was thirteen years her
junior—a fact that no doubt boasted her fertility considerably. They communicated in French, "an immense trust" developed, and so on. Shortly after
turning forty, Fiona flew out to Morocco for five days with the sole purpose
of conceiving; she notes that while they were together Ali had a dream in
which they had a son—a sign they apparently took as auspicious! Ali, who
had never left his country, let alone been in an airplane, arrived in the United
States the day their son was born. Fiona married him and he cared for the
baby while she worked; the baby was eighteen months old at the time of our
last interview. She describes herself as "discontented," even "jaded" concerning her career, but as replete emotionally (indeed she raves about her son and
shows me photos of him taken during their last trip to Morocco, with his
father and Moroccan aunts astride a camel). Thus far, Ali appears to regard
himself as extraordinarily fortunate, but Fiona appears philosophical about
their long-term prospects: he is still very young, she emphasizes. He does not
care for American "consumerism," but has found "soccer buddies" who speak
Arabic or French. She dwells on the almost hallucinatory exhaustion of the
first six months, but also says she has not ruled out having another child with
Ali—though she cannot imagine any second baby being as "good" and "beautiful" as their first.

Betsy is a former ballet mistress with the San Francisco Ballet and now
a choreographer with a splendid office overlooking city hall. The fifty-eight-
year-old mother of seven-year old twins when we meet, she describes herself
as what I would call a postfeminist *avant la lettre*; apolitical, she has
absorbed the advances of feminism, but has no interest in any kind of oppositional stance. Rather, she sees herself as an individual to whom the usual

constraints simply do not apply, who because of personality and genetic endowment transcended biological limitations and traditional scripts. Energy was never an issue—indeed, she exudes energy. She is adamant that she could never have had children when young because she was too focused on her career, and on "traveling to places like the Amazon," and on living life, *her* life, to the fullest. She had written off marriage as unsuited to her temperament. But, in her forties, she met the man who was to become her husband. Coincidentally, like Fiona's partner, he is exactly thirteen years younger—but a CFO. According to Betsy, the setting ("financial and moral") was "right for children." He was eager for a family and at age forty-eight she was game enough to begin fertility treatments; at fifty she had twins "without a hitch" using her own eggs, she declares proudly. It was, she says, "the perfect moment" for her to take on motherhood, and because she had seen and done everything, had fulfilled herself creatively, she was at a point where she could "really enjoy little babies," invest fully in them, and still keep up her career. She travels frequently on teaching stints, and her husband, together with a nanny, cares for the twins. She emphasizes how important "timing" is as a ballerina (marking the difference between "bouncing back" and forced retirement) and notes that her college education gave her more flexibility than most. Her advice to other women: "exhale," "do not rush," and then adopt if you cannot have your own babies (she mentions fellow ballerinas who have done just that and "are very happy").

Of course, the cacophonous ticks of biological and career clocks, of corporate ladders and rapidly senescent eggs, hardly make exhaling easy. Betsy's attitude, however, like that of Fiona and so many of the over-forty mothers, could in some sense be characterized as entrepreneurial: a "can-do" attitude that does not see itself as constrained by a prescribed script. Rather, women like Betsy see themselves as making a family to suit their interests rather than as a way of coping with a work environment that forces a continual deferment of 'mother dreams.' Betsy noted the resentment of a sister who had been more conformist (who had "rushed" into motherhood, led a presumably humdrum life, and who was, Betsy stage-whispered, "a little jealous"). To be sure, Betsy and many of the other women's "can-do" attitude is predicated, however, on a modicum of financial stability, a large dose of optimism, and, above all, somatic fitness. A self-selection process is at work. These women believe they will live longer than most—or at least not die before their time. Indeed, every one of the older women emphasized that they saw themselves as unusually healthy. Betsy, for instance, proudly stated that she had been told by her fertility doctors that she had the body of someone twenty years younger—and Helen always saw herself as belonging to a younger, more enterprising generation than her peers (indeed, she was defensive about her chronological age, which she regards as "irrelevant"). Fiona did not necessarily see herself as healthier than others, but took the possibility of older motherhood for granted because her own mother had been older. As for financial stability, almost all were able to use high-quality daycare or nannies (several had night nurses in the first six months) as a matter of course, though some were driving older cars—an old truck in Helen's case—to compensate for the financial hardship. Hardly insignificant is the fact that a few relied on the financial generosity of supportive albeit elderly grandparents. Finally, all saw the fact of being educated ("hypereducated" in some cases) as crucial; Helen noted that other schoolteachers had viewed her as "formidably intellectual"—which made her feel set apart. Betsy had the least schooling, but made much of the fact that she had more than her peers in ballet.

Eve, a literature professor and feminist activist, was more low-key, less obviously full of energy, than many of my interviewees—though she also mentioned feeling unusually healthy, which she distinguished from "fit" (she was adamant that she was not the latter). She said she and her same-aged male partner of thirty years (they are unmarried) had always felt they would probably have a child, but never felt they "needed" one. In fact, they first started trying to conceive at around forty-four; she was tenured, they lived in the same place for the first time in a decade, the moment seemed right: all the chips were in place, so to speak. And they saw having a child as "no longer restrictive," but, on the contrary, as "enriching" their lives. She muses that taking on older parenthood is a "sign of flexibility" but "also forces you to be flexible"—and she wanted that. It "keeps you young psychologically and mentally," she continues, though, pointing to the dark but not particularly visible circles under her eyes, readily acknowledges that the cost is that she is physically aging more rapidly right when she is going through menopause.

Whereas the women I have mentioned here spoke mostly in the first-person singular about their decisions, she uses only the plural: we decided, we felt, and so on. After several failed attempts using her own eggs (she notes that she naively had no idea fertility ended so much earlier than menopause), she had a daughter at fifty via a donor egg and her partner's sperm. The original plan had been that, thanks to their savings and modest lifestyle, she or he would have the luxury of going half-time after the birth; so far, it has been her because, she explains, her job was secure while they feared his (in the computer industry) was, "for the moment," more precarious. She says this is the first "inequality" in their relationship and notes somewhat cryptically that they are both "very careful" about it, adding that "of course" she benefits insofar as she "gets more time to spend with our daughter." When I interview Eve six months later, she mentions that they are "in therapy" to address the imbalance.

Of course, what's left out is often what is most important; clearly I heard only what my interviewees chose to present as their stories. Plus I saw only those who had succeeded in forging families. Still, these cursory sketches suggest the variety of ways in which women are remaking the family; how new technologies are materializing and normalizing alternate configurations and implicitly challenging old gender constructions. All my interviewees had absorbed the language of rights even if they did not subscribe to feminism per se; they were having children as part of their own carefully articulated interests. For most, late motherhood was to some degree symbolic of their protracted youth, their capacity for growth and flexibility. Which is not to say it was easy—the relentless sleep deprivation, the juggling act, the hardships for single moms who had no immediate fallback partner, the sometimes too-excruciatingly pivotal role of the nanny, the childcare costs were more (and less) than they had anticipated, but, as many were quick to point out, this could be said of younger mothers as well. Eve actually had budgeted $40,000 for childcare and ended up spending an astonishing $60,000 in 2003 for childcare and domestic help (a full-time at-home nanny with training in educational psychology), but this was unique.

The retired professional moms, often lawyers and doctors, typically married to "dot.com-ers" at the top of the income scale, were among those who did not experience any financial hardships; they also seemed to adopt the most conventional lifestyles and gender roles, though obviously from a position of far greater power, privilege, and experience than their younger sisters—for instance, running the PTA as if it were a corporation, as one educator put it. I should also add that I was struck by the number of the younger older mothers (ages thirty-six to forty-two) who mentioned that they had "had" to wait because they did not wish to repeat the pattern of their own childhoods (i.e., negligent fathers, resentful mothers, addiction and divorce legacies, etc.). They needed the extra time to heal and form healthier relationships that were, as a new mother/journalist put it, "consonant with [her] feminist beliefs." As if echoing Rich's dictum, they spoke of needing to make or realize a healthy self first—and many said they had not wanted a child when younger. Some were on a second marriage. Interestingly, several mentioned a shift in the kinds of mates they selected; in their twenties they were prone to repeating their own mother's script (as one woman put it, falling for "the peacock feathers": markers of "virility" or status), whereas in their thirties they favored men with more companionate skills, men they might have overlooked in their youth, and this enabled different kinds of parenting partnerships.

In her book *Creating a Life: Professional Women and the Quest for Children*, author Sylvia Ann Hewlett has argued that the more women achieve in their careers (which she measures purely in terms of income), the less likely they will marry or have children; she does not hesitate to tell her readers that she had a child at fifty-one using "her own egg," but her advice is the opposite of Betsy's. She urges young women today to have babies in their late twenties lest they later be haunted by the empty cradle because of age-related infertility. Subsequent studies, however, have shown Hewlett's sample and methods to be suspect (a case of politics preceding data collection): in short, high-achieving women have children later and do so with their eyes open, as investigative journalist Garance Franke-Ruta has established by drawing on a larger data set. They have children with a partner they can rely on or with the resources to take on single parenthood. And, as sociologists have pointed out, if married, they do not divorce as frequently. Whether family-friendly changes in the workplace or whether fertility technologies of the future (reliable egg freezing, for instance) will further affect the timing of reproduction for such women remains to be seen. My point is that, though the workplace assuredly needs to be more hospitable to families, not just one overriding reason (such as corporate ladders) explains why professional women have children late; the trend is rooted in the whole panorama of postindustrial life: in notions of self realization a la Rich and opportunity costs a la Becker to be sure, but also in lengthening lifespans, the routinization of fertility technologies, the growing elasticity of gender roles, even in different kinds of mate selection—and ultimately in the application of the rhetoric of feminist choice and control to the making of life and families. Ultimately, new reproductive strategies herald new parenting strategies as well.

FEMINIST MOTHERING? MAPPING THE FUTURE

In an article entitled "Invisible Inequality: Social Class and Childrearing in Black and White Families," the sociologist Annette Lareau delineates two types of parenting strategies: "concerted cultivation" of progeny (the deliberate, sustained effort to stimulate children's development and cultivate their cognitive reasoning skills) and a more insouciant, or what she calls "natural growth," model (letting children's development naturally unfold in a non-interventionist manner). Her point is that these parenting strategies set the stage for further inequalities in adulthood. Her research on schoolchildren in the Midwest and Northeast suggests that these parenting strategies are—like reproductive strategies, I would argue—largely class-based rather than race-based. Middle-class parents regardless of race engage in active cultiva-tion by attempting to foster the children's talents through organized leisure activities; working-class parents let their children "hang out." Children of middle-class parents gain an "emerging sense of entitlement" because parents actively foster and assess child's talents and interests, whereas children of working-class parents have wider kin networks but also a sense of constraint with respect to institutions and authority figures, which results in feelings of powerlessness (Lareau 747).

Lareau's paradigms are useful in thinking about older motherhood. Older new mothers invariably practice a concerted kind of cultivation in keeping not only with Lareau's ethnographic study but also with Hrdy's study on pri-mates: a strategy heightened by the fact that older mothers tend to have only one child or two. Indeed, one could argue that the trend toward older moth-erhood, the ever-rising number of first births after thirty in proportion to those before thirty among college graduates,[5] is in itself responsible for the rise of the middle-class parenting strategy delineated by Lareau. The women I interviewed in Silicon Valley were applying the language of the workplace (time management, strategizing, creating opportunity) and of feminist self-realization to their children. They were intent on "fulfilling the promise of birth," to invoke Ruddick's phrase; they articulated this promise in discursive registers rooted in postindustrialism.

As in Lareau's sample, active cultivation took the form of umpteen classes in which children were to discover themselves; develop thier interests, become skilled in sports, art, music, and social interaction. At age seven, Betsy's daughter was already signed up at the San Francisco Ballet School; her son, who "had incredible feet for ballet," was involved in multiple sports; both were "incredible creative writers," and their artwork implied "wonderful creative potential." Parents of biracial children tended to see promise, even a kind of symbolic capital, in their children's multiple heritages. Fiona had "great expectations" of her son's Arabic and Irish heritage; she was intent on his learning Arabic, on his absorbing what she saw as the therapeutic nonfre-netic quality of "time" in his father's country, and on his fulfilling "his destiny" as a global citizen. Debra's daughter, American to the core, already eleven when I last met her, an assertive popular girl with a gift for accents, had a list of weekly activities that included girl scouts, theater, karate, and cotillion in addition to a private bilingual education. This was not unusual. In Debra's case, I questioned cotillion since it seemed at odds with her own persona and Debra replied that she wanted her daughter to be able to master her sur-roundings whatever the situation: tea with a hypothetical queen or the com-petitive world in which, as Debra put it, "average is not okay." One mother spoke of "molding and shaping" her son, but others rejected those words, arguing rather that they were creating opportunity for their child or allowing natural talents to flourish.

Lareau's study suggests that, from an early age, middle-class parents promote in their children reasoning and negotiation skills. This was certainly the case with my sample and arguably exaggerated by maternal age. Typically, the mothers validated their child's opinions or desires before arguing that bending a particular rule was not a good idea. Much older motherhood, though, meant that enlisting progeny in the reasoning process was a necessity. Consider Helen's case. I interviewed at great length and on several occasions Helen's son's preschool's teacher, a man of sixty named Mike, a self-described feminist and former activist, who had been an educator/administrator for thirty-five years, mostly in daycares associated with state colleges. Of one hundred children who had passed through his classroom in the past five years, he estimated that 10 to 12 percent had mothers in their late thirties or over. But both Helen and her son stood out. An exuberant child, Helen's son was nicknamed "Tigger" by this teacher because he had an air of always saying "catch me if you can." "Tigger" was a leader with his peers, husky, blond, charismatic, very articulate for his age. Helen could not catch him. Whereas the working-class parents in the daycare/preschool (attached to a state university, socioeconomically diverse and subsidized) simply picked up their children to discipline them, Helen *had* to rely on "reasoning" skills (or "cajoling" and "pleading"), however ineffective at that age. Somehow the two managed, though after a day of classes she on occasion collapsed "on the couch" in the classroom. The teacher then had to carry the child out to her truck when it was time to leave; the exuberant "Tigger" simply would not obey otherwise. The teacher had spoken to her on several occasions about the necessity of being more firm with her son—and to me he noted that older parents in general rely far more on "voice" than their younger counterparts. Once home, Helen tended to dinner and chores while her son watched nature videos and "only" educational programs, a point she emphasized.

I do not want to overplay this scenario. Aside from the discipline issue, which was of course not trivial, they had by all accounts an "affectionate" relationship, "a strong bond." We do well to remember that many children have been successfully raised by grandparents. And, in addition, my sample, albeit relatively small, clearly demonstrated to me how much "nature" conditioned "nurture." Some toddlers were the diametric opposite of Tigger; for instance, Eve, herself quiet, deliberate in her speech and motions, was graced with a toddler daughter who seemed almost preternaturally responsive to verbal cues. But I think Helen's "story" does raise important questions.

Helen's late-in-life creation of a child was read by the preschool staff as "self-ish"—though the teacher I interviewed also acknowledged that the young working-class parents (in their twenties, typically) were every bit as harried, juggling relationships, classes, jobs, rent, and children—and to boot often themselves had trouble with limits. Helen's condition of motherhood, however, seemed "unnatural"—and it was the combination of unnatural and self-ish that triggered a ripple of whispers. Critics have claimed that older motherhood is about selfishness run amuck, suggesting in some sense that it exposes feminism's ugly underbelly: it sacrifices children's interests to women's notions of self-realization. The fact that Helen would be in her seventies when Tigger was in his teens—and that she did not have other close relatives—seemed "freaky" at first. What struck Mike and his staff most was that she was "going about motherhood as if she were young"; but Mike added that he also felt "awe for her courage" and believed "there was something impressive about her selfishness if that was what it was." He himself mentioned Tony Randall et al. as male counterparts who had "after all" engaged in old parenthood with impunity.

For an older woman, a child is where self-sacrifice and self-interest most acutely meet. For Helen, Tigger was her stake in the future. She was sacrificing herself in every way possible for this child she had so assiduously created. To be sure, because he was so precious, she had trouble "setting limits"—quite apart from the fact that she physically could not. Emotionally, however, she was providing the kind of connection that the psychoanalyst William Pollock among others has argued is the sine qua non of healthy developmental and emotional growth. Whether the inability to set limits would lead to a self-entitled obstreperous adult or a thoughtful one remains to be seen. Helen had sharply curtailed her own standard of living; she ultimately stopped taking classes and temporarily became a full-time mother; she could not afford nannies in the way that many others I interviewed could. She was determined, however, to be in the "right" school district. In these ways, she reminded me of the other 'younger' single mothers who, for instance, spent $300 on theater costumes but could not fix their car's air-conditioning, or even of partnered women like Eve, who was, it seemed, putting a 30-year relationship at risk for the sake of motherhood and spending $60,000 to get the best childcare while living in cramped quarters.

A few other points can be made about parenting strategies. First, older mothers have a keen sense of the passage of time; indeed, timing had played a key role in their reproductive decisions and, simply by virtue of being older, they knew in a visceral sense how quickly five years can pass. I was struck by the degree to which they had mapped out the future of their children; typically, for instance, they carefully timed their child's entry into schools, often holding them back to give them an advantage, opting for a bilingual (Chinese or Spanish) program to prepare them for a global future, and tutoring them in math to help them face a hi-tech future. This issue of timing and of the omnipresent future seemed closely allied to a fierce advocacy of their child—whether that child was advanced or suffering from dyslexia or other learning disorders. Because they were successful professionals (or had been), they knew how to negotiate financial aid or other services, in some sense gaming the system in a positive way to help their child. They insisted on an environment conducive to their child's growth. Two mothers of girls quipped that their partners had gone "from being passive feminists to active feminists"; others were concerned that their toddler daughters not focus on appearance (as a case in point, dressing up as Cinderella was highly problematic for Eve) because they thought fixating on looks, playing into gender stereotypes, would lead to heartache (anorexia, self-hatred, shallow values) in later years. Again, I read this as a form of mapping the future, from the perspective of age and feminist advances: stacking the decks to increase the probability of future well-being. None expressed concern about having a child who might become a homosexual except insofar as this would entail additional social stress. Fiona was relieved her child was a son because she thought it would "too stressful" to straddle Muslim and Western cultures as a girl.

Sociologist Judith Stacey has studied the children of lesbian mothers (these mothers are older on average than comparable heterosexual mothers); she noted no significant well-being differences between them and children of heterosexuals, but she did observe a significant attitudinal difference. Children of lesbians are less rigid about traditional sex roles; daughters feel more entitled and sons are more nurturing. My suspicion is that in a general way this distinction—what amounts to a flattening out of traditional gender differences—may carry over in a muted sense to the children of older mothers, though at present not enough data exists to support a concrete link. In my sample, boys were watching more nature/educational videos than action ones, and were being reasoned with—and, in the case of girls, mothers seemed especially concerned about preparing their child for the future in a competitive world and about the effect of popular culture on healthy self-esteem.

One final point: when I last interviewed Debra, her daughter had just been given an assignment by her sixth grade teacher in which she was supposed to describe how her parents had met—a subject that until then had been taboo from the mother's perspective. Debra realized she had to seize the occasion to talk about how she had selected her child's biological father. She then pointed to another child in the class whose Nigerian mother and

French father had amicably parted ways almost immediately after this boy's accidental conception—but who were equally devoted to his well-being; her point was that children could come into the world, and be raised, in all kinds of contexts. At the same time, she was adamant that she did not want to present a cynical attitude about romance or marriage. The child seemed to take the conversation in stride, though she chose not to discuss 'her story' at school. Debra noted that perhaps it was a good thing that, by chance, the first wedding her daughter had attended had been that of a lesbian couple at their church.

CONCLUSION: A CONSERVATIVE ACT ACHIEVED VIA CULTURALLY DESTABILIZING MEANS

I want to conclude with two points. First, the debate about older motherhood cannot and should not be an either/or one—it is one reproductive strategy among a panoply of other strategies. One monolithic type of family no longer exists; fertility technologies are rapidly materializing alternate configurations; and, indeed, the women in my sample suggest that the family has become a highly elastic construct. Second, older motherhood is a profoundly conservative act insofar as it represents investment in the future, in children, in the family, however defined. When I asked Betsy if hers was a secular household, she promptly replied that it was and that "family" was their "core value." Older motherhood is achieved, however, via culturally destabilizing means; older motherhood destabilizes, indeed loosens, all those inequalities that have heretofore been theoretically and practically grounded in "nature" (in esssentialized sex differences such as differing reproductive life spans).

To be sure, old-old motherhood constitutes a great risk, though at the same time there is more surety of new parents, even old ones, remaining alive for another eighteen years than in any century but the last two. Interestingly, infertility clinics have tried to create loose age cutoffs, but are increasingly focusing not on 'nature' in the form of natural menopause as a limit for motherhood, but on what might be termed the exigencies of social parenthood. When two parents are involved, some clinics use a combined age of one hundred as a cutoff to ensure a reasonable likelihood that one parent will be alive when the child reaches adulthood; others increasingly focus on health indicators rather than a set chronological age.[6]

It may well be that a pressing issue in the future will be a psychological one, as Wendy Mogel has suggested in *The Blessings of a Skinned Knee*. Not only the pressures of inhabiting a competitive world but these children's "unconscious recognition of how preternaturally important they are to their parents" may cause new challenges down the road. But then, as writer Eve McMahon might point out, growing up to some degree is the process of being damaged by those who love you most (228). This returns me to my opening quote from Mona Simpson—and to an issue that trumps Mogel's: the ever-widening gap between the privileged and underprivileged; between Manhattan and the neighborhood fifteen blocks away in which Mona Simpson at thirty-six would have been a grandmother. Clearly, emerging and ever-widening differences in reproductive/parenting strategies herald ever-widening inequalities between classes in the future: between those who can engage in self-birthing and in parenting as a form of feminist self-expression and those who can only survive. In short, older motherhood seems to alleviate sex inequalities but exacerbates class ones. It is this class divide we must consider as well as whether older motherhood is in itself emotionally and indeed medically good or bad for children.

NOTES

1. For example, see the study out of UC Berkeley by Mason and Goulden, which demonstrates the existence of a large gap between men and women who achieve tenure in academia if they have become parents early in their post-PhD careers. Women who have at least one child early in their careers are 20 to 24 percent less likely to get tenure than men who have early babies. The majority of women who achieve tenure do not have children up to that point.

2. Age at first birth is strongly correlated with education. Massachusetts, with the highest concentration of degreed women, is also the state with the highest age of first birth (average age of first birth reached thirty in 1996). In California, according to data from the Department of Health Statistics, births to women over forty-five rose over 92 percent between 1980 and 1998. Since then, in the twenty-first century, births to women over thirty-five have been steadily increasing, often by 3 or 4 percent a year (from 2003 to 2004, for instance)—and births to teens and women in their early twenties steadily decreasing.

3. Census data show that single adolescent mothers are decreasing while single older mothers are increasing. All information on the SMC group comes from the Web site. See also Jane Mattes's book *Single Mothers By Choice* (New York: Random House, 1994, 1997).

4. "Helen" was adamant I not use her real name. I have in fact changed all names except that of "Betsy," the former ballet mistress, who gave permission to use hers and who is easily identifiable. I have made efforts to change a couple of identifying but insignificant markers in the case of the others in the interest of

protecting their privacy—though some narratives were in some sense so unique as to be impossible to alter.

5. See, for instance, census reports such as the *National Vital Statistics Report* 52.10 (December 2003).

6. The American Society of Reproduction Medicine, basically an oversight board, provides data, guidelines, and ethical statements concerning these trends on its Web site, www.asrm.org.

REFERENCES

Becker, Gary S. *A Treatise on the Family*. Cambridge: Harvard University Press, 1991.

Crittendon, Ann. *The Price of Motherhood*. New York: Metropolitan Books, 2001.

Derrida, Jacques. "All Ears: Nietzsche's Ontobiography." *Yale French Studies* 63 (1982): 245–250.

Franke-Ruta, Garance. "Creating a Lie: Sylvia Ann Hewlett and the Myth of the Baby Bust." *The American Prospect* 13.12 (July 1, 2002).

Gaitskill, Mary. "A Woman's Prerogative." *Mother Reader: Essential Writings on Motherhood*. Ed. Moyra Davey. New York: Seven Stories Press, 2001.

Hewlett, Sylvia Ann. *Creating a Life: Professional Women and the Quest for Children*. New York: Miramax, 2002.

Hrdy, Sarah Blaffer. *Mother Nature: Maternal Instincts and How They Shape the Human Species*. New York: Ballantine, 2000.

Lareau, Annette. "Invisible Inequality: Social Class and Childrearing in Black and White Families." *American Sociological Review* 67 (October 2002): 747–776.

———. *Unequal Childhood: Class, Race, and Family Life*. Berkeley: University of California Press, 2003.

Mason, Mary Ann, and Marc Goulden. *The ANNALS of the American Academy of Political and Social Science* 596.1 (2004): 86–103.

McMahon, Eve. "A Little Bit of Loss." *Mother Reader: Essential Writings on Motherhood*. Ed. Moyra Davey. New York: Seven Stories Press, 2001.

"Mean Age of Mother, 1970–2000." *NVSR* 51.1. 14 pp. (PHS) 2003–1120. (see CDC Web site at www.cdc.gov/nchs).

Mogel, Wendy. *The Blessings of a Skinned Knee: Using Jewish Teachings to Raise Self-Reliant Children*. New York: Penguin, 2001.

Pollock, William. *Real Boys*. New York: Holt, 1998.

Rich, Adrienne. *Of Woman Born: Motherhood as Experience and Institution*. New York: Norton, 1981.

Ruddick, Sara. *Maternal Thinking*. Boston: Beacon Press, 1989, 1995.

Simpson, Mona. "Beginning." *Mother Reader: Essential Writings on Motherhood.* Ed. Moyra Davey. New York: Seven Stories Press, 2001.

Stacey, Judith, and Timothy Biblarz. "(How) Does the Sexual Orientation of Parents Matter?" *American Sociological Review* 66 (April 2001): 159–183.

CHAPTER TWO

"No, I'm Not Catholic,
and Yes, They're All Mine"

The Narratives of Feminist Mothering
on the Tenure Track

KECIA DRIVER McBRIDE

I AM ONE OF THE LUCKY ONES: I landed a tenure-track position several years ago at a large state school, a Research I institution in the Midwest. Before classes started, this institution hosted a week of orientation activities and on the first day I met another young woman who was newly hired in the same department. At the first break, we eagerly sought each other out, sharing background stories and comparing areas of specialization.

"Did you bring anyone with you?" This was one of her first questions.

I hesitated. She had already told me she was single, and I didn't want the details of my personal life to create distance between us; in this new environment, I wanted a new friend. But what was I going to do: lie? She would find out the truth soon enough. "Actually, I brought several someones . . . ," I said, trying to sound casual.

"Cats?" she asked with a smile.

"Babies. Three. And my husband."

Her eyes went wide and, without skipping a beat, she blurted, "Damn! Are you Catholic?"

This intelligent, well-educated woman went on to become perhaps my closest girlfriend during my first three years in this job; we benefited greatly

45

from each other's counsel and professional support as we negotiated the scary pre-tenure rapids and adjusted to a small midwestern community that seemed foreign to us both for vastly different reasons. She frequently told this alpha day story and guffawed at her own bluntness, especially after she later accepted a position in the Bible Belt and found her own atheism the frequent target of well-meaning, devout folks who wanted to convert her.

For me, though, this question was an innocent, if blunt, predictor of attitudes to come, attitudes I had not anticipated. Granted, I was the first in my circle of friends to get pregnant in grad school, when I was twenty-four; however, by the time I was a thirty-year-old mother of three and had finished my PhD, many of my friends had a baby or two and it seemed somewhat "normal," (whatever that means) to try to combine a young child with an academic career. There was a supportive local community of women, all of us reading and writing and teaching while also mothering, and the simple act of getting together and sharing stories from the trenches somehow made everything a little easier. What I found in my new tenure-track position, however, was that I had more children than any of my junior colleagues at the time. That whole first year, it seemed to me that my colleagues asked, "How are the kids?" while in contrast they asked my blunt new friend, "How's your work coming?" Were their expectations for my achievement different from their expectations for hers; and, if so, was this a good thing or not? I wasn't sure.

It hadn't really occurred to me that having three children was unusual since both my husband and I come from families of three siblings, but in that first year I started to wonder if the choice to have even a medium-sized family could knock many young women off the tenure track—including, potentially, myself. I was perhaps a bit smug in my ability to manage the rigors of motherhood along with the challenges of my new job, and certainly I was wrong to think that everything would be easier in a couple of years, once my three boys were all in grade school; there were just different, less familiar problems. None of these difficulties improved when I decided two years ago to add one more baby to the mix. My timing was, as usual, crazy; I gave birth to my fourth child in the same year that I was coming up for promotion and tenure review at the college level. Shortly afterward I agreed to serve as assistant chairperson of my large and rather unwieldy department. And then I got pregnant again. But more on that in a minute.

Today, as the recently promoted and tenured mother of four children and with a fifth child on the way, I know that I am unusual, an anomaly in academia; none of my colleagues under the age of fifty currently has three children except for me. I am well aware that the number of children a woman has tends to go down statistically based on her level of education and income, and

I respect whatever choices my colleagues make, including, of course, the choice not to have children at all. I am certainly not advocating that academic women *should* have large families (although I do sometimes tease my colleagues that increasing the average family size would be one powerful way to shift the ratio of red to blue states in the next presidential election). What troubles me, however, are the ways in which the very concept of choice is limited, along with the mistaken idea that it is not possible to choose to combine a large family with a career in academia, or to even recognize that a large family is a choice.

There are many issues surrounding gender politics in the academic workplace, especially the gender politics of mothering, but they have in common one central, overwhelming concern: we (including those of us who are academic mothers and those of us who are sympathetic to their concerns) don't yet know how to balance "professional" work in academia with "personal" work as a mother. Despite all the advances we have made, despite the relative privilege and flexibility of academic life, we still must cobble together bizarre personal solutions to what really are larger social problems. We have agreed that mothers can expand the scope of their focus, that they should be able to have meaningful work outside the home while simultaneously raising their children, but this has not significantly lessened the burden of the ideological baggage of mothering. People say to me all the time, somewhat self-consciously but quite sincerely, "I really don't know how you do it" and this very statement, while it is meant as a compliment, reveals a greater truth: I must still do "it" myself because there is no sense of shared responsibility or even a shared conception, a shared possibility or imagining of how to do "it"; I must negotiate the necessary concessions alone, I must patch together the crazy combination of factors that will allow me to be both a parent and a professor. There will not be a push to find larger, communal solutions to these problems because it is my "choice" to have children, and to have so many of them, and so with that choice comes the responsibility for creative problem-solving (not to mention juggling and, often, adjusted expectations). Practically speaking, I, like all mothers, am already stretched to the limit: it is not possible to squeeze much in the way of grassroots political activism onto my calendar if I am still going to get my four to five hours of sleep each night, at least not while I have a toddler in the house. So, what is to be done?

I propose that one way to extend our conceptions about choice, to challenge the still deeply embedded paradigms of motherhood, is through the sharing of the narratives of our life experiences as mothers. In the act of telling stories, in the gracious openness of hearing them and validating them, we can shape and remake the truth of what it is to be a feminist mother, a working mother on the tenure track, a flesh and blood representation instead of an empty signifier. We already tell such stories to each other all the time. The twist comes, however, in the actual and public act of writing: on the one hand, the pressures to live up to the impossible ideals of motherhood make us wary of displaying our imperfections and revealing ourselves as imposters and poseurs; while, on the other hand, if we have time for writing at all, we are pressured to be sure it is "serious" work, the kind of writing that will be recognized and professionally rewarded.

I have interrupted the writing of this chapter, for example, a thousand times because it is easy to convince myself of the pressing importance of other projects: that academic essay that is necessary for my annual review, the report that my chair has requested, the class lecture for tomorrow that must be prepared, the stack of essays gathering dust on the corner of my desk—not to mention the dirty house, the piles of laundry, the million domestic chores, the children who need their suppers and baths, the teething toddler pulling at my sleeve. How can I prioritize writing this chapter at the expense of pumping up my files for promotion, or at the expense of actually caring for my children? Philosophical speculation about feminist mothering and a call for political action are both abstract and expensive when one must weigh them against the immediate benefits of the security of tenure and the full tummies and clean faces of one's offspring. Even as I write (longhand on a yellow legal pad because one of my sons is using the computer for a school project), my twenty-month-old daughter sits next to me, drawing endless circles (her favorite shape) in the margins of the page, asserting her presence again and again. I know that I am on borrowed time, and if I am able to finish this chapter at all it will be because I have compromised more than one precious commodity this week (gone without sleep, missed someone's basketball game or piano lesson, skipped the deadline for that book review, rushed through tomorrow's class prep) and settled also for the fact that I will never get the wording quite right, will never fully be able to articulate what is so clear to me in my own lived experience.

Although we should know better, we need sometimes to be reminded of the basics: that parenting is unpaid domestic labor, that it is vital for the continuation of our culture, that under capitalism it is unrewarded and marginalized and yet strapped down with the weightiest of ideological burdens. We treat parenting as though it is an individual choice for which we must find complicated, individual solutions when the inevitable problems arise. It is in practice much more than a choice, whatever your position on abortion or working mothers or the gendered division of labor. My expectations for my colleagues are complex: I would like some recognition of the difficulties inherent in combining parenting and academic work, some help in negotiating solutions, but I also don't want to advocate for lowered expectations for working parents that could result in a two-tiered system. We should be working together, as feminist mothers, as scholars, as responsible citizens, to reconceptualize the ways in which we value and define mothering: for ourselves and our partners, for our colleagues and friends, for our daughters and sons. One place to begin to understand the concept of mothering is through the construction and sharing of narratives about it: what are the lived experiences of women who are combining parenting and professorship?

As I said before, I am one of the lucky ones. My colleagues are for the most part supportive; I have managed to stay stubbornly on the tenure track, and have not experienced some of the worst forms of legal discrimination that are out there. At my institution there is even occasional tongue-clucking and head-shaking over the problems that working parents face, and the general feeling is that we should know better, that we should take better care of our working parents (if only to increase our retention rate!). And yet, like many other university systems, there has not been much real change here in the past twenty years: no maternity leave (except for the unpaid leave guaranteed under the FMLA), no support for childcare (and little in the way of adequate childcare in the area), not even coverage through our health insurance for birth control pills or maternity vitamins (although we do have coverage for Viagra and vasectomies). Negotiating campus with a stroller is a challenge, and one would search in vain for a reasonable place to change a diaper, should the need arise. One of our major selling points when we invite new candidates to campus is that this community is a great place to raise a family; local realtors wax eloquent on the low cost of housing, the smalltown values, the abundant green space, and the farmer's market. However, if one actually gets the job, moves the family, and tries to put down roots, one must straddle the divide of town and gown in ways that one's childless colleagues could not anticipate.

To suggest that the combination of work and mothering is difficult is hardly a new idea. However, in the past few months I have come to believe that it is crucial for us to privilege the discourse of and about mothering—for us to stop shoving it aside into the leftover corners and gaps in our lives, the stolen moments and private conversations, and instead haul it unapologetically into the public center. This is real work that deserves real time and focus, serious intellectual engagement, and our undivided attention. Piecing together the crazy scraps of our lived experiences as feminist mothers is a strategy for survival: the telling of these narratives lightens the burden because it is now shared with our fellow travelers, and because the act of

telling gives us some modicum of control (albeit after the fact). We are examples as well to our students and to our own children; what they don't see us
doing they are less likely to envision as possible. I often have bright young
female students come to me for advice about how to manage family and an
academic career and rarely can they imagine the steps by which one chooses
to combine the two. This is a story they need to hear. We can, then, provide
an intervention in the limiting stereotypes surrounding motherhood; beyond
our own personal growth, spinning out these narratives of feminist mothering
expands our conception as a culture of what is possible, and stretches the
limits of what our sisters and daughters can imagine.

And so what sorts of stories should we tell? Honest ones, vignettes of
the crazy and illogical ways in which working mothers are marginalized. For
example: when I fill out my annual reports for promotion and tenure, I am
supposed to erase any evidence that I have carried and am nurturing many
children. Fact: a single, childless colleague who goes to the local elementary
school once a year to help with a literacy program by reading books in the
library is praised for her community outreach, but the information that I
have read to at least one of my own children almost every night for the past
fourteen years means nothing; if I were to include such a "personal" detail on
my vita, the committee would strike it immediately. A colleague who gives a
one-hour presentation at the community center on self-esteem in adolescents gets a line on her vita, but I am not supposed to mention the fact that
I struggle daily with the unfamiliar terrain that my oldest son travels, or that
I will guide four other children completely through the stormy teen years.
Even more strangely, on my own vita I was encouraged to list a community
program I participated in one fall where we offered information to new
mothers before they left the hospital about various subjects: nutrition,
breast-feeding, immunizations, infant CPR, newborn development, colic.
Those who volunteered their time had a one-hour orientation session but
did not themselves sift through all this information—they merely presented
a set of community resources that were available. The fact that I dropped off
a few pamphlets and spent a scant dozen minutes in a stranger's hospital
room was for some reason worthy of recognition from my peers; the fact that
I myself spent countless hours reading and educating myself on these same
subjects and then actually *applying* this knowledge to the care of my own
children is absolutely invisible on the same document. The reasoning is that
when we reach beyond ourselves into the community we are satisfying one of
the "circles of service," that we are being generous with our time and expertise and establishing important ties to the community, which is perceived to
be something outside of and separate from our selves; however, this reveals

once again the illogical split we make between our public and private lives, the strange blurring of lines such that my own children are not considered beyond my self. The simple fact is: the commitment that I have made to raising my children—to nurturing their intellectual curiosity, improving their schools, providing them with the basic necessities of life, and shaping their sense of communal responsibility—doesn't count because we still do not as a society value unpaid domestic labor.

A second type of narrative we need to tell is based in humor, and in loving acceptance of our limitations as both mothers and workers. Part of the problem is the pressure we put on ourselves, the burden of the supermom image that we know logically we should reject but that still haunts most mothers; it's a version of the type of naïve, liberal feminism that dominated the 1970s, when women found strong female role models so important that they suppressed a range of female experiences in pursuit of a limited representation. If I see another mom struggling in a film, for example, I often wince and think: don't make us look weak—stop whining. I might feel empathy, but also impatience, and maybe even embarrassment. My third son was born in September; I had defended my dissertation in August and accepted a postdoctoral teaching fellowship where I taught four classes. After I had him (with a midwife and no drugs, a political decision that I was somewhat evangelical about at the time) I missed two days and then was back at work for the rest of the semester. My partner, who worked opposite hours to mine, would drive down once a day with the newborn and his two brothers in the car, and I would run out to the parking lot to breast-feed between classes. I was exhausted all the time, but felt so lucky that we were able to juggle the babies without having to put them into childcare that it didn't occur to me until a few years later that what I was doing was extreme. I felt like we were getting away with something, cheating the system somehow, because I was able to function as an academic and manage three little ones under the age of five who weren't in group care.

In those early days of motherhood, I reasoned that, with so many highly qualified candidates out of work or underemployed, how could I justify squandering my own chances by having a bunch of kids? No one was making special allowances for me, I thought with pride; I was pulling my weight, working late hours after the kids were in bed, even finding time to send out a zillion job applications for one of those precious tenure-track positions. It was important for me to feel as though my performance in every way measured up, that on the surface all the pieces of my life fit together into a coherent whole. Shamefully, sometimes even now when another parent is complaining I have to stifle my initial impulses toward the kind of clichés one hears in sports-themed films: suck it up. It's hard for all of us. You can't let them see you sweat. It's hard to reach out for support and at the same time maintain the illusion of strength and independence that our culture values above all else. But I have come to believe there is real healing in admitting the gaps that exist in the jigsaw puzzle of my daily life. For me, the experience of recounting through humor the surreal piling up of the ridiculous has been liberating because it is the accumulation of petty annoyances that is so hard to bear.

I handle the big catastrophes pretty well. Once last spring, we had an infestation of about one thousand yellow jackets in our family room; the ceiling was humming with them, and then they bored a hole and started popping through one by one until the windows were covered. One of my children was stung, and I transformed into Ripley from the second *Alien* film, fearlessly crushing anything in my path that might potentially threaten my offspring into a wet yellow smear. It wasn't fun, but I handled it. In the event of emergency—if someone cracks his head open causing copious bleeding, or falls out of a tree and breaks a kneecap, or rips the orthodontic appliance cemented onto his bottom teeth out of his mouth, or breaks his front tooth completely off on the water slide at the pool, or if the sump pump catches on fire one night and fills the house with smoke until it is thrown out in the snow, or the bottom of the water heater rusts out while we are out of town and floods the downstairs (and, yes, all of these things and more happened in my very first year on the tenure track)—then I'm calm, cool, and collected.

But there are mornings when I think I will lose my mind because of the sheer cumulative force of all of the little problems piling up. Mornings in early September when somebody's shoelace snaps in half just as we are walking out the door to school, with no extra shoelaces in the house and no time to spare, and then as I am desperately trying to tie a very tiny bow with the fragments of lace, the owner of the shoe informs me that this is Picture Day and I realize that the kids are all in scrub clothes and I have to find a new checkbook because there are three separate checks to write and envelopes to locate, and so we are probably going to be late to school. I will of course need to staple each of the envelopes with the checks to a form, which is no problem because we have at least fifteen staplers in the house; unfortunately, however, I remember that none of the staplers has the correct size staples and therefore none of them works. And then when I finally manage to herd all the kids out to the car, the buckle on the baby's carseat, the one that worked yesterday, has suddenly stopped working. So I have to drive with all of my children (the youngest one gleefully lifting the broken bar over her head, tempting the gods of safety and traffic, so that her brother must sit beside her and forcefully hold it down) off to the twenty-four-hour superstore to get another carseat before the day can even get started, because of course you can't go anywhere without a carseat, and so we are definitely, definitely going to be late to school. Halfway there, I realize with a jolt (after spilling a drop of coffee and looking down at my lap) that I am wearing white pants and purple panties (although the kids are now sporting color-coordinated, portrait-appropriate outfits, assuming they arrive at school before the photographer leaves for the day). We are so late that it is out of the question to go home and change. In fact, being late or almost-late is a chronic problem for me, a constant battle and source of stress; one of my son's teachers suggested to me at Parents' Night one year in reference to my inability to be on time that I "might have bitten off more than I could chew," and I felt such a rush of anger and frustration (because, I reasoned, she was obviously correct) that I had to leave the room to avoid a scene.

So on this morning in early September, I finally drop off all three of the tardy older kids at school, and the baby at the sitter's house, and I take my lukewarm coffee and scuttle quickly into my office and sit biting back tears because the baby was sobbing when I left her, her round cheeks streaked with tears and syrup. I wince at the appointments on my agenda for the day, the list of people with problems they want me to fix because that is the nature of the assistant chairperson's work. It occurs to me often that the work of a parent and of an academic administrator is similar, and I sometimes find myself using the stern mother voice with recalcitrant or petulant students, even fantasize about doing the same with pouting or selfish colleagues. Then my 8:30 appointment plops down in the chair in my office and starts to whine about how hard it is to come back to teach his two courses after summer break (break? summer?), and I want to throw the stapler from my desk at this person's head but I don't because this is the only stapler I can locate that actually contains the right size staples.

The individual details here are petty things, minor annoyances, and yet my life is cluttered by them in ways that this complaining colleague (who is, after all, a nice enough guy) would not understand. More significant, though, is the fact that I can't express this frustration, at least not in the moment. I pretend to keep everything together, that I can somehow weave a makeshift shoelace out of the unmown grass, build a carseat out of leftover plastic toys in the garage, lash the baby in with a jumprope, and still show up for my administrative position with nary a visible pantyline. I chose this life, so I must prove it's possible, doable, mustn't I? If I admit to sloppiness, aren't I weakening the case for other women who want to combine a career with parenting a family?

The key to my endurance here? I am blessed with a sister in feminist mothering, the woman I can e-mail later in the day and spin a narrative about how ridiculous it all is. She will laugh at the excessiveness, but also offer sympathy. And she will not judge my weaknesses because she is a mother herself. This is not an essentialist connection, but one born out of experience, which is much more powerful. The *telling* of the story of my crazy day (to my understanding partner, to my feminist sister, and ultimately here) makes the day bearable, even though in the moment it was almost more than I could stand. Even imagining the sympathetic ear and the act of changing my travails into something entertaining makes the morning's events controllable *after* the fact, although they most certainly were not at the time. I can reassert myself, poke fun at my bad luck and lack of organization, and yet frame it in such a way that it is contained, organized, limited, and in the end I have survived another day.

Finally, many of the bigger hurdles that we face as feminist mothers are of a different kind: the seductive narratives that position the working mother as somehow lacking an essential component of motherness. And so the third kind of narrative I would like to advocate is a deconstruction of these myths, which are so pervasive that we often unconsciously absorb them, respond to them, without even realizing it. One such dangerous narrative is this whole business of "firsts": not only the experience of first becoming a new mother, but specifically the first step, first word, first smile. Parents often construct such stories together (and of course revise and embellish them) over time. Sometimes there is a dramatic first moment, or at least the tale of one, but the vast majority of time, babies, just like big people, don't move ahead developmentally in huge, quantifiable leaps. A mother first feels the baby move inside her when she is pregnant, but she isn't sure, and then a few days or weeks later the baby moves differently and the mother is positive. However, the first move isn't really a first because the baby has been moving in there all along, well before the mother feels it. So if there is a story about when a mother is first sure, or when a partner first feels the baby from the outside, that is beautiful and sweet and something to remember. But this emphasis on marking the date in the baby book or on her calendar is a fabrication. What it really means is: this is when I was sure, this is when I felt confident narrating my experience of her development, this is when I paused to note the passing of a milestone.

My daughter, like all of my children, started walking early, around nine months. She would take a step here or there, between the couch and the coffee table, without realizing she was doing it. She was capable of walking, she *was* in fact walking, but I didn't tell people for awhile because she wasn't doing so consistently and purposefully, and what she was doing didn't look like those diaper/lotion/long-distance service/life insurance commercials on television in which you experience a performance of "baby's first steps" and the baby toddles sweetly across the room to collapse in mommy's arms. As an experienced mom, I have learned that the real consequence of early walking is merely that there is a bigger mess, or a quicker mess, or a mess that is a little bit taller than it was a month ago—there are, sadly, no cognitive or muscular advantages, although there will be many opportunities to gaze adoringly at those chubby little feet scuttling across the hardwood floor. The larger cultural purpose of the myth of the firsts is to make us attentive, but also to make us feel guilty about every moment we are away, and it is a powerful form of manipulation. Especially in the first two years, babies are constantly doing new things; a stay-at-home mother might just as well miss the first steps or a new word because she is at the grocery store and has left the baby with the father for an hour or because she is in a board meeting most of the morning.

I have a beautiful memory of the first time my oldest son smiled at me in such a huge way that I knew absolutely that he was experiencing joy just because I was in his line of vision; it was an intense moment and it made me cry, even though in the back of my head I couldn't quite block out echoes of Lacan, of Kristeva, of the semiotic, preverbal, baby state. I own that narrative, and I remember every detail about where I was and what it felt like. It wasn't, however, technically his first smile (which probably happened when he was playing with his face muscles in utero and so, even though I was there, I didn't see it). My narrative of his first real smile satisfies a need in me: to slow down time, to mark the moment, to remember a point when I gave him absolute joy just through my presence. It is a way to weave myself into the narrative of his existence and his healthy development—and, further, I can tell this story because I was there, as a mother "should" be, to receive this smile. It is really part of the narrative of my becoming a mother, my moving into his line of vision even while I occupied the position of proud guardian of this tiny squirming infant.

During those early months of his life, the scholar in me battled with the mother. Having been schooled as a good feminist, I believed that environment determined most everything, that gender was semiotics, that parenting was not just women's work. I struggled, then, to sort through the strange sensations of otherness during pregnancy, the intensity of birth, the absolute immersion of breast-feeding when the white ink of the French feminists whom I had been so dismissive of seemed suddenly to take on new meaning. How did I make sense of the fact that I felt this baby in my body, in my bones and my blood, that I felt a physical ache when he was away from me for too long? Before he was born, I vowed that nothing would change, that my life wouldn't be limited in the least; after he arrived, I found myself cut off from freedoms that I had never before realized I had, and most of the time I didn't even mind.

This was the beginning of the schizophrenia: one day I found myself so desperate to get out of the house alone that I lingered as long as I possibly could at the grocery store, touching the canned goods, leafing through the magazine rack, breathing deeply of the fresh produce, sighing at the crisply dressed women around me with flat stomachs. Another day, I spent the entire morning lost in watching my new son flat on his back, kicking his legs and staring at his mobile. When he was safely with someone else for awhile and I could study, I would hurry to the library and lose myself in the stacks, completely forgetting for whole hours at a time that I was a mother. And yet I also spent hours turning over every second of the birth experience in my mind; to this day the moments when my children were born are the most intense and powerful of my life. In those early days of motherhood, I often struggled all afternoon to read a single article for a grad seminar with a squirmy baby in my arms, patting and bouncing and resorting finally to the baby carrier, pacing around the house with the baby strapped to my chest and the article stuck out in front of me at arm's length; but when he collapsed in sleep that night, drunk from breast milk, and I could finally work, I couldn't bear to put him down and be away from him, and so I would let him sleep on my chest, his sweet heavy breath rustling across the pages as I read.

We have lots of stories about those few isolated moments of firsts but not as many about the countless messy hours of childrearing that are undifferentiated, the blurry late night feedings and early morning risings, the endless meals and snacks and diaper changes and baths, the days and days of ugly, boring mess and plastic clutter and terrycloth cotton chaos. The development of our children, like our development as mothers, is not a linear progression—the first year is cyclical, which is great preparation for all the years to come. It's a series of widening arcs, or spirals that move forward, but it is much less tidy than any child development book would have you believe, and it will be that way for (how old I am now?) at least thirty-eight years.

The final type of narrative I think we should tell each other is one of fantasy, of the spectacular possibilities that might exist for the future if we were to allow ourselves to imagine them. To assist with retention and boost morale for working parents, I have a vision that my university establishes a childcare center right in my building, with drop-in care available from hired professionals but also from students, who could work part-time by walking in after their classes. Parents could sign up for co-op hours to work off part of their bills. There would be an area for nursing mothers, parents could eat lunch with their kids, and after school the older siblings could come and help with homework and supervise games (football on the green area in front of the library, or chasing squirrels in the Old Quad). If the writing center tutors were not busy, they could set up Scrabble with the older kids, and our Shakespearean expert could mount elaborate children's theater productions in his downtime. Our colleagues with expertise in art, creative writing, music, and sports could share their interests, and the kids could take field trips to the library, the art museum, the duck pond, the bowling alley, the botanical gardens, the solarium, the gym, and the indoor swimming pool. Parents could work harder and be less distracted because their kids would be nearby and well supervised. If people misbehaved in department meetings or shirked their advising responsibilities, they would be assigned diaper duty or set to scraping the mashed peas and squashed bananas off the high chairs. If people got stressed they could be assigned play therapy and could squeeze play dough or bite the heads off gummy bears or run relay races or play crab ball, or maybe just sit and rock the babies to slow down their heart rates. Art projects could be completed with the mounds of one-sided papers we discard on a daily basis. Our productivity would increase tenfold. Parents of young children would never leave our university, and the news would spread like wildfire at MLA: have you heard about this school in the midwest?

Here and now, in my seventh year as a professor and my sixth month of this fifth pregnancy, I reflect on the experience of feminist mothering thus far. Did my decision to have multiple children affect my productivity as a scholar? Maybe. There are times when I am envious of colleagues with quiet studies and neat stacks of paper, who spend uninterrupted hours researching in the archives or weeks in Oxford gathering information, who could wake up on Saturday morning and stay all weekend at the computer if they wanted, sipping tea and gazing out the window thoughtfully between paragraphs. At least that is how I imagine such a life. But on some level I realize that this, too, is a fantasy narrative, and doesn't represent reality for most of us, or at least not for more than brief periods of time. I could tell myself that I would have been a more prolific scholar if I was childless, but the truth is that my children have a way of forcing me to get my priorities in order. I went up for tenure review with a respectable list of publications to my credit, a reputation as a tough but challenging teacher, a strong record of professional service, *and* four children, including a newborn baby daughter—invisible on my vita, but having richly enhanced my pre-tenure life. I may not be setting the entire academic world on fire with my brilliance, but my performance at this point is solid and my vita is well balanced. I am no slacker, barely squeaking by or trying to pad my credentials; just like in my pre-baby grad school days, I want to be the go-to girl, and I don't play the mommy card when I'm having an unproductive time or am stuck with writer's block. Most of the time, I accept that I am not necessarily busier than my colleagues, but rather busy in different ways.

Theoretically, I have the best of both worlds: I recognize and appreciate the relative flexibility and privilege that I have as an academic and a parent, freedoms that simply would not be available if I were working the third shift at a factory or tied to a desk for forty hours a week. I have a rewarding and challenging career in which I am able to contribute in a positive way to the community and to the future and still participate actively in my children's daily lives.

In practice, however, I am often overwhelmed and frustrated, and I have felt like an imposter in both my professional and my personal lives. In practice, I am sometimes lonely, and I am lacking not only role models but peers who aspire to a similar precarious balance. It seems to me that the real challenge of feminist mothering is not choosing toys and books that are nongender specific or talking to my sons about the problematic representations of women on MTV; the real challenge is to model a mothering style that is fully engaged and confident, both "at work" and "at home" (a crazy distinction in and of itself), with my colleagues at the university and with the other moms on the playground after school. I used to be primarily focused on my sons: their perceptions of women and their ability to admire and respect them, their resistance to negative media depictions and to conventional gendered stereotypes. Since I have given birth to my daughter, however, I am reminded of how very hard it is to struggle through those first few months of a newborn's life. I know she will be watching me for answers, but what has become most clear to me is how important it is to reach beyond my own children, to have conversations with other adults (whether or not they have children themselves) about what parenting is: the functions it serves in our culture, the responsibilities that communities assume in relation to the children, the ways in which we make and remake the images of mothers.

Even as I sit writing this, the baby girl keeps toddling in, tugging on my sleeve, climbing in my lap. My partner can only chase her out so many times before she loses her patience and starts to wail. Right now she doesn't care much for my thoughts on feminist mothering. What she wants is for me to build blocks or color or read to her, to focus my attention on her in the way that only a parent or someone newly in love can.

Even as I write this, I know it is not the kind of piece that will necessarily help my reputation as a scholar, that some colleagues would read it and roll their eyes, that in certain contexts it might in fact even hurt me professionally. Perhaps, I think, I shouldn't be wasting my time on it instead of a hard critical piece, especially if I am going to have to sacrifice family time to write it.

Even as I write this, I am at a crossroads in my career. I have the security of tenure, which signifies at some level the confidence of my peers, and I am beginning a new stage of my career in which I am expected to mentor by example, to step up and take more of a leadership role in my department and my college. If I can't make time to focus on the experience of feminist mothering now, then when will I ever?

At the grocery store one day late last fall semester, I was trundling a towering cart of groceries, my pregnant belly, and all four children toward the checkout lane when I ran into a former student and we exchanged vague pleasantries. As we worked our way through parallel checkout lanes, I noticed she kept watching me out of the corner of her eye as I wrestled with children and milk jugs and laundry detergent and yogurt cups. At the door, as I plopped my daughter on the horse for a penny ride, the student stopped beside me on her way out.

"Are all these kids yours?" she asked. I laughed and admitted they were, and she let out a low whistle. "I had no idea."

It turns out she had recently sent off applications to graduate school, but two weeks later found out she was pregnant. Her husband was ecstatic, but she wasn't so sure.

It turns out that she had a million questions. I told her to come by my office and we would have a nice long chat.

It turns out that, for me, part of the circle of service, even if these particular arcs remain invisible to the untrained eye, is going to be sharing stories about feminist mothering on the tenure track.

CHAPTER THREE

Feminism, Motherhood, and Possibilities in the Writing of Bronwen Wallace

SHELLEY MARTIN

BRONWEN WALLACE'S WRITING represents the fluidity of many of the roles she encompassed during her life: creative writer, newspaper columnist, counselor, teacher, feminist activist, and mother. The stories she discovered in these roles are an integral part of her writing whether the genre is poetry, fiction, or nonfiction. In particular, her identifications with motherhood and feminism motivate and guide the stories she tells. Writing about motherhood is a feminist political statement because not only was she doing it while raising a son as a single mother, she was using it to convey the complex realities of women's maternal experiences—the conflicts and stresses as well as the pleasures. The honesty of her accounts is a refusal of the idealized maternal portraits found in much traditional literature. Instead she depicts the material and emotional realities of uncertainty and violence faced by so many mothers, including herself. Her mothers are at times powerful and powerless, glorious and imperfect, resistant and submissive, but because she writes about them, they are not silenced or ignored. Her writing presents a belief that the inequalities women face are, in large part, results of the ways in which women, especially mothers, are not valued for who they are or what they do. Wallace chooses to tell some of their stories, and her own, to show both their dignity and despair. The goal of doing so is to effect political change by revising the social and cultural attitudes that devalue both the stories and the women who live them. To accomplish this, she writes of women not only in terms of the momentous themes of life like birth and death, but the everyday

61

experiences like raising children and laughing, crying, protesting, and creating with other women.

In order to fully explore how feminism and motherhood inform Wallace's writing, this chapter will explore the intersections of her expressed political beliefs, her writing, and her life, as it is represented in her work. While I acknowledge the perils of applying biographical significance to an author's creative pieces, it is both appropriate and necessary to include elements of Wallace's life in a discussion of her work. Her nonfiction writing offers autobiographical insight, and she is honest about how much of her own life is present in her fiction and poetry. Since she did not write with a distinct line between her creative and her critical work, this analysis will similarly consider the crossovers, with a focus on her poetry and nonfiction, her most prominent genres.

Analyzing Bronwen Wallace's writing in this way, with the connection of issues of motherhood to feminism, is more than a feminist reading of a woman's texts. Wallace insistently labeled herself a feminist in numerous contexts. One example of how she claims feminism for herself is found in an article she wrote on the effects of pornography on women: "I see myself as a feminist writer whose job it is to explore what our culture has previously silenced. For 2,000 years women's stories have not been heard" (1992: 72). She clings to the possibilities of a feminist movement for improving women's lives, though she is also cautious of how it might get too comfortable with itself and become too elitist, thus reproducing some of the exclusionary practices of patriarchy. During a keynote speech for International Women's Day in 1989, Wallace spoke of feminism—of what it gives women and what it needs to give them:

> It seems to me that feminism, as a political force in this culture, is one of the main agents for social change at this time, specifically because it connects the individual and the collective, the private and the political. And, for me, it's important to emphasize both. Individual change is, for me, only one aspect of the process because change for individuals always takes place in a social context. It takes place because of social context. For me that means a commitment to change that recognizes how the politics of class and race affect feminism. How does it shape the questions we ask, the demands we make? If we look at abortion, for example, we can see that by seeing it simply as a matter of "reproductive choice" we are phrasing the question in white, middle-class terms. There are many women for whom choice is impossible, even under very liberal

legislation, because of their poverty and because of their color. Often, the agenda of feminism in this country is still a very middle-class one. (1992: 224–225)

Wallace's focus on the material, emotional, and physical realities of women's lives is, then, tied into her concept of a feminism that considers all women and children regardless of color or race. Her approach to feminism and to her writing centers on diversity, as fellow poet Glen Downie, writing of *Arguments with the World*, a collection of Wallace's nonfiction, describes her "resistance to élitism of all sorts. She remained always a believer in common magic (as one of her poetry titles has it), and in common sense and common speech (as her newspaper columns illustrate). Beyond her death, her writing continues as a force in the common cause" (147). With a feminism that takes such commonalities into consideration and resists exclusivity, she suggests, social changes occur that will give women more choice over the circumstances of their lives.

Her feminism is not easily containable within our existing notions of what feminism has meant and what it continues to mean. Many of her ideas fall in line with those of Second Wave feminism, with its "exten[sion] of the terms 'politics' and 'the economy' to sexuality, the body and emotions, and other areas of social life previously treated as 'personal' only, and the household" and the creation of new political organizations: small antihierarchical consciousness-raising groups" (Humm 251–252). The most effective consciousness-raising groups Wallace presents are often those made up of mothers, or those who understand the value of the maternal in our society. Though we can roughly place Wallace within the Second Wave along a feminist timeline, she also recognizes and embraces the ways in which feminism was evolving. As previously noted, she recurrently articulated ideas about the need for diversity in feminism, an idea that moves her toward what many would label as Third Wave.

Even more complexity is involved in trying to classify what "brand" of feminism Wallace fits into. Her interest in the economic and social conditions of women's lives, for instance, allies her somewhat with materialist feminism and concentrates on how those material conditions result from sociocultural attitudes toward women. She differs, however, in the strategy she takes to change those conditions. Instead of pushing for the women's material realities to be modified in order to change the attitudes that devalue women, she looks to changing the attitudes. If women are more valued, she argues, then the social, economic, and political institutions that disempower them will be changed, thus improving their conditions.

To that end, Wallace describes her disillusionment with partisan politics.
In an article titled "The Politics of Everyday," she says:

> if I look at politics as meaning only what happens every few years in the
> polling booth, then my power is very limited indeed. . . . The politics
> that matter to me are what I call "the politics of everyday." By this I
> mean, basically, that politics involve every aspect of our "ordinary" lives,
> from the food we eat to the choices we make about education or jobs.
> (1992: 38–39)

She goes on to state how political change often happens beyond the "lobbies
and demonstrations," in the conversations occurring in "kitchens and offices
and classrooms and playgrounds and coffee-shops or wherever 'ordinary'
people get together to discuss their 'ordinary' lives" (40). In Wallace's writing,
mothers are a central part of those conversations.

Though she offers the collective images of these mothers developing
themselves in communal dialogues, and places tremendous value on these
female communities, she does so in such a way that their individuality is not
diluted or discounted. Wallace's usual approach, moreover, particularly in her
creative work, is to emphasize the individual women first and then contextu-
alize their place within a collective. She uses the same strategy when depicting herself, as a writer, a feminist, a woman, and a mother. Her sense of these
selves, constituted by her personal past and present, is perhaps at its most
vivid in her poetry, a poignancy that is then expanded in her nonfiction meditations on her position within society.

Furthermore, it is Wallace's explorations of her experiences as a mother
that ground that view of her self in relation to society. Following her divorce,
Wallace raised her son, Jeremy, as a single mother. Her experiences with and
feelings for Jeremy are a frequent presence in her poems. Wallace delves into
the ways in which being his mother affects her as a person and compels her to
seek social and political change. She says in "Fast Cars," for instance:

> I know it was late
> when we reached our own children,
> all of them eager
> to head off into whatever we fear
> will take them furthest from us
> Booze or secrets. Sex. Fast cars.
> How these things worry us, even as we know
> that theirs may be the last generation of kids on earth. (1987: 19–20)

Her poetic motherhood is frequently reflective of uncertainty, of being unsure of how best to parent Jeremy as an individual and a member of a society whose future is threatened by political and social uncertainty. As in the quote, she moves from what may happen between her and her son, to what may happen to him in relation to the rest of the world. In this context of the 1980s that world is at risk of destruction caused by cataclysmic events like nuclear war. It is a fear she revisits in other poems, like the stanza in "Daily News" that reads, "Meanwhile my son says he gets scared sometimes/ on the way home from school/ that they'll drop a bomb/ before he makes it. The worst part though/ is how his voice is/ when he tells me this. How he doesn't ask/ what he can do about it" (1985: 36). Realizing that her own fears of the future are present in her son, but in an even more resigned way, gives her a resolve to afford him a future that he does not believe he will have. She depicts how looking at her son and seeing such a young child already learning not to hope illustrates how much improvement is needed for the world and the human relations that participate in it.

It is the sense of uncertainty in herself, her son, and the world that results in a sort of sublime performance of motherhood in Wallace. Motherhood is presented as compelling—even though it is sometimes alienating because of the isolated place mothers are often put in by society. Even the feelings of alienation are frequently in conflict with the fears she has when her son is pushing away from her, growing in his independence. Wallace characterizes the conflict she feels between her commitment to being a mother and the tremendous stress it lays on her.

The resulting sublimity, the beauty and terror, comfort and doubt of motherhood are tied to the social constructions of it, with certainty not being attainable in a society that devalues mothers and can draw sons toward that belief. Wallace writes of the anxiety of raising a son in a patriarchal culture that may consume him, despite her efforts to prevent it. In "Shaping a Young Male Mind," one of her *Kingston Whig Herald* columns, she wrestles with this anxiety:

> Every parent knows, of course, that there is only so much you can do. After that you have to trust that you have done a good job. But for women like myself, who are the mothers of sons, this trust is a little harder to come by. Beyond the influence of our home, my son feels the enormous pressure of a culture which has a lot invested in the continuation of traditional male role, a culture which offers enormous power and privilege to those who accept that limited idea of what it means to be a man. (1992: 128–129)

Her anxiety is given a cultural context, and reflects many of the feminist concerns about the construction of gender, of the gifts and potential losses mothers face. In a review of *Common Magic*, Margaret Atwood aptly captures the complexity of Wallace's literary portrayal of motherhood, saying "there's grace after loss, many-dimensioned motherhood, and, in conclusion, a beautiful poem on hands, with which we do a great many unpleasant things, but which are also 'what we have instead of wings, / the closest we come to flight.'" (122). Her motherhood depicts the sense of loss and wariness that goes along with it, but maintains the dignity of the mothers going through it.

Nevertheless, this dignity cannot eradicate the uncertainties of motherhood that, for Wallace, are negotiations of the experiences of everyday and the trajectories of life: hers, Jeremy's, and theirs together. This sense of trajectories, of the future and the past, is continually brought up, as in "Joseph Macleod Daffodils," when the planting of lilies of the valley leads her to "thinking *when Jeremy/ is old enough to drive, I'll have to divide these,/ put some under the cedars there; by the time/ he leaves home, they'll be thick as grass*" (1987: 31). What these lines demonstrate is how Wallace privileges the commonplace events like gardening and thinking about her son's future over the philosophical questions of gender. She articulates as much in one her letters to Erin Mouré, published in *Two Women Talking: Correspondence 1985–87*, when she says, in reference to problems of domestic violence, "what seems to me to have to happen . . . is that we begin with what the women themselves are saying and develop our ideas from there, rather than with some political theory about what should happen" (26).

When Wallace speaks beyond her self, of other mother's lives and their endurance of uncertainty, she remains focused on the women's individuality in order to value them as they are and for what they say. While making claims of some of the material and emotional commonalities of women's lives, she is careful not to displace the significance of their selfhoods by simply using them as generalizations for particular purposes. An example of this approach is in one of her columns, "Women's Week 'With Courage and Vision'," in which she addresses the historic erasure of women's voices:

> I turn on the TV and watch "The Cosby Show" or "Family Ties." I let myself believe that the "real family" is like that. Certainly, there is no evidence to the contrary. The battered wife does not get to tell her story. Nor does the incest victim. The single mother on welfare is not heard from. Nor do we want to listen to the lesbian mother whose children have been taken from her because she does not fit our notion of a "normal mom." (1992: 111)

While there are many single mothers, lesbian mothers, incest survivors, and battered wives, she refers to their possessions of individual stories even when giving such broad examples. As scholar Donna Bennett indicates in an analysis of "Isolated Incidents," for Wallace "reality may open us up to the general, but the reality resides in the particular, a particular that is here borne by the reader, who has been located, by the voice of the poem, within the experience itself" (64). For Wallace, particular reality is established within the individual and that reality makes a statement that each woman described has her own meaningful story. Bennett's comment makes the connection with how these beliefs in Wallace's poetry not only bring the subject to the reader but make the reader part of the subject's experience.

This triple engagement in Wallace's work of female subject, poet, and reader functions as a challenge to the cultural silencing of women, especially mothers and the resulting feelings of singular isolation they often endure while doing the marginalized labor of raising their children. She sees that the potential for reversing this isolation and uncertainty is in the connections between mothers, in the small communities they create by talking and listening to each other, instead of situations where they are spoken of or to. In, essentially, getting together to tell each other's stories, Wallace sees the beginnings of change—a move from beyond the insecure place of being relegated to the fringe of society because of their maternal circumstances to being empowered voices shaping society.

Wallace illustrates her point by relating her own memories of new motherhood and the salvation she found in "The Power of a Group of Mothers Getting Together 'Just to Talk.'" She first describes some of what she was feeling:

> Weeks rushed together in a blur of alarm clocks, meals, day care, type-writers, errands, trips to the park, bills, groceries, and laundry, laundry, laundry. This was not what I'd thought motherhood would be. None of the books I'd read prepared me for the nitty-gritty day-to-day of it, any more than they prepared me for the new emotions I was experiencing. How could I feel this angry, sometimes this frustrated, with someone I loved this much? How could I feel so helpless and afraid? Was I always going to be this tired? Any feminist perspective I'd had seemed to collapse with my ability to utter more than a few coherent sentences at any one time. (1992: 146)

Interestingly enough, focusing on the "nitty-gritty day-to-day" of motherhood was, to Wallace, antithetical to being a feminist for a time. Yet she tells us how, with the founding of a "mother's group" that evolved out of a conversation she had with one other mother, she made connections that helped her reconcile her feminism and her maternity. She credits the group for teaching her that she was not the only one feeling "physical isolation . . . at home alone with a small child, cut off from the rest of the world [and] emotional isolation, too, feeling that no other mother was ever as scared or inadequate or as tired as I was" (147–148). She explains that

> this is the power that such groups have, the power that comes when a group of people get together 'just to talk.' In my case, that power expressed itself in many ways. The women in my original group are still friends. Some have formed the Windsor Feminist Theater, working together to perform (and sometimes write) plays that explore women's experience. Others have gone back to school or found the courage to try new jobs. One of us attended the International Women's Conference in Nairobi in 1986. My own decision to take the plunge as a writer came, in part, from the strength I gained in that group. (148)

The diverse personal changes that came out of that group of mothers talking illustrate the power of confidence and community. Wallace shows how mothers who are valued will value themselves enough to insist on being full participants in society—to refuse to be silenced.

Despite the successes of groups such as hers, Wallace's writing demonstrates an awareness of the ways in which countless women are forcibly denied empowerment. Violence against women is a theme present in much of her writing. It is an extreme form of isolation and uncertainty that many mothers face, so, for Wallace, their stories must also be told. She frequently offered narratives based on her encounters with battered women and children when she was a counselor at Interval House.

The intensity of what she saw both compelled her and repulsed her. The stories of so many silenced mothers and their children were stories that, for Wallace, insisted on being told. In "Bones," she writes, "everywhere I went, my work experience/ drew me through confessions I couldn't stop,/ and I couldn't stop talking about them/ so you had to listen" (1987: 81). This compulsion reflects her sense that the violence some families are immersed in has ramifications beyond the families themselves in that it impacts society. In "Intervals," she writes of how a bruise on a client's face becomes "the only currency between us. I carry it home like a paycheque, my fingers smelling of ointment and blood, and when someone asks me how it went today/ it is the bruise that spills from my mouth, uncontrolled, incurable, it stains my son's cheek/ and grows in secret on my breasts and thighs" (59). Violence is a stain, even on those who don't know it's happening—or who don't want to know. She expands on this idea in a column recounting the experience of listening to women's stories of violence, describing how

> those of us who listen realize, as we sit in the circle, that this is our story too, that what happens to any one woman affects us all, that what joins us together is the fact that, in this culture, all women are in danger because we are women.
>
> The power of something like a Speak Out lies in the way it connects the personal experience of individual women to the political context in which it happens. Instead of experts (or party candidates) telling us what the issues are, each woman speaks from her own pain and is believed by those who hear her. In speaking out, we discover what we share. And in discovering what we share, we discover the power to heal our pain, by working together to change the society that causes it. (1992: 142)

Consequently, despite the burden felt by the listener after hearing from those whose lives have been destabilized by violence, Wallace posits that the connections made are ultimately, if not always immediately recognizably, empowering.

She does not try to oversimplify the problems in terms often heard in public debates. She illustrates how easy it is to dehumanize and de-individualize victims of violence and to blame them for staying in abusive situations. An instance of that idea occurs in "Thinking with the Heart" when Wallace describes a police officer's ambivalent attitude towards a battered wife:

> He'd seen it all before anyway. He knows
> how the law changes, depending on what you think.
> It used to be a man could beat his wife
> if he had to; now, sometimes he can't
> but she has to charge him
> and nine times out of ten
> these women who come in here
> ready to get the bastard
> will be back in a week or so
> wanting to drop the whole thing
> because they're back together,
> which just means a lot of paperwork
> and running around for nothing. (1985: 59–60)

Another poem, "Intervals," has a woman, newly arrived at the shelter with her children, wondering "what will happen to them now;/ the brain is adding hydro to food/ to first and last month's rent, phone bills/ and cough medicine, trying to make ends meet" (1987: 64). Wallace presents the tangible factors a victimized woman often has to face when trying to decide about leaving her husband. Concern over not being able to feed one's children or provide them with a home has to be weighed against the violence that potentially must be endured. Economic dependence and the insulated feeling of being alone place women in an impossible and dangerous situation, according to Wallace, one in which attitudes of ambivalence such as that depicted with the officer in "Thinking with the Heart" only help to reinforce the disparity that keeps women in violent relationships. Once again, Wallace stays on the story of an individual woman to transform the attitudes of her readers, a transformation necessary to change the social ideas that lead to violence.

Her emphasis on changing attitudes, furthermore, extends to the men committing the violence. Rather than blatantly condemning them, she suggests that they are as much a creation of society as women. Part of reforming the way mothers are treated is changing the way fathers are constructed. A statement by Mary di Michele, a writer with whom Wallace collaborated, helps to explain Wallace's view of men in relation to her feminism:

> Her feminism was a large-spirited form of humanism. Her concerns about violence against women . . . did not stop her from seeing the men behind the "monsters" she expected to meet, nor did it stop her from feeling compassion and giving support to those wife-batterers who were recognizing their behavior as their own problem, and trying to change. To change is the operative word here, all her writing is imbued with the energy and love and faith which enables you to do things. (J1)

Wallace's world included men, and the vision she had for the future involved them. She suggests that if domestic work and childrearing become more valued, men will be more likely to participate, which is yet another reason why she tells the stories of women's everydays. She knew that in order for women and children to have a truly positive future, men had to be involved in the revision of the attitudes that were withholding possibilities for those women and children.

Even when depicting the horrors of violence, Wallace continually returns to the dignity of the mothers she's describing. Part of their dignity lies in the complexity of their lives, in how they manage to be women and mothers and daughters despite factors like violence, poverty, and shame. She gives a sense of nobility to them, to their carrying on, and to all mothers. In *The Stubborn Particulars of Grace*, she emphasizes the grace that describes her perceptions of her mother and grandmother in the opening poem of the book, "Appeal," and in the closing piece of the book, "Particulars," in which she revisits a childhood memory of Sunday dinners at her grandmother's and how they helped her

> to begin to see, a little,
> what they taught me
> of themselves, their place
> among the living and the dead,
> thanksgiving and the practical
> particulars of grace, and
> to accept it,
> slowly, almost grudgingly
>   [. . .]
> long enough to call out
> all my other loves, locate each one
> precisely, as I could this house
> on a city map or the day I found
> my son, swimming within me. (110–111)

She moves from revisiting the grace of her memories to seeing it outside in a young girl delivering papers to connecting that sight of the external world back to the intimacy of being pregnant with her son. The particulars of everyday are reverential, and with those details of the everyday she is able to connect with and appreciate what is more commonly deemed as momentous, such as creating life and realizing its transience. What she sees of the world outside she is invested in, largely because of her intimate connections inside, especially the one with her son. She holds onto the reverence and dignity of herself, her family, and her history with other women to tell stories and reconsider the aspects of society that have overlooked them. She makes the stories blatant and inescapable. Wallace is compelled by the grace of mothers, of women, to storytelling and to feminism—to the dignity that makes them continue mothering, writing, and trying to change the world, despite the uncertainty those tasks inevitably involve. She envisions a future in which the significance of women taking such actions will no longer be questionable, when what is ordinary for women is viewed with an awe of the extraordinary. Her feminist project and her maternal project, in terms of raising her son, center on validating women maintaining grace every day.

REFERENCES

Atwood, Margaret. Rev. of *Common Magic*, by Bronwen Wallace. *Journal of Canadian Poetry* 2 (1987): 120–123.

Bennett, Donna. "Bronwen Wallace and the Meditative Poem." *Queen's Quarterly* 98.1 (1991): 58–79.

di Michele, Mary. "Author's Large-Spirited Feminism Will be Missed." Rev. of *Arguments with the World*, by Bronwen Wallace. *The Gazette* 29 August 1992: J1.

Downie, Glen. "Forms for Argument." Rev. of *Arguments with the World*, by Bronwen Wallace. *Event* 22 (1993): 143–147.

Humm, Maggie. "Second Wave." *The Dictionary of Feminist Theory*. 2nd ed. Columbus: Ohio State University Press, 1995. 251–252.

Mouré, Erin, and Bronwen Wallace. *Two Women Talking: Correspondence 1985–87*. Ed. Susan McMaster. Toronto: Feminist Caucus of the League of Canadian Poets, 1993.

Wallace, Bronwen. *Arguments with the World: Essays by Bronwen Wallace*. Ed. Joanne Page. Kingston: Quarry Press, 1992.

———. *Common Magic*. Ottawa: Oberon, 1985.

———. *The Stubborn Particulars of Grace*. Toronto: McClelland & Stewart, 1987.

PART TWO

Family

CHAPTER FOUR

Planned Parenthood

The Construction of Motherhood in Lesbian Mother Advice Books

KRISTIN G. ESTERBERG

THE LESBIAN BABY BOOM of the last few decades has changed the cultural climate in which lesbians choose to become mothers—or not. Advice literature, support groups, Web sites, and a variety of other resources for lesbian mothers and those considering parenthood have proliferated. In an unprecedented way, lesbian mothers now face the question of whether to parent or not—and what kind of parent to become.

Like other mothers, lesbians do not do their work in a cultural vacuum, seeking out sources that can provide advice, information, support, and models for parenting. This chapter focuses on the advice literature aimed at lesbian mothers published from 1980 to 2006. I conducted a thematic analysis of advice books aimed at lesbian mothers, supplemented by a close reading of several anthologies and longer works published by and for lesbian mothers and a less systematic analysis of Web sites aimed at lesbian mothers.[1] (See the Appendix for a list of books analyzed.) Although lesbians may come to parenting in many different ways—through a previous heterosexual relationship, through alternative (or artificial) insemination, adoption, or fostering—most of the lesbian mother advice books are aimed primarily at those women who make up the lesbian "baby boom": those who have made (or are making) the decision to parent as open lesbians.[2]

TO BE, OR NOT TO BE:
A CONSUMER CHOICE MODEL OF PARENTING

The importance of choice in shaping lesbian mothers' decisions to parent is paramount. First, because lesbians are assumed to make more conscious choices about parenting than others (due, in large part, to the practical diffi-culties involved in becoming parents), lesbian parents are sometimes assumed to be *superior* parents. As Martin argues, "The children of lesbians and gay men are the most considered and planned-for children on earth. There is no such thing as an unwanted child among us" (15). Further, she claims, "Many years may go into the planning process. We do an impressively careful job of weighing our needs, our resources, and our expectations" (15).

The notion that lesbian mothers are exceptional parents is in sharp con-trast to much early academic research, which was often based on the needs of lesbian parents who were facing custody challenges by former husbands. Early research on lesbian parents attempted to document that lesbian mothers are "normal"—just like other mothers (see Pollack for a thoughtful critique of this research). Thus, academic research attempted to document that children of lesbian parents were essentially no different from children in nonlesbian fami-lies and that lesbian mothers were "fit" parents (see Savin-Williams and Ester-berg for a review of this literature; see also Stacey and Biblarz).[3]

In contrast, advice books aimed at intentional lesbian parents assume that lesbian families have distinctive strengths. Thus, Clunis and Green argue that while they do not believe that lesbians necessarily do a *better* job of parenting than others, "we do think that our families have particular strengths because they are lesbian families" (12). These strengths include the possibility of "more egalitarian relationships, a broader perspective, a more flexible and fluid concept of family and the opportunity for greater sharing of parenting responsibilities and more varied role models for children" (13).

In a similar vein, Martin argues that "what we [lesbian and gay families] have to offer is *exactly what children need* to grow into healthy, happy, and well-adjusted children" (25, emphasis added). Those lesbian and gay parents who have dealt with their internalized homophobia are especially well suited to parenting adopted kids and kids with diverse backgrounds and needs: "because of our experience of being different from the dominant culture, we bring to our commitment to parenting an ability to embrace diversity in our families" (118).

Notably, Pies's workbook, one of the earliest lesbian mother advice books, does not proclaim lesbian families' superiority, a fact that may be explained, at least in part, by the book's publication at a time when most work on lesbian families stressed their abilities to overcome deficits.[4] Although Pies does argue that lesbians face a "unique challenge and exciting opportunity when it comes to building families," her book emphasizes an honest exploration of the pressures lesbian families face. As she puts it, "lesbians are under a good deal of pressure to build healthy families. Our own expectations of wanting to have a close and nurturing family which provides a good place for a child to grow are often challenged by societal expectations that our families will produce sexually and emotionally unstable children at best and a myriad of unknown problems at worst" (71–72). More recent books have cautioned lesbians against the urge to become supermothers. "[N]ot a single one of us is a perfect mother, and even our children, wonderful as they are, are not without fault" (Johnson and O'Connor 23).

Part of the developing lesbian mother script is the necessity of making an *informed* choice about becoming a parent. Pies's book, based on a series of workshops with San Francisco Bay–area lesbians trying to decide whether to become parents, perhaps reflects this issue the most clearly, although the theme is prominent in other texts as well, especially Brill's *Guide to Lesbian Conception, Pregnancy & Birth*. Part of making an informed choice, according to the "experts," involves overcoming the effects of homophobia (and, more recently, transphobia), which tells lesbians, gay men, and transgendereds that they should not have—and do not deserve—children. The flip side of this, however, is the necessity to overcome women's socialization, which tells women that they *should* have children and, indeed, will remain unfulfilled and unwomanly without them.

At the heart of the injunction to make an informed choice is the sense that the individual has multiple options, each of which must be weighed carefully before making a decision. What is most important is that the individual makes her own personal decision and works to actively shape her own future. In addition, the language of choice casts potential lesbian mothers as making explicitly *consumer* choices. Having made the decision to become a parent, lesbians then face myriad other questions about how to effect their plans. Pregnancy or adoption? Sperm donor or father? Known or unknown donor? Although there is some recognition of structural constraints to achieving parenthood—the significant financial costs involved in fertility services or adoption, for example—these tend to be downplayed. "Getting pregnant as a lesbian has never been easier," Martin cheerily proclaims (46).

Martin, who has been described as the "Benjamin Spock of lesbian/gay parenting," is probably most explicit about the consumer model of parenting: "In many parts of the country," she argues, "insemination has become quite a business, and as an informed consumer you are in a position to have it your way, within reason" (55). Thus, lesbians need to consider: which sperm is "best"? Who is the "best" child to adopt? The focus on consumerism becomes even more explicit in her discussion of surrogacy, which she presents as an option for gay men who want to become fathers. Although discussing some of the issues presented by feminists who oppose surrogacy, ultimately, she argues, women should be allowed to make the choice to bear children for others for pay. "The surrogate is making a choice to use her time, her body, and her energies to accomplish an end" (108).

Obviously, surrogacy is not an issue for most lesbian couples (for whom a more pressing issue may be which of the two will physically bear or legally adopt the child). Still, lesbians who use fertility services clearly enter into a consumer model of reproductive choice, sorting through catalogs of sperm donors that list a variety of social and personality characteristics and making choices about which genetic traits to pass onto their children.[5] The costs of fertility services can be substantial, ranging from $300 to more than $1,000 a cycle, depending on whether the insemination takes place in a clinic or at home and the specific insemination technique chosen. Not surprisingly, fertility services are well beyond the reach of most poor and working-class women.

What are the implications of the consumer choice model? Some feminists (such as Robyn Rowland and Barbara Katz Rothman) are clearly opposed to new reproductive technologies, arguing that the commodification of reproduction within capitalist patriarchy ultimately harms women. The impact on lesbians is less clear. The spread of sperm banks and alternative forms of insemination has enabled many lesbians to become parents. This is not, by itself, a bad thing. Still, the advice literature does not dwell on thorny issues of class and gender or the larger social questions, focusing instead on the technical aspects of donor selection, charting fertility, and insemination techniques. In line with a model of consumer choice and with self-help books more generally, the advice books stress making a choice that is right for *you*, given your own particular proclivities and life circumstances. Women are exhorted to become educated consumers. As Pepper writes, "Ultimately the only expert you can count on in this process is yourself. The better educated you are, the more likely you are to feel that you, the paying customer and hopeful parent, are in control of this process" (47).

Having the proper feelings about one's parenting choices is also important. Hochschild argues that the anecdotes in advice books contain what she calls "magnified moments," which magnify the feeling that a person has within a particular situation, typically contrasting how she expected to feel with how she actually felt. In this way, magnified moments tell readers how (and what) to feel in particular situations. In the lesbian parent advice literature, women are expected to feel and overcome doubts and fears. Anecdotes portray the various dilemmas women experience in attempting to become parents, including the pain of infertility and loss of a child. Ultimately, however, the joys of childrearing (and even pregnancy) win over. Once one has embarked on the process of becoming a parent, Clunis and Green exhort, "Take pleasure in your creation! And appreciate the loving work required to translate your vision of lesbian family into reality" (59).

LOVE MAKES A FAMILY

The achievement of pregnancy or adoption doesn't only transform women into mothers. It also, according to current sensibilities, creates a family. Yet lesbian families are not "natural" families, according to law or custom. That is, unlike heterosexually married couples with children, who are automatically assumed by law and otherwise to form a family, lesbian families have to proclaim their existence. Advice books have much to say on family formation.

Perhaps what is most notable is the message that lesbians are consciously—and creatively—constructing new family forms, apart from the constraints of biology or the narrowness of the nuclear family. As Clunis and Green summarize,

> Our chosen families represent a very different approach to kinship than the idealized myth of the 'nuclear family' or the reality of the extended family which is characteristic of many ethnic cultures. As lesbian families, we challenge the very foundation upon which the notion of family has been based, namely heterosexuality. Blood relationships and legal ties are not the defining factors for inclusion in our families. (10)

If law and biology are not presented as the defining features of lesbian family life, individual choice is. That is, lesbians are presumed (and exhorted) to select deliberately among a wide variety of potential family members, including friends, partners, ex-lovers, sperm donors, and fathers. Lev argues, "There are many paths to becoming a parent, and each one has its own built-in joys and challenges. It is important to remember that there is no one right way to become a parent. In fact, many families choose to utilize a different path with each child brought into the family" (50). And Pies notes, "We can create the family style that suits our needs and those of the individual family members best. We can take on aspects of other families that we have liked and aspects of our past experiences in forming families that will work well" (71).

This model of choice in some respects echoes the issue of consumer choice involved in becoming a family. Although lesbians are not depicted as *purchasing* family members, they are encouraged to think deliberately about family life and to create a family that best suits the individual's needs. So, for example, lesbians are advised that "each family has its unique way of growing and accommodating to the individualities of its members. There is no perfect way to do this, and what may be ideal for your family wouldn't work for another" (Martin 295). Exercises in Pies's workbook explicitly encourage readers to consider how they want to structure their family: as a single parent with child, as two women who are lovers (or not) with one or more children, as a cooperative or extended family, and so on. Readers are encouraged to fantasize about what it might be like to live in each of the various forms outlined in the book and come to a decision based on their own unique needs and desires.

Family boundaries are thus depicted as more flexible than those in other, nonlesbian families. Because lesbian families explicitly need to consider how children will be brought into the family, motherhood is not automatically equated with biology. All the texts deal with the issue of how to define the roles of the biological or legal adoptive parent and the nonlegal parent.[6] While individuals are encouraged to make informed choices, they are explicitly encouraged to define motherhood apart from biology (or, perhaps, in addition to biology) and to make choices that will solidify the nonlegal mother's relationship to the child. So, for example, readers are given advice on how to negotiate the medical system so that both mothers' roles will be affirmed, and parents are cautioned to spell out their roles in a legal document in the event of death or dissolution of the relationship. Potential parents are warned of the difficulties involved in being the parent who is not socially recognized.[7]

Other potential family members may be included within the boundaries: known sperm donors may take on a variety of roles, ranging from distant uncle to hands-on dad. While acknowledging the legal difficulties that bringing a sperm donor-father into the picture may create, readers are encouraged to bring a variety of other adults into their families: honorary aunts and uncles, godparents, mentors, and other role models. As Martin notes, "For lots of gay men and lesbians who like children but don't want the role of parents, forming relationships with the children of other gay men and lesbians is a way of affirming and supporting all of us" (43).

Despite the insistence on new family forms, the core of family life, according to these texts, is still children. Thus, having a child through birth or adoption is typically referred to as "creating a family" rather than extending a family, and prospective parents are encouraged to examine the different ways by which one can construct a family. Single adults or couples without children are typically not seen as families in their own right, unless they are related as family to an individual or couple with children.

Finally, lesbian families are also portrayed as on the cutting edge: as role models for a more flexible and equitable family life and as families that are more suited to today's circumstances. Thus, Clunis and Green explicitly state, "Especially in these times of high-speed change, parents need to design flexible yet solid family structures and to approach parenting challenges with consistency and creativity. We encourage you to keep experimenting until *your* system works; don't worry that it may not look like anyone else's. Remember, your solution of today could be a role model in ten years" (17).

The lesbian mother advice literature thus depicts a number of progressive ideals for family life. By choosing family members wisely, lesbians are seen as expanding the possibilities for contemporary family life. Most important, lesbian mother advice books attempt to frame lesbian families as "beyond" biology, consciously choosing new roles based not solely on biological imperative but on individual choice. However, lesbian mothers are limited in their abilities to create truly novel mothering scripts. Rather than create wholly new and different forms of family life, lesbian mothers draw selectively on and recreate, to varying extents, dominant ideals for family life.

THE PLEASURES OF PARENTHOOD

Like nonlesbian mothers, lesbian mothers are assumed to gain deep pleasures from raising children. Indeed, because lesbians are presumed to make more conscious choices about parenting, they are perhaps expected to gain greater pleasures than heterosexual women. Whether a family is formed by birth or adoption, parents are expected to go through a process of falling in love with their children. Children's development is described as "a magical process to observe and be a part of" (Martin 242). Despite the challenges, including physical and emotional exhaustion, financial burdens, and the difficulties involved in negotiating the heterosexual world, parenthood is described as ultimately worthwhile: "your heart and soul have been forever changed. Your life will never be the same again, yet the parenting journey is really just beginning. You will probably never be so challenged or so rewarded by any other job" (Clunis and Green 202).

The pleasures of parenting described in advice books are many. New mothers especially are expected to be infatuated with their babies. One mother, for example, is described as "smiling beatifically at her tiny daughter" (Clunis and Green 192). Another woman's separation from her sixteen-month-old daughter is described in this way: "her heart ached for her baby and their time alone together" (199). Even toddlerhood, often a difficult period, is described as "really magical." Children help adults become "young and silly," more in touch with the world. As one mother quoted in Martin noted, "It's very difficult to be serious when you have this delightful bundle of joy running around just being amazed at every little leaf that drops" (Martin 242). Other parents cited "the job of watching a person become a person" (Martin 242) and the bonds of love they feel for their children.

One of the texts, Lev's *Complete Lesbian & Gay Parenting Guide*, is notable for its cautions to prospective parents about the challenges of parenting. The author describes, sometimes humorously, the realities of colicky babies, leaky diapers, and lack of sex and sleep. Despite the less than glamorous reality, however, the message is that parenting is still worthwhile. Lev insists, "the fewer expectations you have [for parenting], the easier it will be to let them become themselves and watch their growth with openness and awe" (128).

Despite differences in family configuration, lesbian mothering scripts seem essentially like dominant scripts for white, middle-class women in regard to the feelings mothers are expected to have toward their children. Indeed, lesbian advice books seem little different from other childrearing manuals in their descriptions of parent–child interactions. Although child rearing is seen as physically and emotionally taxing, it is also described as among the most important work a person can undertake. In this way, lesbian mother advice books essentially put forward a child-centered view of parenting, placing children's needs and desires at the center of lesbian family life.

DISCUSSION AND CONCLUSION

The analysis of lesbian mother advice books revealed a number of important cultural ideals. First and most notably, lesbian mothers are encouraged to see their mothering in terms of a consumer choice model in which planning is paramount. Certainly no one would argue that planning parenthood is a bad thing. An important question remains, however. Is seeing motherhood as a consumer choice good for women? To what extent does a consumer choice model push lesbians into a commodified version of family life? Is having more consumer choices necessarily freeing? For whom? Although this chapter cannot fully address the debates around the new reproductive technologies, one fact is clear: fertility services are clearly out of the financial reach of most poor and working-class women—lesbian or heterosexual.[8]

I argue that the consumer choice model is, at best, a mixed blessing. To the extent that lesbians can truly exercise reproductive choices, perhaps lesbians can provide a model of optional, truly voluntary motherhood. Given the compulsory nature of motherhood for most women,[9] a model of choice and planning can challenge the notion that womanhood equals maternity and the imperative that women become mothers. This, surely, is a good thing. Yet to the extent that the choices are available primarily to middle-class and professional women, this choice is clearly a class-inflected one. Given limited access to fertility and adoption services, some lesbians can choose motherhood more freely than others. And given the injunction that practically all women face to bear children, it's not clear that lesbians are, really, making a choice. No choice is truly individual, outside the bounds of the social.

Second, unlike dominant scripts for mothering, lesbian mothering scripts reflect an ambivalent attitude toward biology. The emphasis on bearing a child through pregnancy and breast-feeding inevitably privileges the biological aspects of motherhood. Still, lesbian mother advice books attempt to counter this focus by providing strategies for deemphasizing the biological links between mothers and children and preserving the bonds with the non-biological parent through whatever means are available. "Love makes a family," proclaim many lesbian and gay family advocates—not biology. To the extent that biology becomes disconnected from mothering, an understanding of motherhood as involving labor can develop (see also Rothman). If mothers are those who do the work of mothering—caring for sick children, worrying about nutritious meals and clothing, and acting in all the ways that mothers are presumed to act—then the link between biology and motherhood can diminish. Seen this way, as labor, anyone—even perhaps men—can mother. Lesbian mothers (like adoptive heterosexual mothers) thus have the potential to challenge essentialist beliefs about the nature of the mother–child relationship.

Third, lesbians are presumed to have more flexible and perhaps more egalitarian family structures than heterosexual families. Lesbian mother advice books exhort prospective parents to create a unique support system of family, friends, and community. Although the extent to which any particular lesbian family actually does this may be questioned, it is notable that lesbian mothers are encouraged to seek support outside of a nuclear family system. Unlike heterosexual mothers, who are expected to mother in relative isolation (Chodorow and Contratto), lesbian mothers are expected to need—and create—their own, personalized community supports.

Again, the question remains: to what extent do lesbian families actually attain flexible family structures? To what extent do lesbians reject biological imperatives? Although little research has focused primarily on family structure, lesbian families seem somewhat less likely to create truly novel family structures than, perhaps, the advice literature suggests. Such structures may occur, but they seem relatively rare. This is at least in part due to the legal system, which offers only a small window for lesbian couples to create legal ties to their children, as well as the strategies of the lesbian/gay movement itself, which has tended in recent years to emphasize similarities between lesbian/gay couples and heterosexual ones. In some states, lesbian and gay families are able to use a legal strategy known as second-parent adoptions to secure a legal relationship of both mothers to their child(ren). In these adoptions, both mothers are seen as the legal parents to the child. Yet, significantly, sperm donors or biological fathers must not claim legal parental rights to the child in these cases; nor may a third or fourth mother be considered. Thus, in the view of the courts, a child may have two, and only two, legal parents.[10] (See Polikoff for an important critique of this notion.) In addition, strategies to legalize lesbian/gay marriage or to celebrate gay/lesbian unions tend to privilege two-parent families over more alternative family structures.

Whether lesbian families draw on heterosexual family scripts in other ways seems less certain. According to some research, lesbian families are more likely to rely on their families of origin for support than nonkin, thus privileging biological over community connections (Lewin). Yet others, such as Ainslie and Feltey, Weston, and Dunne have found that lesbians rely significantly on friendship networks and lesbian community members for support. In addition, lesbian families tend to arrange more egalitarian divisions of household labor than other types of couples, although at least some research indicates that biological lesbian mothers are more likely to spend time in childcare than nonbiological mothers (Patterson). And, as Gillian Dunne argues, lesbian families challenge the heterosexual model in other ways as well: by incorporating sperm donors and fathers in more flexible ways than heterosexual families, by integrating mothering and breadwinning, and by simply making visible an alternative.

Finally, although lesbian mothering scripts may be overlaid on top of dominant mothering scripts, there still are multiple points of contact. Perhaps most important is the emphasis on child-centered parenting. Although lesbian mothers are typically not exhorted to become full-time at-home mothers, they are expected to make children the center of their emotional lives. Like the middle-class heterosexual women McMahon and others have written about, lesbian mothers are expected to see motherhood as an "essence-making" process (158). In this view, mothering is not just a job, but a lifelong creative endeavor.

Ultimately, lesbian mothers both challenge and conform to existing arrangements for caring for children. While lesbian mothers may provide a more egalitarian alternative to traditional gender roles, they do not challenge the privatized and increasingly commercialized model of parenthood currently dominant. Children, especially young children, are laborious. In the prevailing social arrangements, individual women (and, increasingly, men) are seen as responsible for their care—but not the larger society. In this regard, lesbian mothers are little different from other mothers. Because lesbians are seen as making an *individual* choice, a consumer choice, they do not challenge the privatized arrangements by which individuals are expected to care for "their" children. Changes in individual family composition will not necessarily translate into supportive family policies—support for education, for livable wages and work schedules, affordable health care, and other family policies that will truly support mothers and children. Like all other mothers, lesbians are expected to do the work themselves—or, for middle-class and wealthy women, to arrange to have the work done by others. Indeed, the very planned nature of lesbian motherhood may even exacerbate this tension. After all, is this not what planning is all about?

APPENDIX ONE: LIST OF WORKS ANALYZED

Advice books aimed at lesbian mothers, 1985–2006:

Cheri Pies, *Considering Parenthood* (Spinsters Ink 1985)

April Martin, *The Lesbian and Gay Parenting Handbook* (HarperPerennial 1993)

D. Merilee Clunis and G. Dorsey Green, *The Lesbian Parenting Book* (Seal 1995; second ed. 2003)

Jill S. Pollack, *Lesbian & Gay Families: Redefining Parenting in America* (Franklin Watts 1995)

Rachel Pepper, *The Ultimate Guide to Pregnancy for Lesbians* (Cleis 1999, second ed. 2005)

Stephanie Brill, *The Queer Parent's Primer* (New Harbinger Publications 2001)

Suzanne Johnson and Elizabeth O'Connor, *For Lesbian Parents* (Guilford 2001)

Kim Toevs and Stephanie Brill, *The Essential Guide to Lesbian Conception, Pregnancy, and Birth* (Alyson 2002). Revised edition published as Stephanie Brill, *The New Essential Guide to Lesbian Conception, Pregnancy & Birth* (Alyson 2006).

Arlene Istar Lev, *The Complete Lesbian & Gay Parenting Guide* (Berkley 2004)

Anthologies by and about lesbian parents:

Gillian Hanscombe and Jackie Forster, *Rocking the Cradle* (Alyson 1981)

Sandra Pollack and Jeanne Vaughn, *Politics of the Heart* (Firebrand 1987)

Katherine Arnup, *Lesbian Parenting: Living with Pride and Prejudice* (Gynergy 1995)

Jess Wells, *Lesbians Raising Sons* (Alyson 1997)

Harlyn Aizley, *Confessions of the Other Mother: Nonbiological Lesbian Moms Tell All!* (Beacon Press 2006)

NOTES

1. By advice books, I mean those books that are written by professionals (psychologists, social workers, childbirth educators, and so forth) and aimed at a general audience of lesbian parents or those who are considering parenthood. Unlike general advice books for parents, which are typically written by pediatricians, advice books aimed at lesbian mothers are often written by psychologists or social workers who are lesbian mothers themselves, and often published by feminist presses.

2. Linda Silber (1991) refers to these women as "deliberate lesbian mothers."

3. This research stream is ongoing; see Patterson 2006 for an overview.

4. The first edition was published in 1985; the second in 1988. Both editions are substantially earlier than the other advice books, which came out in the 1990s and after.

5. When women inseminate using sperm from a sperm bank, they are typically given a catalog that gives basic information about the donors available. Although sperm banks vary in the amount of information given, they typically offer height and weight, coloring, and ethnicity. Information about health and family health history may be available, as may be a variety of social and personality characteristics, including occupation, recreational pastimes, religion, and so forth.

6. I use the term *nonlegal parent* or *nonlegal mother* to refer to the parent who does not have a legal relationship to the child, either through birth or adoption. Increasingly, lesbians who are not the birth or original adoptive parent of the child are gaining a legal relationship to the child by a process known as second-parent adoption, which is available in about twenty-five states.

7. In this regard, see also Harlyn Aizley's edited volume, *Confessions of the Other Mother: Nonbiological Lesbian Moms Tell All!* (Beacon Press 2006).

8. In Massachusetts, state law mandates that certain kinds of fertility services (in vitro fertilization, for example) be covered under workers' health insurance

policies. While this policy makes fertility services available to a broader range of women, those who are not covered by health insurance are still left out.

9. Unlike middle-class women, however, poor women are, significantly, exhorted *not* to have children—or at least not to have children that they cannot afford to support by their own efforts. Similarly, disabled women are also seen as ineligible for motherhood.

10. This is similar to the case of adoption of a stepchild in a heterosexual family. The biological father or divorced father must give up rights to the child for the adoption to occur.

REFERENCES

Ainslie, Julie, and Kathryn M. Feltey. "Definitions and Dynamics of Motherhood and Family in Lesbian Communities." *Marriage & Family Review* 17:1–2 (1991): 63–86.

Aizley, Harlyn, Ed. *Confessions of the Other Mother: Nonbiological Lesbian Moms Tell All!* Boston: Beacon Press, 2006.

Brill, Stephanie. *The New Essential Guide to Lesbian Conception, Pregnancy & Birth.* New York: Alyson Books, 2006.

Chodorow, Nancy, and Susan Contratto. "The Fantasy of the Perfect Mother." *Rethinking the Family: Some Feminist Questions.* Ed. Barrie Thorne with Marilyn Yalom. New York: Longman, 1982.

Clunis, D. Merilee, and G. Dorsey Green. *The Lesbian Parenting Book: A Guide to Creating Families and Raising Children.* Seattle: Seal Press, 1995; 2nd ed., 2003.

Dunne, Gillian A. "Opting into Motherhood: Lesbians Blurring the Boundaries and Transforming the Meaning of Parenthood and Kinship." *Gender & Society* 14:1 (2000): 11–35.

Hochschild, Arlie Russell. "The Commercial Spirit of Intimate Life and the Abduction of Feminism: Signs from Women's Advice Books." *Theory, Culture and Society* 11 (1994): 1–24.

Johnson, Suzanne, and Elizabeth O'Connor. *For Lesbian Parents.* New York: Guilford, 2001.

Lev, Arlene Istar. *The Complete Lesbian & Gay Parenting Guide.* New York: Berkley Books, 2004.

Martin, April. *The Lesbian and Gay Parenting Handbook: Creating and Raising Our Families.* New York: HarperCollins, 1993.

McMahon, Martha. *Engendering Motherhood: Identity and Self-Transformation in Women's Lives.* New York: Guilford, 1995.

Patterson, Charlotte J. "Children of Lesbian and Gay Parents." *Current Directions in Psychological Science* 15:5 (2006): 241–244.

Pepper, Rachel. *The Ultimate Guide to Pregnancy for Lesbians.* San Francisco: Cleis, 1999; 2nd ed., 2005.

Pies, Cheri. *Considering Parenthood* (2nd ed.). Minneapolis: Spinsters Ink, 1988.

Polikoff, Nancy. "This Child Does Have Two Mothers: Redefining Parenthood to Meet the Needs of Children in Lesbian-Mother and Other Nontraditional Families." *Georgetown Law Review* 78 (1990): 459–575.

Pollack, Jill S. *Lesbian & Gay Families: Redefining Parenting in America.* New York: Franklin Watts, 1995.

Pollack, Sandra. "Lesbian Mothers: A Lesbian-Feminist Perspective on Research." *Politics of the Heart: A Lesbian Parenting Anthology.* Ed. Sandra Pollack and Jeanne Vaughn. Ithaca: Firebrand Books, 1987. 316–324.

Rothman, Barbara Katz. *Recreating Motherhood: Ideology and Technology in a Patriarchal Society.* New York: Norton, 1989.

Rowland, Robyn. *Living Laboratories: Women and Reproductive Technologies.* Bloomington: Indiana University Press, 1992.

Savin-Williams, Ritch C., and Kristin Esterberg. "Lesbian, Gay, and Bisexual Families." *Handbook of Family Diversity.* Ed. Katherine Allen, Mark Fine, and David Demo. New York: Oxford University Press, 2000.

Silber, Linda. *Dykes with Tykes: Becoming a Lesbian Mother.* Unpublished PhD dissertation. University of Minnesota, 1991.

Stacey, Judith, and Timothy J. Biblarz. "(How) Does the Sexual Orientation of Parents Matter?" *American Sociological Review* 66.2 (2001): 159–183.

Toevs, Kim, and Stephanie Brill. *The Essential Guide to Lesbian Conception, Pregnancy, and Birth.* New York: Alyson, 2002.

Weston, Kath. *Families We Choose: Lesbians, Gays, Kinship.* New York: Columbia University Press, 1991.

CHAPTER FIVE

The Voice of the Maternal in Louise Erdrich's Fiction and Memoirs

AIMEE E. BERGER

> Lives do not serve as models, only stories do that. And it is a
> hard thing to make up stories to live by. We can only retell and
> live by stories we have heard. . . . Stories have formed us all:
> they are what we must use to make new fictions and new
> narratives.
>
> —Carolyn Heilbrun, *Writing a Woman's Life*

ANY WRITING MOTHER is engaged in an essentially subversive act. Not only
does she fly in the face of psychoanalytic theory, which has traditionally told
us that the creative instinct flows naturally into the maternal drive and so
should find outlet in raising babies rather than in writing books, but she also
problematizes and even disproves fundamental cultural assumptions, such as
the system of binary "oppositions," which "conceive of woman and writing,
motherhood and authorhood, babies and books, as mutually exclusive" and
competing impulses (Susan Friedman qtd. in Jeremiah 7). The writing
mother is engaged in an essentially feminist task—challenging patriarchal
thought and conceptions of "right womanhood" inasmuch as "mothering and
literary production—both profoundly relational practices—can be linked and
deployed as challenges to traditional western ideals of rationality and individuality" (Jeremiah 7).

But if she writes *of* mothering and takes on a maternal perspective in her
writing, the writing mother embodies feminist thought and engages in

feminist practice on yet other levels; as Carol Hult observes in "Writer in the House: Mothering and Motherhood," "As mothers become "speaking subjects" and add their perspectives to the literary stream, the limiting conceptions of a dying patriarchy begins to be replaced with the realities of mothers' lives" (Hult 28–29). In other words, to borrow from Adrienne Rich,[1] giving voice to the experiences and emotions of mothers in writing helps to redefine mothering in terms set forth by mothers, and as something apart from the patriarchal enterprise of motherhood. The stories of mothers in fiction and autobiographical writing, then, are "key tool[s] in the redefinition of maternity in which feminists are engaged" (Jeremiah 7).

While writing may serve to elucidate mothering, it can also be said that "the act of writing continues the act of mothering" (Daly and Reddy 16). If one function of mothering is understood to be instructing the child and transmitting values, then the reader is positioned to be in a sense mothered by a writer whose stories serve to bring the reader into her worldview. This is especially important for a writer like Louise Erdrich who is writing from a worldview that differs from that of mainstream Western thought and who takes as her subject the forgotten stories and distorted histories of a subsumed culture.

As Jace Weaver writes, Native writing "prepares the ground for recovery, even re-creation, of Indian identity and culture. Native writers speak to that part of us the colonial power and the dominant culture cannot reach, cannot touch. They help Indians imagine themselves as Indians" (44–45) (Weaver qtd. in Little 497). Though she enacts this role more distinctly after 1995, Erdrich has long been conscious of her role as cultural mother. As she states in "A Writer's Sense of Place," "Contemporary Native American writers have before them a task quite different from that of non-Indian writers. In the light of enormous loss, they must tell the untold stories of contemporary survivors, while protecting and celebrating the cores of cultures left in the wake of the European invasion" (41). This sentiment is clearly an expression of maternal thinking, specifically the attitude that Sara Ruddick in her well-known 1980 essay titled "Maternal Thinking" refers to as "holding": "A mother, acting in the interest of preserving and maintaining life . . . develops a metaphysical attitude [called] "holding," an attitude governed by the priority of keeping over acquiring, of conserving the fragile, of maintaining whatever is at hand and necessary" (217). Erdrich's writing is increasingly an attempt to "hold" her culture and to mother it by preserving its life.

Though the centrality of mother figures in Erdrich's work has been noted in much of her writing, *The Blue Jay's Dance: A Birth Year* (1995) is a watershed text that signals and perhaps even brings about a significant shift in Erdrich's fictional portrayal of maternal subjectivity and representations of mothers in her later novels. Through the writing of this memoir, Erdrich not only claims her own maternal subjectivity, but also comes to terms with a central paradox of mothering, power/powerlessness, that structured representations of maternal experience in her earlier texts and led to generally ambivalent portrayals.[2] The memoir, as well as the novels written most immediately before and after it, map Erdrich's struggles with this paradox and perhaps her own ambivalence, but also suggest ways in which the framing of maternal subjectivity and recognition of the motherline can be seen as writerly acts of feminist or empowered mothering.

Reclaiming her maternal I/eye through the writing of this memoir also leads Erdrich to assume the role of cultural mother in pronounced ways. Specifically, in the period following publication of *The Blue Jay's Dance*, Erdrich writes three children's books (new territory for her), which overtly trace her cultural and familial history[3] and she increasingly incorporates the Ojibwe language into her storytelling framework; in multiple ways, then, her stories become vessels for holding and transmitting cultural values.

Also significant is the foregrounding of the stories of women[4] as told by women in the period. The novel published most immediately after the memoir, *The Antelope Wife* (1998), is primarily about the motherline in which the stories of abandoning mothers are told from their own points of view, and their presence restored to both the narrative and to their children's lives. In addition, male othermothers are not seen as preferable to females, a trend that was evident in Erdrich's earlier fictions. This novel also builds around traditional Ojibwe stories of Oshkikwe and Matchikwesis, stories Paula Gunn Allen reports were told for the singular purpose of educating young women so as to aid their spiritual development (141). In the period immediately before and after *The Blue Jay's Dance*, then, Erdrich's writing becomes, in multiple and distinct ways, a continuation of her maternal thinking and practice, and an act of feminist mothering.

Though maternal thinking and experience informed Erdrich's creative practice and shaped some of the representations of mothering in her earliest fiction, her ambivalence toward the figure of the mother is nonetheless evident in the tetralogy,[5] and many characters and narrative situations seem to represent distinctly the power/powerless paradox of motherhood. In these novels, Erdrich often represents maternal experience in terms of communal or othermothering, mirroring the values of many Native American cultures. In her chapter on Erdrich's work in *Mother Without Child: The Crisis of Contemporary Fiction*, Elaine Tuttle Hansen points out: "motherhood was understood in many Native American tribes as a spiritual and social condition separable from biological identity or sexual behavior" (116–117). Mothers might be aunts, grandmothers, or even people, male or female, in the community unrelated by blood to the children they mother. Communal mothering also mirrors feminist values, configuring mothering as a verb and recognizing mothering as a chosen practice rather than a biological destiny and, further, by demonstrating that the patriarchal institution of traditional motherhood is an isolating and limiting expression of maternal experience.

But the reasons for the dominance of othermothering in Erdrich's tetralogy are often linked, textually and aesthetically, to the power/powerless paradox. First, children are mothered by others because of the absence of the biological mother, often because she has abandoned them, sometimes inexplicably. Second, by representing mothering primarily in terms of othermothers, Erdrich is able to displace and thereby defuse maternal power. Even the powerful Fleur Pillager, a central figure in Erdrich's oeuvre, is not allowed to maintain both her power and her child. As long as the figure of the mother remains shadowy and voiceless, her power is not recognized, but neither is her powerlessness highlighted. Othermothering and the silence of biological mothers in these texts to some degree mask the underlying paradox but belie the author's ambivalence toward the figure of the mother.

Thus, biological mothers often appear as carefully framed absences in the texts, casting long, speechless shadows over their offspring, each of whom can only invoke her memory from the perspective of the child he or she had been. Mothers, in particular June Morrissey and Fleur Pillager, haunt the landscape of the Matchimanito novels, hovering just beyond the scope of the narrative eye. Lacking narrative subjectivity, they are continually constructed, demolished, and reconstructed by their offspring and others who offer to tell their stories, and these characters reappear time and again, popping up incidentally or integrally in novel after novel. Because one or both of these figures appears in each of the Matchimanito novels, and because they demonstrate in many ways Erdrich's awareness of the power/powerless paradox, they are the best subjects for this abbreviated discussion of Erdrich's early (fictional) representations of mothers.

In general, the paradox shows itself in representations of the mother as both or either the fearsome, powerful mother (controlling, demanding, devouring) or the frighteningly powerless mother (victimized, cornered, silent). While the ambivalence that derives from living this paradox touches all mothers, it is perhaps most pronounced in the literatures of a colonized people with an imperiled culture and silenced language, and has special implications in colonial and neocolonial contexts. Native American mothers certainly fall into this category. Mothers throughout Erdrich's fiction are located in the troubled interstice of power and powerlessness, placed there by circumstances out of their control, unable to protect their children or themselves from encroaching threats or erasure, and so left with few choices about how or even whether to mother, though it is easy to ignore this context and focus on individual mothers as blameworthy, as some critics have done.

In Erdrich's novels, family relationships and cultural identity have been largely destroyed. Mothering has been rendered painful or even impossible as evidenced by Fleur's decision in *Tracks* to send her beloved daughter Lulu to the indian boarding school in response to the loss of their land. Erdrich returns to this event more than a decade later in *The Last Report on the Miracles at Little No Horse* and *Four Souls* and it is integral to, and maybe even the exigence for, both. As Hertha Wong writes, "Fleur didn't really abandon Lulu—she simply can't prepare the girl for a life that threatens to be so different from what Fleur herself knows. The Anglo-dominated world has crushed Fleur's culture and her life. . . . [Fleur] suffer[s] cultural alienation, which makes mothering almost impossible" (186). Yet Lulu refuses forgiveness, feeling that Fleur should have made a better choice, a view that assumes her mother's power even as the narrative demonstrates Fleur's powerlessness. Similarly, other characters invest Fleur with supernatural power even as the narrative shows her to be a nomadic, silent old woman inhabiting the periphery of the intratextual world. Fleur's situation exemplifies the condition of mothering under colonization, which gives an extreme and so more obvious view of the situation of all mothers who must necessarily be inscribed within the paradox of the mother's power and simultaneous powerlessness.

Another key mother figure is June, who "may be dead, but her sadness lives on, not unconscious or repressed, but as a fundamental subtext" (Hansen 120) throughout the Matchimanito novels. June Morrissey Kashpaw walks into the snow to her death in the first few pages of Erdrich's first published novel, *Love Medicine* (1984, 1993), and from that point on haunts each of the subsequent Matchimanito texts (with the exception of *Tracks*, which is set in the historical past and focuses on Fleur). Sometimes June is a memory, but other times a ghost, acting for or most often against those who loved her. She is consistently represented as one whose inability to accept the love offered her over the course of her life is a direct result of her own mother's failures. For example, June rejects the maternal love of Marie Lazarre, who recognizes, "it was a mother she couldn't trust after what had happened" (1993: 92). June goes on to abandon (and maybe attempts to kill) her own child, Lipsha Morrissey, a central character in the tetralogy. Over the course of the Matchimanito novels, Lipsha is engaged in numerous mother-related quests: to come to terms with his mother's ghost; to find mother-love through his romantic relationship with Shawnee Ray Toose, recognizing that his love for her "is mixed up with the love" she shows her young son (1994: 154); and finally, abandoned in a blizzard by his father, Gerry, who has been lured away by June's ghost, Lipsha is left with the infant he has inadvertently kidnapped and exposed to harm, but he is able to break the cycle of failed mothering by determining that the baby boy now in his care will be someone "who was never left behind" (1994: 259).

And Lipsha is not the only male character in Erdrich's works to assume a mothering role; in fact, abandoning mothers are often replaced in the tetralogy by nurturing male figures. Nanapush parents the orphaned Fleur and tells her story in both *Tracks* and *Four Souls*, and of course, there is also Scranton Roy of *The Antelope Wife*. After participating in the massacre of an Ojibwe village on the Otter Trail River and fleeing the carnage because, as he bayonets an old woman, Roy receives a vision of his own mother, he follows a dog carrying a baby girl. He cradles the baby to his chest and then, in answer to her hungry cries, "opened his shirt and put her to his nipple" (6), nursing her with "his own watery, appalling, God-given milk" (8).

While mothers and othermothers are important figures in all of Erdrich's novels, they command special attention during the period surrounding the writing of her birth memoir. *The Bingo Palace*, published the year before *The Blue Jay's Dance*, indicates a new awareness of the mother's story, which will become a focus in the later novels. The text not only offers June's story for the first time in a chapter titled "June's Luck," (though told by an omniscient third person narrator and not by June herself), but also offers her forgiveness through her son Lipsha who realizes that June had only done to him "what was done to her" (217). Further, the communal narrative voice of this novel is often focused on Shawnee Ray Toose and aware of the paradox she experiences in her role as a single Native American mother to a young son. She holds power to mother Redford in her own way, but she is also powerless, as she lives under the control of others, including her surrogate mother, Zelda, and Redford's father, the wealthy and influential Lyman Lamartine. Further, the narrative voice situates the mother as both analogous to culture and as the receptacle and bearer of that particular culture, and so remarks, "The red rope is the hope of our nation. It pulls, it sings, it snags, it feeds, it holds. How it holds" (6). The image of mother-love as a powerful rope for holding things together is recast in an equally eloquent passage in *The Blue Jay's Dance*, when the speaker ponders "our human problem . . . how to let go while holding tight, how to simultaneously cherish the closeness and intricacy of the bond while at the same time letting out the raveling string, the red yarn that ties our hearts" (69). The power of mother-love and the powerlessness of the mother to hold on to her offspring as they pass through time and the world are brought together in this image, which speaks to the earlier image as many central images in the memoir respond to significant images of earlier texts.[6]

Writing in 1997, Elaine Hansen observes, "Erdrich's novels to date consistently engage the possibility of recovering the role of the mother and revaluing the status and power of Native American women" (Hansen 121). But until the paradox that structures the experience of mothering can be resolved, the ambivalence that structures representations of her cannot be overcome, and she must remain a silent screen onto which others cast their own projections. And so, speechless and shape-shifting yet powerfully present even when textually absent, the mother haunts Erdrich's tetralogy as a literal representation of the paradox and the ambivalence it produces. But in writing *The Blue Jay's Dance*, Erdrich finds a unique resolution; by simultaneously accepting her limitations and powerlessness, while reconnecting with important sources of empowerment and maternal power, the motherline and Mother Nature, she becomes able to represent maternal subjects in complex ways that defy reductive reading through either the "Angel in the House" paradigm or relative to its binary opposite, the Bad Mother.

In this way, she demonstrates characteristic subversion of binary logic, refusal to accept the neat separation offered by the oppositional breakdown of these contradictory but ultimately indivisible aspects of maternal experience. Actively resisting the power/powerless split for herself enables her to represent similarly empowered, resisting mothers whose experiences include both moments of power and moments of powerlessness, but whose lives are not structured by either realm of experience and whose stories can thus be told more fully.[7] *The Blue Jay's Dance* is written years after the experiences detailed in the book have taken place, and initiates a conversation between Erdrich's writing self and her mothering self, or, as she puts it, "This book is a set of thoughts from one self to the other—writer to parent, artist to mother . . . writing is reflective and living is active—the two collide in the tumultuous business of caring for babies" (1995: 6). Through narrative recreation of her own experiences of mothering, Erdrich comes to render and perhaps experience maternal subjectivity in new ways.

The construction of the text highlights the fragmented, semiotic experience of early motherhood, and also explores the interstices of a variety of paradoxes. Divided into four parts, each containing multiple short sections, it begins with winter and ends with fall. Winter establishes the "household map" as well as the dominant themes of the text: maintaining a sense of self while parenting; the contradictory but confluent impulses toward writing and mothering; the place of humans and animals in each others' worlds as well as in the world at large and the wondrous complexity of it all; the exhilarating but heartbreaking experience of holding life in your body and bringing your baby into the cycle of time, into the wonder, terror, joy, and despair of life.

As much as this is a memoir of birth, it is paradoxically a death-haunted text in which losses are many and diverse, the story of a year of which the speaker writes, "we have a baby . . . our older, adopted children hit adolescence like runaway trucks. Dear grandparents weaken and die" (4). Erdrich is aware of the ways in which her narrative rocks back and forth between the reflections of a mother mothering and those of a child losing loved (m)others, growing into herself through the experience of these two ends of life's spectrum: "beginnings suggest endings and I can't help thinking of the continuum, the span, the afters and befores" (8). Later, looking at a bird's nest into which the hair of each of her daughters has been woven, Erdrich is again confronted by the inescapable duality and painful cycle of living. She writes, "Life seems to flow by quickly, taking our loves quickly in its flow. In the growth of children, in the aging of beloved parents, time's chart is magnified . . . with each celebration of maturity, there is also a pang of loss" (69).

Throughout *The Blue Jay's Dance*, images of new life are closely paired with images of life fading or ended; each scene of intense beauty mirrors one of intense violence or terrible loss. Power is held in balance with helplessness, life with death, love with loss; the reader is suspended throughout on a pendulum that swings between seeming contradictions over a landscape of repeating but subtly shifting images through which we come to see the inseparability of these aspects of human experience, and to realize that it is only the binary analytic that renders them oppositional and therefore seemingly paradoxical. Dualities emerge as part of a cyclical whole rather than as opposing forces.

Many images and figures repeat through the text (nests, both empty and too full; birds, particularly screaming jays and gentle finches; wild animals, watching and watched; cats, which stalk through the text trailing time in the form of progeny and progenitors; moths/butterflies, predominantly the tragic Luna whose visit evokes some of Erdrich's most powerful and poignant writing as well as the Mourning Cloaks that represent Erdrich's coming to terms with her place in the motherline; food—lovingly prepared, ritualistically consumed), but central to a consideration of Erdrich's resolution of the maternal paradox are houses and gardens.

House and garden appear early on in the text, and are drawn and redrawn throughout, their symbolic significance as individual and relational images shifting. Both are ultimately, complexly, seen as maternal metaphors and represent, at various junctures, the time-and-earthbound body of the mother, and her timeless essence as part of the cycle of life. Gardens seem to grow paradoxes—the one the author dreams in winter is both "spiritually definitive and of the earth" (27), filled with possibility, but it also "exceeds the reality of what will, in truth, turn out to be my garden" (33). The dream garden "includes a child lying on a blanket, entranced by the spectacle of light" (34) and, of course, this is not reality either, as we come to know clearly in Part II: Spring. The garden, like a child, contains seeds of possibility, which the mother then cultivates in the hopes of avoiding the "usual blights and mistakes" and thwarting the "ruinous parasites" (32–33) that would beset her finest flowers. So the garden is seen as a world that contains beautiful and delicate lives, but also shelters parasites and offers no protection from blights and acts of nature. The mother dreams the flowers, plants their seeds, protects them as she can, but then must stand by powerless and watch them grow or die, according to the whims of nature and the dictates of time.

But the placement of this section, "Wintergarden," in the text enables us to also read the garden as metaphor of maternal power—specifically, the power of the mother's body to create and bring forth life. "Wintergarden" immediately precedes "Famous Labors," in which Erdrich states, "we are all stronger than we think when we are put to the task" of bearing our children and wonders, "Why is no woman's labor as famous as the death of Socrates? Why don't women routinely receive medals for giving birth?"(35). The remaining sections of Part I, with one significant exception, focus on the ways in which "birth is intensely spiritual and physical all at once" (44), with the longest section, "Women's Work," detailing the physical tasks engaged by the laboring body. The final section, "Archery," introduces the well-known analogy "You are the bows from which your children as living arrows are sent forth," which Erdrich recalls finding written on a scrap of paper in her father's handwriting during a troubled time in her young life. Erdrich interprets the metaphor in a way that her father most certainly could not, relating it to birthing labor, wherein "a woman bends the great ash bow with an unpossessed power. . . . Each archer feels the despairing fear it cannot be done. But it will" (50). The valorized image of the powerful, laboring mother who is deserving of medals for her active, conscious participation in bringing forth life is clearly the inverse of the mother tending the garden that is ultimately beyond her control. The surrounding sections' focus on the laboring body reminds us that the mother is both the garden and the gardener, a being perched on the border between power and powerlessness.

So gardens planned in winter, representing both the powerful laboring body of the mother (in winter, Erdrich is pregnant and the section ends with the birth of her baby) and the mother/gardener's powerlessness to ensure against "blights, mistakes, ruinous beetles and parasites" (33), bloom in spring, sheltering the nests and the offspring of Eastern phoebes and beloved finches. But in the section "Fiddlehead Garden," the image of the life-giving and life-sheltering garden finds its counterpart as Erdrich relates the story of John McCauley whose

> wife loved to eat fiddleheads. He lost her in a senseless accident. Together they had also planted a front yard crocus patch in letters that spelled Welcome Spring. After she died, John stamped the early blooms into the frozen dirt. But he kept the fiddleheads. . . . The young, brilliant, still-coiled heads of ferns are a spring tonic that also taste to me of grief. (85)

Images like this one play on contrast: the early blooms and the frozen dirt; the loving planting of the crocuses by the couple in anticipation of spring juxtaposed against the violent destruction of the plants by the survivor in the aftermath of loss. And the fiddleheads themselves contain contradiction, at once a tonic (restorative, life-giving) and a bitter reminder of death. This is only one example of the way in which the images and metaphors of gardens enable Erdrich to demonstrate the coexistence of contradictory aspects of human experience as well as her growing acceptance of them as intertwined and cyclical.

The house is another site through which Erdrich investigates such interconnections. In the section titled "Wild Kitten," in Part II: Spring, Erdrich hears the piteous crying of a lost kitten, which is an echo of the "banshee quaver" of the kitten's mother, Tasmin, who blames Erdrich for the death of her lover, Chuck, in winter's "Passions" section. Erdrich enters the crawlspace beneath the farmhouse to rescue the kitten, which retreats into a bearing wall and nearly becomes trapped. This is one of the few instances in which the narrator interferes with the animals she is bound up with throughout the text and relative to which she is constantly shifting between the subject position of spectator and the object position of the watched. Not only does her interference almost cause the kitten to become entombed beneath the house, but also through rescuing the kitten, Erdrich inadvertently causes the death of the beloved female goldfinch. The finch is presented to Erdrich by the admiring kitten in the section titled "Love Gifts" in summer. Similarly, in trying to rescue the besieged female duck in "Duck Rape," the narrator is horrified to realize that her interference has frightened the duck back into the water where her pursuers again attack her. The narrator's struggle to hold back when she wants to interfere with happenings in the animal world are analogous to the struggles of the narrator-mother to understand that her child is no longer part of her body but of the world beyond it, and the need to let go.

In the book's final section, Erdrich reckons with her understanding that she is in many ways increasingly a spectator in her infant daughter's life: "She sweeps on with her life. I cannot gather back one moment, only marvel at what comes next" (212). Maternal power and powerlessness are bound together in these instances, as the narrator recognizes that she has the power to interfere, but not, ultimately, to inhibit violence and death in the world; her seeming power only leads her into confrontation with her true powerlessness in the realm of lived experience.

While pursuing the kitten, Erdrich is conscious of her position as both mother and child, as well as the power/powerless paradox. Trapped beneath the house, which throughout the text is figured alternately as the metaphorical body of the mother and as a space that shelters mothering, the narrator experiences herself as both fetus and maternal body. As the darkness presses against her in a dream-memory of the event, she observes, "What the body remembers of birth it anticipates as death" (102), relating the experience of lying under the house to the experience of both giving birth (which she speaks of in "Famous Labors" as containing the possibility of maternal death) and being birthed. In the subject position of the child, she continues, "I fear in particular the small space, the earth closing in on me, the house like a mother settling its cracked bones and plumbing. . . . It was like being dead or unborn" (103). These lines inscribe the power/powerless paradox in a subtle way, especially if read in light of an episode in *Tracks* wherein Pauline Puyat tries to kill her unborn child by closing her legs during labor to prevent it from being born. In labor, the mother holds power of life or death, even as she hovers uncomfortably close to the line between them, powerless to anchor herself. This section of *The Blue Jay's Dance* ends with the narrator imagining "the husk of myself, still buried against the east wall . . . a kind of house god, a woman lying down there, still, an empty double" (104). The language here, describing the woman's body as a husk and an empty double, suggests the power of the maternal to contain and produce life, as well as the power of maternity to shape, if she so chooses, a woman's life. Importantly, though, it also suggests the essential powerlessness that comes from being defined by or in relation to another such that one is empty without the presence of that other. The mother here is at once a powerful protective force (a house god) and a fragile, discarded shell (a husk, an empty double).

The following section, "Fairy Tales. Love, Grief and Invisible Seeds," continues Erdrich's reflections on these ideas. She begins with the question,

"How many women lie buried beneath their houses?" and goes on to contemplate a mother's "helpless and devouring love" (104) for her children and the fact that "we cannot choose who are children are, or what they will be—by nature they inspire a helpless love, wholly delicious, also capable of delivering startling pain" (105). Love is a primary point of reflection early in the section, but, as is typical of the structure of the writing here, the focus turns to loss.

The image of the garden is the lynchpin of the section, joining the themes of love and loss, extending the metaphor of the garden and tying together the previously disparate threads in the text that relate nature and the motherline to individual experiences of mothering: "In the tended garden of the personality or soul, love is the weed of startling loveliness. . . . but even love is not the story here, nor what will survive us or me. The tale that will live on is the same that survives the other woman, the narrative of flowers" (107). The "other woman" is the long-ago occupant of the house with whom Erdrich experiences and expresses connection through care of the house and garden. The woman, Mrs. B., is a pivotal figure who links Erdrich to the past and to the community of women, and the narrator pays homage to these connections by tending the "stately foxglove" in the garden. The last line of the spring section reads: "it is the foxglove . . . that I keep for her and multiply with slow perseverance, as if in the presence of the foxglove the ghosts are not so much laid to rest as still able to partake of the rich and rooted fullness of this life" (110). Thus, Erdrich again frees herself from the either/or paradoxes produced by binary logic, and the dualities of life and death, love and loss, are shown as naturally (and even supernaturally) bound together.

The next part of the book, Summer, makes explicit the narrator's growing awareness of the importance of her connections to other women, especially other mothers, and her own motherline. The short consecutive sections titled "The Veils," "Three Photographs," and "The Precious No" contain the narrative's most direct statements on these connections and suggest the power of such connections to help individual women resist the naturalized segregation of maternal power/powerlessness and structure their experience in less oppositional terms. The three photographs of the section title are of Erdrich's grandmother on the day of her first communion, Erdrich's mother on her wedding day, and the author herself: "Me at seven. And that's my mother's [veil] cut down and tacked onto a lacy headband. And I might as well be holding my grandmother's candle, too. It is exactly the same" (139). These images obviously underscore Erdrich's recognition of her connection to her motherline, but the surrounding sections enable us to read deeper. Each photograph contains a veil; in the preceding section, "The Veils," Erdrich describes the veil as "the mist before the woman's face that allows her to limit her vision to the here, the now, the inch beyond her nose" (138). Here, the veil cuts women off from one another, from their individual motherlines and from the motherline that connects all who mother. But, at the same time, as expressed by "Three Photographs," the veil, like the "red rope" in *The Bingo Palace*, also holds and connects.

Throughout the text, Erdrich delves into these important motherline connections. In "Nests," for example, the narrator is at her wit's end with her crying baby and reaches down for the child, hands "trembling with anger" but then feels herself "somehow physically enlarged . . . invested not with my own thin, worn endurance, but with my mother's patience" (71). The text contains many such reflections on the author's mother and grandmother, their place in her life and their lessons in mothering, but goes further and attests to solidarity among the larger community of women who mother (both biological and othermothers). For example, in "All Mothers," the narrator voices her sense of being enlarged or added to by her experiential connections to other women, concluding "Some days, I am made up of a thousand mothers" (161). But it is in the section titled "The Precious No" that the writer ties together many threads of the text, and offers a transformative vision of feminist mothering, so it is to this section that I now turn.

Picking up the image of the veils from the two previous sections, Erdrich locates the source of both maternal power and powerlessness: women's relationships with other women. Earlier, the veil is described as "an illusion of safety, a flimsy skin of privacy" and "a violent grace is required, to lift the veil all on your own" (137–138). The veil separates women from one another, and through this separation, we are diminished. It is only through "wild blue dancing" (140) that we can hope to shed them so that we might finally "look each other in the eye, our faces clear, nothing between us but air. And what do we do with the nets, the sails that luffed, that tangled our feet? What do we do with the knowledge and the anger?" We transform the veils that once separated us, knot them between us "like sheets for escape . . . ropes between us. Primary cords" (141). Paradoxically, then, the source of powerlessness becomes a source of power as the flimsy veils are twisted together and used to draw us one to the others so that we might all climb safely out of entrapment in patriarchal structures of isolated motherhood toward the experience of empowered mothering. The wild blue dance is our first step in this direction, and this is, of course, the dance of the title, the blue jay's dance.

Explained in one of the book's final sections, "The Blue Jay's Dance" is a survivor's tactic, "cocky, exuberant, entirely a bluff, a joke" (194), undertaken when all is all but lost; it is powerful protection in a situation of material powerlessness. And so, in this context, it is a mother's dance, a dance of violent grace that is evidence of a desire to "clench down hard on life" (195). It is the dance that our mothers danced for us while we "were still in the process of differentiating." Here, in writing of dancing with her daughter, Erdrich writes, "my acts are hers, and I don't even think, yet, where I stop for her or where her needs, exactly, begin. I must dance for her. I must be the one to dip and twirl in the cold glare and I must teach her, as she grows, the unlikely steps" (195–196).

In Erdrich's maternal vision we must recreate this experience of oneness and dance for our children and each (m)other and ourselves, dance to survive, to throw off the veils so that we can gather them together into a powerful rope that ties us to one another, enables our participation in the fullness of time by connecting us to the past and future and frees us to embrace all aspects of maternal experience:

> We are all bound, we are all in tatters, we are all the shining presence behind the net. We are all the face we are not allowed to touch. We are all in need of ancient nourishment. And if we walk slowly without losing our connections to one another, if we wait, holding firm to the rock while our daughters approach hand over hand, if we can catch our mothers, if we hold our grandmothers, if we remember that the veil can also be the durable love between women. (141)

Although abandoning mothers proliferate in the early novels, seen always through the eyes of their abandoned children, this trend alters in the novels written in the period immediately before and the years after publication of *The Blue Jay's Dance*. Through reclamation of the maternal eye/I and by overcoming the oppositional separation of power and powerlessness through acceptance of these aspects of maternal experience as interconnected, Erdrich is able to make peace with the divided spectral mother who had haunted the periphery of her novelistic world. In the novels that follow this remarkable memoir, mothers begin to speak for themselves, lost mothers find their children and the way home, and the durable love between women takes center stage. Thus, *The Blue Jay's Dance* touches off a shift in Louise Erdrich's voice, style, and vision, providing readers with a beautiful and profound exploration of early mothering and a vision of empowered mothering that can transform the experience for all women.

NOTES

1. Adrienne Rich in *Of Woman Born* (1976) draws a distinction between mothering as a potentially empowering experience for women and motherhood, an institution governed by patriarchal thought and geared toward its reproduction. The term *mothering* is distinguished from *motherhood* in other ways as well, primarily in that the former is often used to describe the caring labor associated with being a mother and not just the biological fact of having given birth.

2. Sharon Abbey and Andrea O'Reilly observe, "Mothering is profoundly an experience of both powerlessness and power, and it is this paradox . . . that helps explain women's ambivalence about motherhood" (*Redefining Motherhood* 78).

3. In the "Thanks and Acknowledgements" section of *The Birchbark House* (1999), a book for young readers, Erdrich writes, "This book and those that will follow are an attempt to retrace my own family's history." The book includes a glossary of Ojibwe words and incorporates the language into the text much more heavily than Erdrich's earlier works, making explicit the connection between story/history, culture, and language, and suggesting that part of her project is to keep the language itself alive by teaching it to a young audience. *Books and Islands in Ojibwe Country* (2001) participates in this project as well, though it is written for an older and more general audience, and includes several chapters that reflect on the importance of language in keeping a culture alive and on the Ojibwe language in particular.

4. In an interview with Robert Spillman regarding *Tales of Burning Love* (1996), the first novel to be written after the publication of *The Blue Jay's Dance*, Erdrich says, "for this one, I wanted the core of women."

5. I'm referring here to Erdrich's planned tetralogy of novels centering on four central Ojibwe families. These novels have commanded many awards between them and critical work on Erdrich has generally, though not exclusively, focused on them: *Love Medicine* (1984, revised edition in 1993), *The Beet Queen* (1986), *Tracks* (1988), and *The Bingo Palace* (1994). Peter Beidler and Gay Barton coin the useful designation, "the Matchimanito novels" in *A Reader's Guide to the Novels of Louise Erdrich* to refer to the tetralogy, as well as later novels that focus on the same families (whose reservation was situated in proximity to Matchimanito Lake) such as *Tales of Burning Love*. Because I see significant shifts in Erdrich's writing after 1995, I regard the tetralogy of earlier works as more or less unified in their representation of mothers and later Matchimanito novels, including *The Last Report on the Miracles at Little No Horse* (2001) and *Four Souls* (2004) as significantly different, redressing many of the same issues through slightly different lenses that sometimes wrestle with and sometimes transcend the paradoxes of ambivalence that characterize her earlier portrayals of maternal characters.

6. Another interesting variation on a theme is the image of nests and hair. A central image in *The Beet Queen* is that of the spider making its delicate nest in

the hair of the infant, Dot Adare, while her mother Celestine watches. Celestine recognizes that it is "a complicated house" (176) and can't bear to destroy it. This image is inverted in *The Blue Jay's Dance* when Erdrich finds a bird's nest made of her daughters' hair and can't bear to "hold the nest because longing seizes [her]," (69) a simultaneous longing to stop her girls from outgrowing her arms and to be with her own mother.

7. I am thinking here of Dot Adare Mauser and Marlis Cook Mauser in *Tales of Burning Love*; the mothers in *The Antelope Wife*, particularly Blue Prairie Woman and her descendants, Rozin Roy Whiteheart Beads Shawano and Sweetheart Calico; and of Fleur Pillager in *Four Souls* (2004).

REFERENCES

Abbey, Sharon. "Researching Motherhood as a Feminist: Reflecting on My Own Experience." *Journal of the Association for Research on Mothering* 1.1 (1999): 45–55.

Abbey, Sharon, and Andrea O'Reilly, Eds. *Redefining Motherhood: Changing Identities and Patterns.* Toronto: Second Story Press, 1998.

Allen, Paula Gunn. *Grandmothers of the Light: A Medicine Woman's Sourcebook.* Boston: Beacon Press, 1991.

Allen, Paula Gunn, Ed. *Spiderwoman's Granddaughters: Traditional Tales and Contemporary Writing by Native American Women.* Boston: Beacon Press, 1989.

Bloom, Lynn R. "Heritages: Dimensions of Mother-Daughter Relationships in Women's Autobiographies." *The Lost Tradition: Mothers and Daughters in Literature.* Eds. Cathy Davidson and E. M. Broner. New York: Frederick Unger, 1980. 291–303.

Bushnell, Jeannette. "Tribal Mothering as Portrayed in Paula Gunn Allen's *Spider Woman's Granddaughters.*" *Journal of the Association for Research on Mothering* 1.1 (1999): 130–136.

Caeser, Terry. "Motherhood and Postmodernism." *American Literary History* 7.1 (Spring 1995): 120–140.

Chase, Susan E. *Mothers and Children: Feminist Analyses and Personal Narratives.* New Brunswick, NJ: Rutgers University Press, 2001.

Daly, Brenda O., and Maureen T. Reddy. *Narrating Mothers: Theorizing Maternal Subjectivities.* Knoxville: University of Tennessee Press, 1991.

Davidson, Cathy, and E. M. Broner, Eds. *The Lost Tradition: Mothers and Daughters in Literature.* New York: Frederick , 1980.

Erdrich, Louise. *The Antelope Wife.* New York: HarperFlamingo, 1998.

———. *The Beet Queen.* New York: Henry Holt, 1986.

————. *The Bingo Palace*. New York: HarperCollins, 1994.

————. *The Blue Jay's Dance: A Birth Year*. New York: HarperCollins, 1995.

————. *Books and Islands in Ojibwe Country*. Washington, DC: National Geographic, 2003.

————. *Four Souls*. New York: HarperCollins, 2004.

————. *The Last Report on the Miracles at Little No Horse*. New York: Harper-Collins, 2001.

————. *Love Medicine*. 1984. New York: Henry Holt, 1993.

————. *Tales of Burning Love*. New York: HarperCollins, 1996.

————. *Tracks*. New York: HarperPerennial, 1988.

Glenn, Evelyn Nakano, Grace Chang, and Linda Rennie Forcey, Eds. *Mothering: Ideology, Experience, and Agency*. New York: Routledge, 1994.

Hansen, Elaine Tuttle. *Mother Without Child: Contemporary Fiction and the Crisis of Motherhood*. Berkeley: University of California Press, 1997.

Hult, Carol. "Writer in the House: Mothering and Motherhood." *Journal of the Association for Research on Mothering* 1.1 (1999): 25–31.

Jeremiah, Emily. "Troublesome Practices: Mothering, Literature and Ethics." *Journal of the Association for Research on Mothering* 4.2 (Fall/Winter 2002): 7–16.

Ladd-Taylor, Molly, and Lauri Umansky. *"Bad" Mothers: The Politics of Blame in Twentieth-Century America*. New York: New York University Press, 1998.

Little, Jonathan. "Beading the Multicultural World: Louise Erdrich's *The Antelope Wife* and the Sacred Metaphysic." *Contemporary Literature* 41.3 (Fall 2000): 495–524.

Lowinsky, Naomi. "Mother of Mothers, Daughter of Daughters: Reflections of the Motherline." *Mother Outlaws: Theories and Practices of Empowered Mothering*. Ed. Andrea O'Reilly. Toronto: Women's Press, 2004. 285–292.

O'Reilly, Andrea, Ed. *Mother Outlaws: Theories and Practices of Empowered Mothering*. Toronto: Women's Press, 2004.

Ruddick, Sara. "Maternal Thinking." *Mothering: Essays in Feminist Theory*. Ed. Joyce Trebilcot. Totowa, NJ: Rowman and Allanheld, 1984. 213–230.

Spillman, Robert. "The Creative Instinct." *Salon* online. www.salon.com/weekly/interview960506.html.

Stokes, Karah. "What about the Sweetheart?: The "Different Shape" of Anishinabe Two Sisters Stories in Louise Erdrich's *Love Medicine* and *Tales of Burning Love*," *MELUS* 24.2 (Summer 1999): 89–105.

Stookey, Lorena L. *Louise Erdrich: A Critical Companion*. Westport, CT: Greenwood Press, 1999.

Suleiman, Susan Rubin. "Writing and Motherhood." *The (M)other Tongue: Essays in Feminist Psychoanalytic Interpretation*. Eds. Shirley Nelson Garner, Claire

Kahane, and Madelon Sprengnether. Ithaca: Cornell University Press, 1985. 352–377.

Wong, Hertha D. "Adoptive Mothers and Throw-away Children in the Novels of Louise Erdrich." *Narrating Mothers: Theorizing Maternal Subjectivities.* Eds. Brenda O. Daly and Maureen T. Reddy. Knoxville: University of Tennessee Press, 1991. 174–192.

CHAPTER SIX

African American Mothers

Victimized, Vilified, and Valorized

SHIRLEY A. HILL

SOCIALLY CONSTRUCTED IMAGES of motherhood and norms about the priority it should have in the lives of women have been issues of intense debate
among many social actors, not the least of them feminists. The historic mandate was for women to bear as many children as possible, and their status and
well-being often hinged on their ability to do so (Hartmann; Kitzinger). This
procreation ethic, however, was breached in the United States during the
1800s by the rise of the industrial economy, modernization, the nation's first
birth control movement, and new family and gender ideologies. The linchpin
of these new ideologies was the breadwinner–homemaker family, which advocated the removal of white middle-class women and children from the labor
market and a public–private gender-based division of responsibility. Most
white women embraced these new ideologies as elevating their status and
economic security and enabling them to become mistresses in their own
homes (Walsh). Still, it is noteworthy that the First Wave of feminism
emerged during that era. Early feminists challenged the exclusion of women
from the public arena and lobbied for the right of women to control their
own sexuality, practice birth control, and become mothers on a voluntary
basis (Berg; Kline).

Feminist activism, industrialization, the abolition of slavery, and, to some
extent, the efforts of eugenicists reduced the rate of fertility in United State in
the late 1800s, a trend that was not reversed until the post–World War II
baby boom generation. Peace and economic prosperity proved an ideal

context for the creation of breadwinner–homemaker families, and the 1950s
were often seen in America as the "golden age of the family." Yet before the
decade had ended, married white women had begun to enter the labor market
in unprecedented numbers, where they were mostly relegated to dead-end,
low-wage jobs based on the notion that family and motherhood were their
real priorities. Thus, with the 1960s Second Wave of feminism, motherhood
became a topic of much debate. Some white feminists criticized motherhood
as an institution embedded in patriarchal and economic systems of domina-
tion (Andersen), yet others described it as potentially empowering (Kahn;
O'Brien). The experiences of African American women resonated with the
later view; indeed, their long history of broadly defining mothering made
them especially critical of the motherhood-as-oppression thesis.

African American feminists have played an especially important role in
bringing fresh insights into the analysis of motherhood by showing how its
meaning and demands are structured by race and class position. Based on
images of motherhood that originated in West Africa and were reinforced by
slavery, these theorists contended that fertility and motherhood are often
sources of power and esteem for women. They also challenged the construction of mothering work as isolated, privatized, devalued labor that reinforces
the secondary status of women (Collins 1990). Drawing on the experiences of
black mothers, they pointed out that women have headed their own families,
defined mothering work to include childcare, employment, and social
activism, and relied on extended family ties to help with the demands of childrearing (Polatnick; Stack). Their work suggests that motherhood is neither
inherently oppressive nor diminutive of women's position and power in society. Patricia Hill Collins, for example, pointed out that while motherhood is a
contradictory institution that is experienced in diverse ways by black women,
it can be empowering:

> [m]otherhood can serve as a site where Black women express and learn
> the power of self-definition, the importance of valuing and respecting
> ourselves, the necessity of self-reliance and independence, and a belief in
> Black women's empowerment (1990:118)

This analysis of African American motherhood invokes intersectionality
theory, which sees race, class, and gender as interlocking systems of oppression (Brewer; Zinn and Dill). Intersectionality theory is a useful approach for
understanding the significance of childrearing not only as gendered labor but
also as shaped by the historic and cultural experiences of poor and/or women
of color. It has broadened the feminist discourse on motherhood by recogniz-

ing that its meaning among black people has been different from the dominant cultural ideology, and in a sense has been more liberating.

I begin this chapter by looking at racialized constructions of motherhood in American society. In colonial America, black and white women were expected to produce as many children as possible; neither had much control over their sexuality or reproductive work. Enslaved black women, because they theoretically gave birth to "property," were seen as especially victimized by motherhood; however, they often used their childbearing ability as an instrument of personal fulfillment and as leverage in their relations with white slave owners. Although their progeny was valued during slavery, once slavery was abolished African American women were quickly vilified as "reckless breeders," "welfare queens," and the heads of pathological families, yet they asserted their rights as mothers through personal and organized social activism. During the civil rights era, revisionist historians and black feminists began to rearticulate the meaning of black motherhood, highlighting their struggles, efficacy, and activism on their own behalf. These images of motherhood served as a corrective for decades of negative stereotypes; however, they also valorized motherhood in ways that obscure the diverse experiences of African American mothers today. I conclude the chapter by looking at how the postindustrial economy has produced class polarization among African Americans that is slowly altering their mothering work.

THE STRENGTHS OF
"VICTIMIZED" ENSLAVED MOTHERS

> Children are a woman's constituency within the narrow political world of the family; the more she has, the stronger her clout. If she is infertile, her status plummets, and she often falls victim to polygamy, desertion, or divorce.
> —Betsy Hartmann, *Reproductive Rights and Wrongs*

Whether based on choice, powerlessness, ineffective birth control, labor demands, or the need to perpetuate the species, women have long had their identities and value tied to the production and rearing of children. In colonial American society, all enslaved black women and married white women were expected to produce as many children as feasible, as children were economic assets needed in the agricultural labor force. Black and white women shared a legally sanctioned lack of control over their own bodies, sexuality, and children, since white men felt entitled to have sex with and children by whomever they pleased. Moreover, white married men and slave owners were the legal custodians or owners of all children—whether they were born as legitimate heirs or held the status of being property. Enslaved black mothers have often been seen as especially victimized by childbearing. Angela Davis, for example, has argued that motherhood for them was a fragmenting and alienating experience, as they had little control over their own children:

> Birth mothers could not therefore expect to be mothers in the legal sense. Legally these children were chattel and therefore motherless. Slave states passed laws to the effect that children of slave women no more belonged to their biological mothers than the young of animals belonged to the females that birthed them. (358)

Yet whatever laws and customs governed the relationships between black mothers and their children, it is still the case that motherhood was likely one of the few sources of personal gratification available to black women, and there is evidence of intense motherly devotion to children. Despite their work demands, enslaved parents were responsible for training their children, and they often taught them values that differed from the dominant values of white slave owners, and did their best to shield them from the shock of bondage (Blassingame). Scholars have documented the stubborn resistance of enslaved black women to the sale of their children (Frazier), along with their "legendary efforts to preserve the lives of their children, to nurture them, and to encourage their development" (Shaw 300). One of the most important aspects of black mothering was providing their children with a higher standard of living than offered by slave owners (Shaw). Mothers who had lost their children through sale often made heroic efforts to see them, as noted in Frederick Douglass's account of slavery. Douglass, who was separated from his mother during infancy, pointed out that she traveled twelve miles by foot at night to see him, often after a long day of working as a fieldhand.

In addition to the gratifications they received from mothering, childbearing could enhance the status and value of black women. As Thomas Jefferson, one of the founding fathers of American society, once famously explained, "I consider a woman who brings a child every two years more profitable than the best man of the farm" since her childbearing added to slave owners' capital (qtd. in Booker 7). Childbearing held some potential for expanding the rights and privileges of enslaved black women; for example, it might reduce her chances of being sold, increase her social standing and work status, give her greater access to resources such as food, result in a more lenient work schedule, and, for a few, even serve as a route to freedom. On the other hand, black women could exercise leverage by their refusal to bear children: many drew on African folk knowledge to avoid or abort pregnancies, leaving one physician to explain to a frustrated slave owner that these women simply "are possessed of a secret by which they destroy the foetus at an early stage of gestation" (Ross 145).

Finally, the mothering work of some black women was highly appraised and co-opted by white families, as seen in the stereotypical image of the black mammy who (although often separated from her own children) was depicted as ferocious in the care and protection of white children (White 1985). As Deborah Gray White has explained, the mammy was a stereotypical image of a powerful black woman who, because of her domestic knowledge and abilities, could excel at doing everything. From slavery to modern times, white families relied heavily on the mothering work of black women.

EMANCIPATION AND THE "VILIFICATION" OF BLACK MOTHERS

The growth of the industrial economy in the nineteenth century radically altered family life, race relations, and gender expectations in American society. The demise of the agricultural economy was a significant factor in the eventual abolition of slavery and the exclusion of white women from productive labor. While most former slaves moved from slavery to sharecropping—a system that continued to insist on the economic labor of black women—a new breadwinner-homemaker family ideology prescribed exclusive roles of domesticity for white women. The care of children took on new significance as motherhood was elevated as the central occupation for white women. During the era of scientific motherhood, "the good mother" was seen as an angelic, self-sacrificing being who devoted her full-time energies to caring for children and availed herself of the advice of childrearing experts (Apple and Golden). Not surprisingly, black women were vilified as the antithesis of the good mother, as they often had children without the benefit of marriage, failed to be sufficiently subordinate to patriarchal authority, worked outside of the home, violated gender rules, and relied on other women for childrearing help.

Racialized constructions of motherhood helped spark the First Wave of feminism among black and white middle-class women, both of whom challenged the ideology of pious motherhood, but also used the premium placed on being a good mother to advocate for birth control, better prenatal care, and education for women (Berg). Black middle-class women saw birth control and smaller families as key to "racial uplift" because it could dispel notions that black women were sexually promiscuous and irresponsible child-bearers. Thus, despite insurmountable racial barriers between the two groups, the reproductive goals of middle-class black and white feminists often converged: they lobbied for the reproductive rights and autonomy of women, and in the process they undermined the efforts of eugenicists who urged middle-class white women to have more babies and decried the fact that "racial inferiors" were having any children at all.

Rates of fertility declined significantly with modernization and industrialization, yet the efforts of middle-class women to control childbearing often reflected their class biases and privileges, and failed to resonate with the life experiences of working-class or poor women. Only a small percentage of African Americans, for example, had achieved middle-class status, and the lure of motherhood as a route to adulthood, marriage, and a more fulfilling life loomed large (Hill 2005). Moreover, despite the exploitation of black women's sexuality and childbearing during centuries of slavery, the value of fertility and motherhood as a source of status and power remained strong. During the early twentieth century, African Americans began to defend themselves against the growing criticism of "pathological" and "matriarchal" families (Frazier). They also found a way to evade eugenicists who called for the sterilization of poor women and black nationalists (mostly men) who saw any form of birth control as black genocide.

Black women used their roles as mothers to lobby for racial uplift and freedom for African Americans. Perhaps one of the most dramatic examples is found in the insistence by the mother of Emmett Till, a fourteen-year-old African American boy who was tortured and lynched in Mississippi in 1955, that the "whole world" witness her maternal grief and the badly mutilated body of her son (Feldstein). At an open casket funeral, Mamie Till Mobley took the podium and declared that she would spend her time pursuing justice rather than hating. A more collective assertion of the maternal rights of black mothers was seen in the National Welfare Rights Organization, which had more than 20,000 members by the late 1960s—mostly women of color (Neubeck and Cazenave). It challenged the long-standing exclusion of black mothers from welfare rights and urged them to apply for the same benefits available to other single mothers.

THE RISE OF THE "VALIANT" BLACK MOTHER

By the late 1960s, the political activism and histories of black mothers were being captured by scholars who refuted the notion of pathological black motherhood and sought to provide a more culturally relevant and accurate perspective on black families. Andrew Billingsley's *Black Families in White America* was pivotal in providing the framework for a broader analysis of African American families, and Carol Stack's *All My Kin* highlighted the childrearing efficacy of mothers in poor black families. Stack explained patterns of childswapping and norms of reciprocity between women that fostered strong social bonds and aided in the work of caring for children. Other scholars also emphasized how the mothering work of African American women differed from that of white women; the former unfolded in a matrifocal family system composed of an "extended line of female kin: mothers, daughters, and their children pooling resources and often sharing a household" (Dickerson xv). Because African American mothers usually engaged in labor market and family work, they had evolved a distinctively different organization of mothering—one in which othermothers played a crucial role in the work of raising children (Collins 1990, 1994).

Beyond developing a shared system of motherhood, the meaning of motherhood was also shaped by race. For example, motherhood among black women was often seen as a route to achieving adulthood, and the concept of legitimacy, which was based mostly on property and inheritance rights, had less relevance among black people (Ladner). The roots of these mothering traditions were also traced to West African cultures, which added further credence to the idea that slavery had neither stripped black families of their cultural heritage nor completely defined them. Despite the diversity found among African societies, the value of procreation was widely agreed upon because cultural and religious ideologies saw one's eternal spiritual existence as nullified by the absence of descendants. As Barbara Christian explained, "The African mother is a spiritual anchor; thus she is greatly respected in African societies. By giving birth to children, African women ensure their people's continuity, both here and in the hereafter" (96). Fertility and childbearing provided African women a status that belied strongly held patriarchal ideologies.

Besides religious ideology, the most salient structural factor in the organization of mothering in gender-segregated colonial African societies was that women were usually responsible for both rearing and providing food for children. To fulfill this responsibility, they built strong coalitions with other women that, along with their roles in economic production, enhanced their status, power, and independence (Burgess). Thus, while polygamy and other restrictions on women suggest that patriarchy was the ideological norm, the impact of patriarchy was mitigated by the premium placed on women's fertility, the priority of blood over marital ties, the strength of female-centered kinship groups, and mothers' economic responsibility for their children

(White 1994). Slavery both reinforced and degraded these mothering traditions, as it forced black women to perform arduous labor and of necessity rely
on other women for help in the rearing of their children.

Based on the proliferation of research during the civil rights era on the
historic and contemporary experiences of black families emerges the image of
valiant black mothers—an image that was clearly at odds with motherhood
discourse articulated by most white feminists. In her analysis of two feminist
organizations that were active in the 1960s—one composed of mostly low to
working-class black women and the other of middle-class white women—
Polatnick pointed out that views on motherhood were starkly different. Both
groups firmly demanded reproductive rights for women, but motherhood
among white middle-class women was associated with the loss of sexual privileges and careers, social isolation, and narrow futures of domesticity and
dependence. On the other hand, African American saw mothers as strong,
authoritative figures; for them, Polatnick noted, motherhood "encompassed
caring for all the children of their community and fighting for a better future
for the community" (Polatnick 680).

BLACK MOTHERS IN POSTINDUSTRIAL AMERICA

The work of revisionist and feminist scholars in articulating how race and
class affect the experience of motherhood is to be applauded, especially in its
efforts to dispel negative and erroneous stereotypes about African American
mothers. Still, like most counterdiscourses, it risks inadvertently fostering the
notion that motherhood has a single meaning among black women and pro-
ducing stagnant images that belie the impact of evolving social and economic
forces. Appreciating the heroic struggles of valiant black mothers may also
obfuscate the challenges they face, and even unwittingly support myths that
view them as reckless breeders or innately equipped for the work of childrearing. In reality, the success of the civil rights movement, the rise of a postindustrial economy, and the passage of new public policies have all affected
African American families and the status of mothers. Invoking intersectionality theory—which contends that gender, race, and class are interlocking systems of inequality—is a useful tool for critiquing valorized images of black
mothers and highlighting the increasingly diverse family and mothering
experiences.

First, intersectionality theorists assert that, while gender is a social construct, it is a dimension of inequality that has important consequences for
perpetuating inequality. The work of raising children has always been espe-

cially gendered, as women cross-culturally are assigned the major responsibility for children. African American cultural norms have conceptualized mothering work as a collective rather than individual enterprise, yet focusing on the efficacy of shared mothering has often overshadowed the fact that raising children remains highly gendered among African Americans. Valiant black motherhood rarely demands gender equity in childrearing work, even though low-income and especially unmarried black men are often only minimally involved in caring for their children. In other cases, the normalization of childrearing as women's work ignores the contributions of fathers who actively engage in the work of raising children, some eager to become the fathers they never had (Hill 1999), and of other black men who deserve the title of "other fathers" for the support they provide to black children (Haney and March). That single mothers can effectively raise children is also challenged by poverty and research associating single motherhood with adverse child outcomes (McLanahan and Schwartz).

The intersectionality approach suggests that class also shapes experiences, and in the past few decades class diversity has grown remarkably among African Americans. As a result of the civil rights movement and greater opportunities, the rate of poverty among black people has fallen from 75 percent in the 1950s to about 25 percent today. Although black poverty remains more than twice as high as white poverty, and the racial gap in income (Brown) and especially in wealth (Oliver and Shapiro) is notable, many black Americans have achieved class mobility and their patterns of childbearing reflect their class position. The fertility rates of black and white women have converged, and social class competes with race in shaping how they mother their children (Hill 1999; Lareau). Middle-class black mothers engage in childrearing practices and face challenges similar to those of their white counterparts—the lack of adequate childcare, the demands of balancing work and family responsibilities—but also continue to racially socialize their children and teach them to deal with racial discrimination. Class mobility has reduced their reliance on family connections for support in raising their children, and many turn to private and public daycare centers. While they often enjoy strong family bonds, these bonds are less obligatory and revolve around an exchange of emotional and psychological resources rather than material support or economic assistance (Hill 1999).

Economic mobility has clearly not been shared by all African Americans; indeed, the rise of the postindustrial economy has deepened the poverty and despair among many black people. During the 1970s, job loss in major black urban areas not only undermined the opportunity of many African Americans to marry and form stable families, but was accompanied

by a surge of violence, homicide, and illicit drug use (Wilson). Most theorists have focused on the adverse impact of these forces on young black men,
yet African American women were affected as victims of violence and drug
abuse and by receiving even less aid in raising their children. Thus, black
mothers who need help the most—those who are single and poor—are often
experiencing less support from their extended families, and higher levels of
social isolation and depression (McLoyd). While there is no doubt that patterns of shared mothering can still be found (Higginson), myriad studies
have now documented the decline in extended family resources among
African Americans. Black grandmothers, once referred to as "guardians of
the generations," have become much more reluctant to make the sacrifices
necessary to care for children (Kaplan). Grandmothers today are often young
and employed; many feel disrespected by their children and are eager to
pursue ventures other than childrearing. As Ladner and Gourdine pointed
out more than two decades ago:

> Grandmothers complain about unmet emotional and social needs. They
> appear to feel powerless in coping with the demands made by their chil-
> dren. They comment frequently that their children show them no
> respect, do not listen to their advice, and place little value on their roles
> as parents. (23)

Finally, race and racism intensify social class disadvantage and further sap
the resources of poor mothers. Much of it is institutionalized in social policies
that provide inadequate health care for poor mothers and in welfare policies
that have stripped black women of the resources that once supported their
central roles in families. The growing participation by black women in the
social welfare system has been a key factor in the creation of the "welfare
queen" image of poor mothers. Fear over growing welfare expenses escalated
during the 1980s, when the significant minority of black families traditionally
headed by single mothers became a majority, making the separation of marriage and parenthood the statistical norm. By 2000, only one-third of African
American women were married and living with a spouse, and most children
(nearly 70 percent) were being born outside of marriage (Hemmons). Black
welfare dependency led to punitive policy changes throughout the twentieth
century, such as reductions in subsidized housing and the curtailment of
nutritional programs. Finally, the major welfare program (i.e., Aid to Families
with Dependent Children) was scrapped in favor of a more restrictive program (Temporary Assistance to Needy Families), a move interpreted by many

as racially motivated (Neubeck and Cazenave). All of this has fostered a decline in the power and authority of African American mothers (Scott) that is often ignored by studies that see extended family ties and shared mothering as features of black families.

Motherhood today is a diverse experience for black women, shaped largely by their marital status, social class position, access to resources, and public policies. Studies routinely highlight these class differences by showing that motherhood for economically disadvantaged women seems a surer route to creating families and achieving adulthood than does marriage (Edin). Many think of marriage and motherhood as two separate things, and do not believe the economic benefits of marriage would compensate for the loss of their independence (Blum and Deussen). Many women assert their right to have children regardless of their marital status, and most do an effective job of raising them. But it is important to recognize that black mothering traditions such as organizing childrearing collectively and sharing resources are in a state of transition due to evolving political and economic forces and greater class polarization among black people.

CONCLUSION

In this chapter I have provided an overview of three images of black mothers, showing how they were seen as victims of slavery, were vilified once slavery ended and black children lost their value, and finally were viewed as valiant by feminists and other scholars who rejected images of pathological black families. I have also invoked intersectionality theory to highlight how changes in gender, class, and race position are now challenging images of valiant black motherhood. In the past, structural forces such as slavery, racial segregation, and economic marginality contributed to the retention a model of shared mothering characteristic of African society and slavery. Now, new structural forces like class diversity challenge traditional patterns of mothering, leaving the "it takes a village" philosophy with more symbolism than substance.

The challenge facing African Americans today is to develop new strategies for supporting mothers and their children. Given the strength of self-help and community action-oriented ideologies among African Americans, there are numerous possibilities. Black churches, for example, could actively match mothers who lack adequate support with other mothers and families able to provide help. Communities might organize more effectively to bring needed resources (e.g., childcare centers, lunch programs) to the area. While "wedfare" policies that attempt to solve poverty among mothers through the promotion of marriage demand scrutiny, the efforts of African American fathers to become involved in their families must be encouraged and supported. What is evident is that the task of raising a child must not be relegated solely to a mother; it clearly demands the efforts of a team.

REFERENCES

Anderson, Margaret L. *Thinking About Women*. Boston: Allyn and Bacon, 2000.

Apple, Rima D., and Janet Golden. *Mothers and Motherhood: Readings in American History*. Columbus: Ohio State University Press, 1997.

Berg, Allison. *Mothering the Race: Women's Narratives of Reproduction, 1890–1930*. Urbana and Chicago: University of Illinois Press, 2002.

Billingsley, Andrew. *Black Families in White America*. Englewood Cliffs, NJ: Prentice-Hall, 1968.

Blassingame, J. W. *The Slave Community: Plantation Life in the Antebellum South*. New York: Oxford University Press, 1972.

Blum, Linda M., and Teresa Deussen. "Negotiating Independent Motherhood: Working-Class African American Women Talk About Marriage and Motherhood." *Gender and Society* 10.2 (1996): 199–211.

Booker, Christopher B. *"I Will Wear No Chain!" A Social History of African American Males*. Westport, CT: Praeger, 2000.

Brewer, Rose. "Theorizing Race, Class, and Gender: The New Scholarship of Black Feminist Intellectuals and Black Women's Labor." *Theorizing Black Feminisms: The Visionary Pragmatism of Black Women*. Eds. Stanlie M. James and Abena P. A. Busia. London and New York: Routledge, 1993. 13–30.

Brown, M. *White-Washing Race: The Myth of a Color-Blind Society*. Berkeley: University of California Press, 2003.

Burgess, Norma J. "Gender Roles Revisited: The Development of the 'Women's Place' Among African American Women in the United States." *Journal of Black Studies* 24.4 (1994): 391–401.

Christian, Barbara. "An Angle of Seeing: Motherhood in Buchi Emecheta's *Joys of Motherhood* and Alice Walker's *Meridian*." *Mothering: Ideology, Experience, and Agency*. Eds. Evelyn Nakano Glenn, Grace Chang, and Linda Rennie Forcey. New York: Routledge, 1994. 95–119.

Collins, Patricia Hill. *Black Feminist Thought: Knowledge, Consciousness, and the Politics of Empowerment*. Boston: Unwin Hyman, 1990.

————. "Shifting the Center: Race, Class, and Feminist Theorizing About Motherhood." *Mothering: Ideology, Experience, and Agency.* Eds. Evelyn Nakano Glenn, Grace Chang, and Linda Rennie Forcey. New York: Routledge, 1994. 45–66.

Davis, Angela Y. *Women, Race, and Class.* New York: Random House, 1981.

Dickerson, Bette J., Ed. *African American Single Mothers: Understanding Their Lives and Families.* Thousand Oaks, CA: Sage, 1995.

Douglass, Frederick. *Narrative of the Life of Frederick Douglass, An American Slave.* Cambridge: Belknap Press, 1960.

Edin, Kathryn. "What Do Low-Income Single Mothers Say About Marriage?" *Social Problems* 47.1 (2000): 112–113.

Feldstein, Ruth. "'I Wanted the Whole World to See': Race, Gender, and Construction of Motherhood in the Death of Emmett Till." *Mothers and Motherhood: Readings in American History.* Eds. Rima D. Apple and Janet Golden. Columbus: Ohio State University Press, 1997. 131–170.

Frazier, E. Franklin. *The Negro in the United States.* 1939. New York: Macmillan, 1957.

Haney, Lynne, and Miranda March. "Married Fathers and Caring Daddies: Welfare Reform and the Discursive Politics of Paternity." *Social Problems* 50.4 (2003): 461–481.

Hartmann, Betsy. *Reproductive Rights and Wrongs: The Global Politics of Population Control.* Boston: South End Press, 1987.

Hemmons, Willa Mae. *Black Women in the New World Order: Social Justice and the African American Female.* Westport, CT: Praeger, 1996.

Higginson, Joanna Gregson. "Competitive Parenting: The Culture of Teen Mothers." *Journal of Marriage and the Family* 60 (February 1998): 135–149.

Hill, Shirley A. *African American Children: Socialization and Development in Families.* Thousand Oaks, CA: Sage, 1999.

————. *Black Intimacies: A Gender Perspective on Families and Relationships.* Walnut Creek, CA: AltaMira Press, 2005.

Kahn, Robbie Pfeufer. *Bearing Meaning: The Language of Birth.* Urbana and Chicago: University of Illinois Press, 1995.

Kaplan, Elaine Bell. "Black Teenage Mothers and Their Mothers: The Impact of Adolescent Childbearing on Daughters' Relations with Mothers." *Social Problems* 43.4 (1996): 427–443.

Kitzinger, Sheila. *Ourselves as Mothers: The Universal Experience of Motherhood.* Reading, MA: Addison-Wesley, 1995.

Kline, Wendy. *Building a Better Race: Gender, Sexuality, and Eugenics from the Turn of the Century to the Baby Boom.* Berkeley and Los Angeles: University of California Press, 2001.

Ladner, Joyce A. *Tomorrow's Tomorrow*. New York: Anchor Books, 1972.

Ladner, Joyce A., and Ruby M. Gourdine. "Intergenerational Teenage Motherhood: Some Preliminary Findings." *Sage: A Scholarly Journal on Black Women* 1 (1984): 22–24.

Lareau, Annette. "Invisible Inequality: Social Class and Childrearing in Black Families and White Families." *American Sociological Review* 67 (October 2002): 747–776.

McLanahan, Sara, and Dona Schwartz. "Life Without Father: What Happens to the Children." *Contexts* 1.1 (2002): 35–41.

McLoyd, V.C. "The Impact of Economic Hardships on Black Families and Children: Psychological Distress, Parenting, and Socioemotional Development." *Child Development* 61 (1990): 311–346.

Neubeck, Kenneth J., and Noel A. Cazenave. *Welfare Racism: Playing the Race Card Against America's Poor*. New York and London: Routledge, 2001.

O'Brien, Mary. *The Politics of Reproduction*. Boston: Routledge and Kegan Paul, 1981.

Oliver, Melvin L., and Thomas M. Shapiro. *Black Wealth/White Wealth: A New Perspective on Racial Inequality*. New York: Routledge, 1995.

Polatnick, M. Rivka. "Diversity in Women's Liberation Ideology: How a Black and a White Group of the 1960s Viewed Motherhood." *Signs: Journal of Women in Culture and Society* 21.3 (1996): 679–706.

Ross, Loretta J. "African American Women and Abortion: 1800–1970." *Theorizing Black Feminisms: The Visionary Pragmatism of Black Women*. Eds. Stanley M. James and Abena P. A. Busia. New York: Routledge, 1993. 141–159.

Scott, Kesho Yvonne. *The Habit of Surviving: Black Women's Strategies for Life*. New Brunswick: Rutgers University Press, 1991.

Shaw, Stephanie J. "Mothering Under Slavery in the Antebellum South." *Mothers and Motherhood: Readings in American History*. Eds. Rima D. Apple and Janet Golden. Columbus: Ohio State University Press, 1997. 297–318.

Stack, Carol. *All Our Kin: Strategies for Survival in a Black Community*. New York: Harper and Row, 1974.

Walsh, Lorena. "The Experiences and Status of Women in the Chesapeake." *The Web of Southern Social Relations: Women, Family and Education*. Eds. Walter Fraser, R. Frank Saunders, and Jon Wakelyn. Athens: University of Georgia Press, 1985. 1–18.

West, Cornel. *Democracy Matters: Winning the Fight Against Imperialism*. New York: Penguin Press, 2004.

White, Deborah Gray. *Ar'nt I A Woman? Female Slaves in the Plantation South*. New York: W.W. Norton, 1985.

————. "Female Slaves: Sex Roles and Status in the Antebellum Plantation South." *Unequal Sisters: A Multi-Cultural Reader in U.S. Women's History.* Eds. Vicki L. Ruiz and Ellen Carol DuBois. New York: Routledge, 1994. 20–31.

Wilson, W. J. *The Truly Disadvantaged.* Chicago: University of Chicago Press, 1987.

Zinn, Maxine Baca, and Bonnie Thornton Dill. "Theorizing Difference from Multiracial Feminism." *Feminist Studies* 22.2 (1996): 321–331.

CHAPTER SEVEN

Mothering as Relational Consciousness

AMBER E. KINSER

IN THIS CHAPTER, I explore some of the ways that feminist living, and in particular feminist mothering, is irresolvably messy. I explore mothering and its struggles as subjectively meaningful in an effort to answer the call by some feminist writers, such as Brenda Daly, Maureen Reddy, and Andrea O'Reilly, and to be responsive to the example of other feminist writers, such as Valerie Jean, Lynda Marín, Jeannine Howitz, and Noelle Oxenhandler, to pay more pointed attention to *what mothering is like from the mother's point of view.* Moving away from discussions about how mothering results for children, I confront some of the ambivalence, confusion, and turbulence that may characterize its practices. Specifically, I discuss a mother's struggle to reconcile, or reconcile herself to, the blurriness of boundaries that delineate her various selves and the relational and identity tensions that emerge in motherwork.

A goal of my writing here is to resist the "master discourses" (Kaplan) that suggest clarity and certainty in mothering practices, coming from both the patriarchal institution of motherhood and feminist writings on mothering. I want to add my voice to those who, in O'Reilly's words, "speak truthfully about motherhood," to "tell my (m)other side of the story" (30). Another, equally important, goal is to try to make some sense of me *for me*, to give my own life, as Gloria Anzaldúa has said, "a handle, so I can grasp it"; I believe she was right when she said that "the act of writing is the act of making soul, alchemy" (169). For failing to face the messiness of feminist mothering, of confronting what Susan Maushart calls the "mask of motherhood" and its "semblance of serenity and control that enables women's work to pass unnoticed in the larger drama of human life," surely will result in self-betrayal (Maushart 5–6).

Mothering practices intersect the multiple relationships of which I am part, the multiple selves I embody at home, at work, and in my community, the multiple family subsystems and suprasystems that overlap in my life. There is a simultaneous connectedness among these relationships and selves, and yet, often enough, there is a fragmentation about them. They are parts of a unified whole that seldom feel unified, both connected and fragmented, both seamless and split. There are times, plenty of times, when these multiple and often divergent selves, contradictory selves even, rub against one another. There are times when the rubbing against of my mother self and my feminist self, for example, create such a friction it is a wonder I don't get burned. Then again, I suppose I do. Every moment of mother-relating for me also is a moment of relating-in-multiplicity, of trying to reduce the friction of opposing demands of multiple selves and relationships. Survival in feminist mothering necessitates coming to see this rubbing against, this friction, this tension, not as purely oppositional and therefore needing to be resolved, but as inherent, and necessary, and not in need of fixing. It means embracing what dialectical theorists call a "unity of oppositions" (Baxter and Montgomery 9). Such *dialogic consciousness*, such *relational consciousness*, as Brenda Daly and Maureen Reddy argue, would help us to live with "both/and" thinking as subjectively meaningful in feminist mothering (12).

Drawing in part from *symbolic interactionist* and *relational dialectics* perspectives, I begin with the assumption that individuals have no single, stable self but rather that we each represent a weaving together of multiple selves that are always in flux (Baxter and Montgomery; Mead). Our selves emerge from and are continuously shaped by and ascribed meaning within interpersonal relations. As a mother, I never am only constructing definitions of mothering; I also am simultaneously constructing definitions of partner, teacher, daughter, neighbor, mentor, community member, and more, and all of these selves overlap with, crash into, inform, undermine, strengthen, and create friction for each other. So any treatment of my mother self necessarily implicates my other selves. Further, such treatment also implicates a central tension of social life: the simultaneous need to connect with and separate from others (Baxter and Montgomery). The multiplicity of selves with which I contend at any given moment each are wrestling with this tension, and this wrestling is further complicated by the fact that one self's efforts to connect or disconnect will often undermine another's efforts.

To illustrate, a regular tension for my family and me emerges from our need to connect with and separate from our neighbors. As a neighbor self, I want to be seen as someone worth acknowledging and being friendly to, someone whose children are good playmates and friends. But as a feminist and a liberal self, I don't care much for strong affiliations with my particular neighbors, or the neighborhood summer cookout, which is populated largely by ultraconservative families. And I don't care much for the conservative party political campaign signs that populate the yards where we live; it is tricky being one of the only people to post yard signs for liberal candidates, although we do it anyway (and when one gets stolen, we replace it with another). At the summer cookout last year, I was delighted to come across some people who communicated, though cautiously given our immediate environment, a liberal mind-set. It was affirming to connect with them through our mutual separation from the others in the group even as we connected to those others through our presence at the cookout. My family's attendance at this gathering facilitated our sense of belonging—a sense especially lacking for us given our location as agnostics and atheists in the Bible Belt—but then of course connected us in ways that encouraged church invitations and questions about who we are and what we do, the answers to which would ensure our disconnection from the group and our children's exclusion from potential social circles.

This fusion-separation tension, identified by dialectical theorists as the contradictory necessities of centripetal and centrifugal forces, is the stuff out of which the self is constructed (Bakhtin 272; Baxter and Montgomery 25). Motherwork, and the ongoing creation of one's mother self, is laden with perpetual efforts to manage the fusing (centripetal) and separating (centrifugal) forces that characterize, but find different form in, each of a mother's other selves. While I do not provide a proper dialectical analysis here because I focus more on self and identity than relationship interaction, I do draw loosely from dialectical theory to illuminate tensions emergent when oppositional forces interact.

In this chapter, I consider relational influences on motherwork and mothering identity. Specifically, I discuss ways that *having been* mothered or othermothered, ways that past and present partner relationships, and ways that issues of class overlap with and create potentially unresolved tensions in mothering choices, experiences, and identities. I draw here from my own experience as a mother in relationships with persons other than my children, as a person who, like other persons, is always relating-in-multiplicity. Because, as O'Reilly points out, mothering does not "require self erasure" (153), my effort here is directed at illustrating how any discussion about motherwork is never just about mothers and children, and often enough is not even primarily about children, but is also, and I would argue more so, about women navigating their way through the sometimes serene but mostly choppy, and often treacherous, waters of multiple relations at once. Such navigational efforts are characterized by the rather relentless pulls toward meeting the contradictory and simultaneous demands to connect with and to separate from multiple relationships and selves.

DAUGHTER-PRACTICE IN RELATIONAL CONSCIOUSNESS

Feminist writers on mothering do not have to choose between, on one hand, writing that is wholly daughter-centric, and on the other, writing that isolates mothers from relationships beyond their children. We can, as Daly and Reddy argue, and as Farr, McDonnell, Wong, and several other writers in their volume have shown, "move through the daughter's experience to the mother's" and remain focused on a subjectivity of mothering (Daly and Reddy 2–3). And we can do this in ways that center the mother, in ways that avoid, to use Marianne Hirsch's terms, "othering the mother" (136, qtd. in O'Reilly 94). I seek neither to transcend my daughterness nor to write around it, but rather to consider my motherness in light of it. I write not only as a mother but also as a daughter who still is becoming, at forty-four years, the woman my mother and I raised me to be. What this means for my mothering practices is that even as I make parenting decisions, establish rules for public and private, encourage some behaviors and discourage others, teach about food and rituals of eating, and whether I allow this clothing or that tone of voice, respond to someone else's mood or am too immersed in my own to notice, I act not only as the mother of my daughter and son, but also and simultaneously as the daughter of my mother. My interrelatedness with my mother overlaps with my interrelatedness with my children. Through my own motherwork I continue the journey of learning who I am and what I believe in that I began as a daughter four and a half decades ago; I am rarely engaged in motherwork except that I am, at some level, also engaged in daughter-practice. By daughter-practice, I refer to a woman's adult thinking and action that she uses to work through and think through the lessons, experiences, memories, and observations of her past or present relationship with her mother, or othermother(s), or mothering figure(s). My point here is not to say that relations with one's mother are always salient, or overarching, or primary, but that they are present to varying degrees in, and ought be considered relative to, motherwork. As Leslie

Baxter and Barbara Montgomery articulate, "there are no 'clean slates' in relationships; no relationship 'starts fresh' or 'begins over'" (161).

Daughter-practice is complex and often enough emerges out of struggle; it can run a gamut (or a gauntlet) of emotional, psychological, spiritual, and somatic responses; it can permeate a variety of contexts and relationships, and likely operates at various levels of consciousness. It is complicated by the likelihood that in many given moments, one is wrestling with what it means to be, to have been, or to feel like one should be connected with a mother figure, and simultaneously with what it means to be, and how to go about being separate from and different from her. One's motherwork and daughter-practice exist in dialogue with each other. Their complexity and struggle are magnified when a woman's daughter self rubs up against her mother self in ways that produce friction for her.

ON HEAD OF HOUSEHOLD

I have loved my mother fiercely my entire life. She is strong and tender, demanding and forgiving, self-sacrificing and self-made. She taught me how to create all of this in me, lessons I hope I learned well. She also seems generally disdainful of men, works herself to a frazzle, and is a devoted Baptist who supports the teachings of the church even though they often enough betray her, from my perspective, and even though, in her world, the only man who may have ever effectively headed any household was her father. In our extended family, the women run the households, though typically they ascribe figurehead "leadership" to the men. While I feel resolute about not having anyone "head" my household, and argue this stance in my teaching and writing, I find that I nevertheless place *myself* at the head on most factors affecting children and domestic life. This is clearly quite tricky for me as a feminist because, ideally, my partner would share equally with me in these matters. Indeed, egalitarian households are what I "believe" in, and the gospel I preach in my classrooms. I suppose that, for many intents and purposes, and though I'm hedging as I'm typing this because I hate seeing it in print, I head our household. It is an unresolved tension that I am still learning to reconcile myself to, part of a larger "negative capability" that Barbara Schapiro argues, borrowing from and extending Keats, is inherent to motherhood. Living with this tension means acceptance of "being in uncertainties, Mysteries, doubts, without any irritable reaching after fact and reason" (Keats qtd. in Schapiro 180). Though I do pine after a more seamless connection between my selves, and the simplicity and clarity it seems this would produce, I also know that, as relational dialectics theorists point out, "disparity and contradiction [are] ever present between and among these different selves" (Baxter and Montgomery 159).

DINNER AS ALBATROSS

One of the sites of greatest struggle for me as a feminist mother revolves around dinnertime. I have heard myself recite many times that the only part of my life that I hate is dinner. It is relentless. I cannot reconcile, for example, my ambivalence about having "home-cooked" meals for my family. My mother always made them, from scratch, even though she worked full time; she prepared them during her "second shift" (Hochschild) while my father read the newspaper and watched the news. While as a feminist I am proud that I was able to resist at some level, though perhaps only intermittently, perceiving myself as obligated toward a second shift given that I had no exposure to any other way until I was an adult, I also rather like *eating* home-cooked meals, and smelling the fusion of love and food and care in the air in my home, and seeing my family enjoying meals I have created, with my own hands and affections, for them. This is tricky for me because, though I like *having cooked,* and feel, frankly, inadequate as a mother when I don't, I finally am less interested in cooking activity than my mother was, am less adept at it, and am less willing to devote time to it. Still, even knowing and articulating all of this, even knowing that I am, and my priorities and passions are, different from her and hers, I cannot seem to feel good about how I feed my children, despite the feminist intellectual acrobatics I do to make sense of my choices.

It is my hope that my inconsistent meal preparations nevertheless avoid some of the discomfort that was coupled with dinner in my childhood. Children were to be seen and not heard at the table, where rules of eating etiquette abounded and tension mounted. Dinners were very stress-inducing, as we feared a sibling might make us laugh, or we might clank one serving bowl against another or, worse, spill something, all of which put us at risk for some kind of thrashing, verbal or otherwise. I vowed very young that dinners would be different in my adult life. Yet, sitting at the table with my children now, I find to my discomfort that my tolerance for anything but adult-sounding talk is low, and my expectations for polished behavior high. I have broken vows that my child self made to my future adult self about what I would undo of my parents' patterns, about how I would differentiate myself from my mother, my marriage from hers. Despite my plans, it seems I haven't undone dinnertime constrictions much, except to extend adult-level talk to include children and to consider laughter and bowls clanking and things spilling as part of the meal. And there certainly are no thrashings of any kind at my table or any threats of them. I still feel tense though, sitting at my own dinner table. I wonder if my children do.

It also is my hope that, because I don't cook dinners regularly—we go out or order in (an economic privilege my mother never had), or have what my mother called and I still call "whatever" (where everyone fends for themselves) or my husband makes something (though no more interested in cooking than I am)—my children actually see the effort I put into meals and appreciate it in ways I never did of my mother. I don't believe I ever truly valued the fact that my mother prepared meals for us. I've always known her to be an excellent cook, I ate her meals heartily, and I praised the taste when she prepared a favored dish, but I don't remember ever truly valuing *the fact that she created our meals.* I missed the lesson somehow that my mother's food rituals emerged from conscious choices she made, and plans she executed with much effort. Because this aspect of my mother's work and efforts—which I now understand was so consuming of her time and energy—was not clearly visible to me, I did not have a sense of her as a complete person. As Anne Morris explains:

> When mothers' contributions to their children's lives are barely seen, let alone valued, it is hardly surprising that other aspects of mothers' lives, which give mothers a presence as people in their own right and which provide a context for understanding their actions, are also invisible to sons and daughters. (230)

My mother's relative invisibility to me in my childhood feels painful for me now. Much of who my mother is remains, I fear, invisible to me still. And now, I no longer feel positioned to render her more visible, given the intense life work I have done to cut my own path in ways that are not directed by the race and gender and religion paradigms that direct the rest of my family of orientation.

In my family of creation, however, one of the results of complex daughter-practice for me has been, I believe, that my children have a more holistic sense of my person and my life. I have resisted mightily being defined solely as a mother; I have demanded my right to develop as a professional; I have wrestled guilt from not attending cross-country meets or fourth grade field trips regularly. I taught my children to pack their own lunches and keep up with their own schedules. And this despite the fact that, in their social circles here in the mountain South, such practices are an anomaly, providing my children a tenuous frame of reference for viewing them other than suspiciously. I have worked to live and to practice mothering "from a position of agency, authority, authenticity, and autonomy," as O'Reilly argues feminist mothering ought enable me to (45). And still, my capacity for feeling empowered by my choices and practices is weak. This tension ruffles my identities as a mother and as a feminist. Furthermore, when I consider Alease Ferguson and Toni King's insight that Third Wave–era daughters have not found their feminist mothers' lives particularly liberating or enviable, and resent the ways in which feminist movement has robbed them of their mothers, and so have no intention of using their mothers' examples as models for living, I catch myself wondering just what I think I am accomplishing for my children in the end.

UNITY OF SEPARATENESS AND CONNECTEDNESS

Clearly, one of the frictions that arises when my mother self and daughter self rub up against one another is that between trying to *undo in me* and trying to *recreate for me*, what I saw in my mother, to disconnect and reconnect, as I mother my children. This friction is particularly heat-producing because I am not sure what my feminist obligations are on this front. Feminist living is especially messy because it is not prescriptive, so I never quite know if I am connecting with/conforming to feminism or dissociating myself from it in a given moment. In constructing my identity as a mother, ought I honor what my own mother, as a woman doing the best she knew how while working within a patriarchal order, and as a woman whom I adore and always have, was able to carve out for her family? Or ought I rail against the practices whereby she participated in her own oppression, the practices she embodied—not the least of which is a dismissive attitude about men that let them off the hook but kept her serving them—that I struggle daily to move against in my own family life? Surely there is both feminist connection and dissociation no matter which direction I choose; either option brings me closer to feminism in some way and farther from it in another. It seems reductive to think of the most powerful and respected woman in our family, the one who ran nearly the entire show, as oppressed. My mother was hardly a dupe; she made conscious choices that served her purposes. Indeed, as O'Reilly and Porter suggest, "Oppression does not equate to the absence of agency" (9).

In my own motherwork, I struggle simultaneously to resist the thinking that kept my mother deferring and working two shifts a day and mediating between us children and my father's rage, *and* to reproduce for my family the good my mother created for us, the warmth and courage and pride she modeled and the stability she provided. I struggle even to distinguish what *was* good from what *felt* good, to me and in the moment, aside from what it did for me or to me in the end, and aside from what it may have done to my mother. My experience as a mother is shaped by daughter-practice and its struggles to both resist and recreate my mother's teachings—those she intended and those she didn't—and the ambivalence this produces.

Understanding mothering to evolve from relational consciousness means not only acknowledging daughter-practice as an important component of many women's motherwork, but also acknowledging how subjective experience of one's own mothering practices emerge out of, and in tension with, other relationships as well. While I believe it is true that, as O'Reilly has argued, it may be impossible to mother fully outside the institution of motherhood (23), this institution does not stand alone, and is not the only force directing mother choices. As George H. Mead's work illustrates, we each have "all sorts of different selves answering to all sorts of different social reactions" (142). Partner relationships, too, among others, are implicated in a relational consciousness of mothering. And, often enough, these also can relate to daughter-practice at some level.

PARTNER RELATIONSHIPS AND LONE PARENTING

My mother divorced my biological father and married my stepfather, whom I have considered my father most of my life (and refer to him as both my father and my stepfather in this chapter; I do not refer to my biological father). He was a great "provider" in my mother's eyes, working two jobs most of my childhood. He loved my mother deeply and still does, as she does him. He and my mother, who worked as a cocktail waitress and later a breakfast cook and then a voc-tech school-trained medical office manager, molded a lower-middle class existence for our family from decidedly working-class clay. He was authoritarian and what my therapist aptly named a rage-a-holic, which, coupled with my mother's deference, afforded him much authority in our home, despite his complete detachment from the everyday grind of raising children and domestic work. This was my model for living with one's children and their stepfather. This is the model that I am, perpetually, connecting to and separating from, struggling with the tension that comes out of doing these simultaneously. And though my day-to-day mother practices look different from my mother's, my struggle to move against some of her patterns situates me squarely in the middle of others. While I have learned from various resources, feminism among them, to explore alternative patterns, and while few of the people who know me would ever believe it, at any given moment in any given day I am working to resist the male authoritarian model provided by my parents. This surprises and continues to perplex even me. Neither feminism nor, I suspect, anything else, has the power to fully liberate my thinking and feeling.

My children's father, in contrast to my own, is of very mild spirit. When I was married to him, I was happy to be raising my children with someone who was so unlike my father in spirit; it was almost ten years before I realized that he was very much like my father in many other respects. Somehow I had reproduced with him a model wherein the mother is responsible for all thinking and activity related to the children and the home. But he didn't ever yell and didn't ever watch football (which I loathed and still do, partly because of the reverence for it that was demanded of us as children) and loved to shower the children with affection, so I had reason to believe that I had undone what needed to be undone. After we divorced, I married someone who is not mild-spirited. Because I have primary custody of my two children, these differences in spirit remain, six years later, thorny for my son and daughter as they continue to adapt to our current family system. My partner, my children's step-dad, has a voice that is deeper and stronger; he is well-read and opinionated and has a slicing wit that some find off-putting but I relish; he has two adult sons whom he raised not only as intellectuals but also as star athletes, including in football. Because my mothering in each of these two family systems cannot be considered fully outside of the relational others with whom/against whom I parent, understanding what it is like to mother from the mother's point of view necessitates an interrogation of what I am moving against as I construct my own definitions of motherhood, definitions that are, then, never truly my own.

My partner fathered his children in notably different ways than I want mine fathered, but I consider his relationship to my children secondary to his relationship to me; my choice to partner with him was one I made, quite resolutely, for me and not for my children. This choice of course simultaneously fused me with him and, in several ways, functioned as a wedge between me and my kids. This is difficult for me to live with and this difficulty is magnified because the research literature grounds the breakdown of subsequent marriages in difficulties with children from previous marriages (Clamar 160; Salwen 124 qtd. in Downe 174). That I chose their father in the same way—as a partner for me rather than as a father for them—is a factor that I would guess eludes them. Still, in making the choice to be with my current partner, I was quite clear on the fact that I would not afford him the kind of authority over my children that my own stepfather had over us. So I have chosen to manage on my own the day-to-day activities of parenting.

Problems emerge when I consider that, on this note, I did *not* evolve my second partnership significantly from my first, as childrearing remains my responsibility, and this rubs up against my feminist—and feminist mothering—identities. I struggle with the fact that, after all I've done in terms of evolving my own thinking, after resisting many dimensions of my mother's example and learning from my previous partnership, divorcing and remarrying in an effort to disentangle some knots in my life, I have managed still to be bound as the primary childrearer, a bit of a lone parent. I struggle with whether to "fix" the childrearing inequity, or to learn to respond to my partner in ways that keep from punishing him for *not* doing what I won't *authorize* him to do with my children, or to expect that he will discard the only parenting practices he knows, given the neglectful example that was set for him by his own family. I imagine that this struggle will never be quite resolved. Some knots, it seems, are not going to be untangled. Even as I resist my parents' model, I reproduce it at some level, and this illustrates the kind of both/and thinking that relational consciousness provides, or even requires. Further, even as I associate with feminist thinking by claiming my own authority on childrearing matters, I dissociate from it by carrying an unequal share of the work. These are choices I make knowingly and willfully as a feminist and though I struggle through the tensions that emerge, I embrace them.

My relationship with my mother and my relationships with my partners, and their necessary overlap, offer up comparatively concrete tensions as their various oppositional forces rub against one another, demonstrating the complexity of relating-in-multiplicity. My evolving issues with class identity and how it intersects with mothering are less concrete, in part because, while the boundaries that delineate various relational selves are quite blurry, those that surround changing class identity seem more so for me.

MOTHERING AND CLASS IDENTITY

Among the many lessons my mother taught me, several were especially identity-shaping: I should act independently, live simply and frugally but fully expect to work, never assume someone would take care of me and so do and make what I need for myself, and be committed to my family. Such are often the lessons of the working class. I earned my college degrees on significantly fewer resources than anyone I knew and received precious little from my parents (or anyone else) in that effort. Lest I overstate, however, the heroic and romantic quality of this simple and frugal life, I should say outright that I didn't like it. Part of the difficulty I think was that, since we were working-class people devising a middle-class existence, I was surrounded by families and friends who were in fact not like ours, so I was painfully aware of the differences in our socioeconomic status, as, I suspected, were they. Even in graduate school, I had no student colleagues who lived as meagerly as I did.

In my youth, we lived in a decent middle-class home in a decent middle-class neighborhood and, eventually, worked our way up to decent middle-class vehicles. But I never had a dime in my pocket, a tradition I carried with me until well after graduate school and its $50,000 student loan debt on top of credit card debt, none of which did much, finally, to fill the voids in my pockets, nor those in my soul, the latter ever-deepening as a result of perpetually feeling financially inadequate. No candy and soda at the convenience store with young girlfriends; later no lunches with friends unless they paid; drinks with men, including professors, whose company I didn't care for, because they paid; still later, exceptionally meager grocery bills for my daughter, husband, and myself of sixty dollars, which exceeded my ridiculous forty-five dollar budget. The floorboard of my 1964 Nova, which I drove until the early 1990s, had rusted clean through and my shoes and long skirt got wet when I drove to school in the rain. And though plenty of other people have similar and worse stories to tell, stories from which I might have gathered strength and solidarity, I wasn't connected with them. I lived and worked among people whose debts and cars and grocery store trips and pocket change were decidedly more comfortable than mine. I persistently felt out of my league, always aware of how I did not, and could not, measure up. I feel nauseas even typing it now, but seeing it in print helps me to understand why I was agitated by my read of Curtis Sittenfeld's recent best-selling novel *Prep*. I identified too readily with the desperation of Lee, the working-class protagonist on scholarship at the prep school, whose tenuous but meticulously crafted persona stood always on the brink of shattering, until one day it did shatter. Interestingly, "teetering" is a term I still to use to describe multiple aspects of myself.

Perhaps my years of feeling financially inadequate fed my sense in graduate school of being intellectually inadequate, a clear case of "imposter syndrome" no matter the context, rooted in my childhood working-class/middle-class tensions. We had no discussions about going to college in our house as I grew up; I had not the faintest idea what a bachelor's degree was until over two years into college courses. At every juncture in my educational career, I was resolute that *THIS was the point at which they would figure out that I did not know what I was doing*, tag me as an imposter, and at best redirect my pursuits to something better fitting my station, but at least peg me as a fraud.

My years of working-class struggle produced a person of both assured character (my mother was right about that) and uncertain identity; I have lived much of my life responding to persistent internal tensions between confidence and diffidence. This tension is grounded in large part, I believe, in issues of economic and educational class and seeps into my parenting in multiple ways. Mothering for me is characterized by a perpetual pull between my working-class, imposter-self emergent in my childhood and surviving still, and my upper-middle-class accomplished self emergent in my adulthood, and wrestling still; and all of this knotted up with daughter-practice. My point is not to say, of course, that there isn't accomplishment in the working class; I've seen such accomplishment my whole life—but to say that in my own life my sense of feeling accomplished coincided with my moving into, no longer teetering precariously on the edge of, the middle class.

I feel propelled toward and, simultaneously, mightily resist movement in two primary directions in this regard: seeing my childrearing as a new means by which my fraudulent self might be detected, and seeing my children's comfortable lives as a source of envy for me, dare I say resentment, even though I am quite purposeful in my efforts to ensure that their lives are in fact different from, better than, mine was. Interestingly, the two themes seem to be gender-divided. The theme of envy emerges most in my relationship with my sixteen-year-old daughter, which may be more a function of her age, of seeing her come into herself as a young woman with much greater resources than I had. The theme of fraudulence emerges most with my son, which, again, may be a function of his being nine and the "piercing societal gaze that is projected onto mothers," especially those with young children (Downe 165), and something about which I also was sensitive with my daughter when she was younger. But the gendered division of these themes, which only become clear to me as I write this, is certainly something to consider.

I fret a good bit about how much money my son should have—trying to fill the emptiness in my soul created by memories of the emptiness of my pockets, no doubt. Elementary school field trips give me cause to agonize: how much lunch money is too much or not enough on these trips? How much souvenir money? I struggle to find a way to teach the necessary lesson of frugality, to teach him how to be pennywise, and still to feel comfortable and not have to distress about every dollar spent, and all of this without subjecting him (me) to judgments about his family as too miserly or too out of touch with what is appropriate for young children. Similarly, I fretted over his soccer uniform, which called for black shorts, the team T-shirt, and foot and shin gear. I bought a standard pair of boys' sport shorts and took him to his first game only to discover, to my (overly) great disappointment (and shame) that the other boys wore short shorts, compared to his now basketball-looking shorts. I could hear old tapes playing: *THIS is the point at which they figure out that I don't know what I'm doing.* Subsequently, I looked everywhere for shorter shorts and found none for the longest time, only to learn that when I did get them he didn't wear them; he preferred the long ones. I should have asked him what he thought, but I suppose I didn't think I could bear it if he told me that he felt out of place in the long shorts—what could be worse, I guess I was thinking, than making your own son feel like a fraud. (I confess that, as an intellectual, I can see the problem in that thinking, but as I read this over I think, *Well, there probably isn't much that's worse than that.* Some knots don't get unraveled.)

"Our" performance at the science fair, which I'm learning to make less about "us" than I did when my daughter was doing them, is, like much of what I've explored in this chapter, about more than the children and more than the institution of motherhood. For me, it also is about, among other things, issues of class and class identity. It is about not just being a good enough mom, but also about working to avoid being pegged as a person who can't figure out the educational system, who can't navigate private school parenting, who doesn't know much about science at all. Maybe *THIS is the point at which they'll figure out I don't know what I'm doing.*

The second place where my working-class self and my middle-class self rub against one another, and where my mothering identity and class identity rub against one another, emerges from envy. At some level, though I am loathe to admit it, I envy my daughter: her sense of entitlement, her great sense of belonging in this world, her fabulous bedroom, her savings account. These are all advantages that I have worked exceptionally hard to provide for her, and advantages that I longed for in my own life and have access to now, though not without a bitterness of which I am not proud. I am happy to be able to offer this life for her and continue to be amazed that I can, but I can't honestly say there are no strings attached. These are strings that are like fishing line—not readily visible, but strong and rarely relenting. The problem lies in the fact that I want her to appreciate her life in the same way that I would have, had I had a shot at it when I was sixteen (or any time before forty, for that matter). Having vending machine soda money in your pocket doesn't mean, probably can't mean, the same thing for her as it did (and oddly continues to do) for me. She probably never will feel sheer ecstasy over a cold Diet Coke; I made sure that such a thing wouldn't have to matter that much in her life. It is a (perhaps pathetic) joy that only comes from having lived without, and, for a majority of her years, she hasn't. At restaurants I communicate that, within reason, she should choose what she wants from the menu, but then I feel a pang of something nondescript when she doesn't choose the cheap item. I say nothing, but not because I feel nothing. Maybe I want her to respond with some kind of working-class humility so that I can counter with some kind of upper-middle-class extravagance: "Get whatever you want, Honey!" Maybe this interaction would provide better proof that I'm not an imposter to the middle class. Maybe it would even offer the bonus of not having to envy her sense of entitlement. I do hope I will be able to get my daughter through college debt-free, ideally through all of it but at least (and more likely) through her four-year degree. And she will never be able to grasp what a gift that is—and this unsettles me. But she can't feel the liberation from having a burden lifted that she's never had to bear. Neither will she risk carrying the bitterness I do for having had to bear it alone and for so long.

I wish I knew of a way, as I suppose many, many mothers do, that my children could learn, without so much struggle and toil, what it seems one only learns through struggle and toil. And I wish I knew of a way that I could feel better about that fact that my children, and especially my daughter right now, have access to the privileges, but not the lessons, never mind the work ethic, that emerge therefrom. As I raise my children, I always am pulled between connecting with and separating from my working-class identity, always struggling to embrace the both/and thinking of my working-class self and my middle-class self, to find ways to let them both inform my mothering while trying to reduce the friction of their opposing demands, to "hold two opposed ideas in mind at the same time," as F. Scott Fitzgerald is often quoted as saying, "and still retain the ability to function."

CONCLUDING THOUGHTS

Feminist mothering consists, in part, of turbulent practices. Exploring what mothering is like from the mother's point of view implicates, among its liberations, confidences, and clarity, a host of constraints, doubts, and haze (Kinser). As feminist mothers, we venture forth with resolve and work toward resolutions through our revolutions. But this is not to say that we do so without reservation, in the absence of confusion, devoid of contradiction. In fact, the latter complexities may more accurately characterize feminism generally and mothering specifically than resolve or clarity. And this is a definitive feature of the lives we have chosen with which we need to get more comfortable.

As I've said elsewhere, even "through our ambivalence, we [have] some feminist things to say about mothering in these times" (Kinser, forthcoming).

Diane Speier suggests that, "because mothering is a trial and error experience, we need to respect that at best it will be 'imperfect'" (149). I am
coming to see that evolving my own parenting practices from those of my
parents has meant, for me, maintaining a similar level of maternal responsibility and burden and authority over the children's everyday affairs that my
mother had. In daughter-practice and partner relationships, I converge with,
even as I diverge from, my mother's mothering practices. And regardless of
what I vowed I would undo and still try to undo, it may not be necessary to
reconcile these tensions, but rather to reconcile myself to them. The tensions
emerging from my working-class and middle-class selves illuminate for me
the complexity of identity in general and class specifically and the ways in
which multiple selves overlap to inform mothering experiences. I'd like to
keep the fear and bitterness that was born in my working-class struggle from
seeping into my mothering, and allow only the courage and persistence and
appreciation of simple things to permeate. But I know it doesn't quite work
that way; that these all get tangled up into lifeknots. And I'm beginning to
get more comfortable with them. I'm beginning to see how I might settle into
the oppositional pulls and demands of my working-class self and middle-class
self. Conceptualizing feminist mothering as relational consciousness is
encouraging me to embrace the "unity of oppositions" in my life.

Honest examinations of mothering experiences and practices, and their
emergence from relating-in-multiplicity, work against what Shari Thurer calls
the "cultural conspiracy of silence" (xiv) on mothering truths. Not only feminist mothers working to make sense of their own lives, but also feminist writers seeking to "make soul, alchemy" (Anzaldúa 169) in their work must
continue to courageously explore the irresolvable tensions of feminism and
the family. Confronting the messiness of feminist mothering is the beginning
of getting comfortable with the discomfort of knots that won't come untied.

REFERENCES

Anzaldúa, Gloria. "Speaking in Tongues: A Letter to 3rd World Women Writers." *This Bridge Called My Back: Writings by Radical Women of Color*. 2nd ed.
Eds. Cherríe Moraga and Gloria Anzaldúa. Watertown, MA: Persephone,
1983.

Bakhtin, Mikhail. M. *The Dialogic Imagination: Four Essays by M. M. Bakhtin*. Ed.
Michael Holquist. Trans. Caryl Emerson and Michael Holquist. Austin:
University of Texas Press, 1981.

Baxter, Leslie A., and Barbara M. Montgomery. *Relating: Dialogues and Dialectics.* New York: Guildford Press, 1996.

Clamar, Aphrodite. "Stepmothering: Fairytales and Reality." *Handbook of Feminist Therapy: Women's Lives in Psychotherapy.* Eds. Lynne Bravo Rosewater and Leonore E. Walker. New York: Springer, 1985. 159–169

Daly, Brenda O., and Maureen T. Reddy. Introduction. *Narrating Mothers: Theorizing Maternal Subjectivities.* Knoxville: University of Tennessee Press, 1991.

Downe, Pamela J. "Stepping on Maternal Ground: Reflections on Becoming an 'Other-Mother.'" *Mother Matters: Motherhood as Discourse and Practice.* Ed. Andrea O'Reilly. Toronto: Association for Research on Mothering, 2004. 165–178.

Farr, Cecelia Konchar. "Her Mother's Language." *Narrating Mothers: Theorizing Maternal Subjectivities.* Eds. Brenda O. Daly and Maureen T. Reddy. Knoxville: University of Tennessee Press, 1991. 94–108.

Ferguson, S. Alease, and Toni C. King. "Going Down for the Third Time." *Mothering in the Third Wave.* Ed. Amber E. Kinser. Toronto: Demeter. (Forthcoming.)

Hirsch, Marianne. *The Mother/Daughter Plot: Narrative, Psychoanalysis, Feminism.* Bloomington: Indiana University Press, 1989.

Hochschild, Arlie Russell, with Anne Machung. *The Second Shift: Working Parents and the Revolution.* New York: Avon, 1989.

Howitz, Jeanine O. "Reflections of a Feminist Mom." *Mothers and Children: Feminist Analyses and Personal Narratives.* Eds. Susan E. Chase and Mary F. Rogers. New Brunswick: Rutgers University Press, 2001. 81–85.

Jean, Valerie. "Successions." *Doublestitch: Black Women Write about Mothers and Daughters.* Boston: Beacon, 1991. 146–147.

Kaplan, E. Ann. *Motherhood and Representation.* London: Routledge, 1992.

Keats, John. John Keats to George and Tom Keats, 21–27 December 1817. *The Letters of John Keats 1814–1821.* Ed. Hyder Edward Rollins. Cambridge: Harvard University Press, 1958. 21–27.

Kinser, Amber E., ed. *Mothering in the Third Wave.* Toronto: Demeter. (Forthcoming).

Marín, Lynda. "Mother and Child: The Erotic Bond." *Mother Journeys: Feminists Write about Mothering.* Eds. Maureen T. Reddy, Martha Roth, and Amy Sheldon. Minneapolis: Spinsters Ink, 1994. 9–21.

Maushart, Susan. *The Mask of Motherhood: How Becoming a Mother Changes Everyting and Why We Pretend It Doesn't.* New York: The New Press.

McDonnell, Jane Taylor. "Mothering an Autistic Child: Reclaiming the Choice of the Mother." *Narrating Mothers: Theorizing Maternal Subjectivities.* Eds. Brenda O. Daly and Maureen T. Reddy. Knoxville: University of Tennessee Press, 1991. 58–75.

Mead, George Herbert. *Mind, Self, & Society*. 1934. Chicago: University of Chicago Press, 1967.

Morris, Anne. "Naming Maternal Alienation." *Motherhood: Power & Oppression*. Eds. Andrea O'Reilly, Marie Porter, and Patricia Short. Toronto: Women's Press, 2006. 223–236.

O'Reilly, Andrea. *Rocking the Cradle: Thoughts on Motherhood, Feminism, and the Possibility of Empowered Mothering*. Toronto: Demeter Press, 2006.

O'Reilly, Andrea, and Marie Porter. Introduction. *Motherhood: Power & Oppression*. Eds. Andrea O'Reilly, Marie Porter, and Patricia Short. Toronto: Women's Press, 2006. 1–22.

Salwen, Laura. "Myth of the Wicked Stepmother." *Women and Therapy* 10 (1990): 117–125.

Schapiro, Barbara. "Mothering . . . 'Without Any Irritable Reaching after Fact and Reason.'" *Mother Journeys: Feminists Write about Mothering*. Eds. Martha Roth, Maureen T. Reddy, and Amy Sheldon. Minneapolis: Spinsters Ink, 1994. 179–188.

Speier, Diane S. "Becoming a Mother." *Mother Matters: Motherhood as Discourse and Practice*. Ed. Andrea O'Reilly. Toronto: Association for Research on Mothering, 2004. 141–153.

Thurer, Shari L. *The Myths of Motherhood: How Culture Reinvents the Good Mother*. Boston: Houghton Mifflin, 1994.

Wong, Hertha. "Adoptive Mothers and Thrown-Away Children in the Novels of Louise Erdich." *Narrating Mothers: Theorizing Maternal Subjectivities*. Eds. Brenda O. Daly and Maureen T. Reddy. Knoxville: University of Tennessee Press, 1991. 174–192.

PART THREE

Childrearing

CHAPTER EIGHT

Feminist Family Values

Parenting in Third Wave Feminism and Empowering All Family Members

COLLEEN MACK-CANTY AND SUE MARIE WRIGHT

> I remember putting adults on a pedestal. . . . But, for my kids,
> from the first grade on, they call their teachers by their first
> names. They've known so many of my friends (and I don't
> remember my dad having any friends) . . . they meet my
> friends and have fun with them just like they do with me. So
> we've really broken a lot of barriers . . . that's important to me.
> That, to me, is a feminist value.
>
> —Greg, a single, gay, feminist parent

TODAY MANY FEMINISTS believe we are in a Third Wave of feminism, one
that challenges the ideas of hierarchy itself while recognizing diversity, partic-
ularity, and embodiment. This feminism, rather than working from established and usually abstract foundational theories, arises from the situated
perspectives of different(ing) women. In this chapter, we consider how the
feminist family is an example of Third Wave feminism. Like the practice of
Third Wave feminism generally, we begin by listening to how members of
diversely structured feminist families describe their family practices. We start
with a brief overview of feminist analyses of the family, both the idealized
family and actual families.

During the Second Wave of feminism, women began addressing how family life was maintaining the sex hierarchy (Johnson; Okin). Feminists recognized that the idealized traditional family of the 1950s, as symbolized by such icons as the television character June Cleaver, a happy women cleaning her suburban home in high heels and pearls, totally identified as mother and wife with no other interests, and the finances to sustain that lifestyle, was neither ideal nor traditional (Coontz). The instruments of popular culture informed younger women that the only true vocation lay in marriage and motherhood, but they observed that their mothers' realities were often different or unhappy.

Feminist scholarship in this period, in addition to exposing the now well-known feminist mystique, began to analyze how the family was structured to sustain general disparity between the female and male members within traditional families. Political theorist Susan Moller Okin (1989) asked, "If families are not themselves governed by principle of justice [between their female and male members], how can they morally educate citizens fit to sustain a just society?" (16). Sociologist and family scholar Miriam Johnson (1988) maintained that the husband–wife relationship was male-dominated. The organization of work and the male provider role pushed women to both need and want their husbands to be superior. Women were constrained to "choose" an asymmetrical relationship: to "marry up," which, in fact, reinforced the societal expectation for husbands to be dominant (7–8). Many feminists began to see the family as a sort of gender mill or place where people's identities as either female or male were maintained and reproduced.

Over the past two decades, family scholars, including feminist family scholars, have increasingly included nontraditional or alternative families as the subject of research. Many of these studies have focused primarily on the ways gendered roles and interactions between heterosexual married couples in the family are shifting. Some of these studies have involved dual-income families, families in which wives are also employed in the paid labor force, but, for the most part, these families have not been found to be egalitarian either in terms of power or the division of domestic and childrearing tasks (Hook; Zipp, Prohaska, and Bemiller).

Couple-focused studies have also explored the relational dynamics of "peer marriage" and "post-gender couples." Pepper Schwartz defines "peer marriage" as marriages in which the division of household labor remains within a sixty/forty split, power in decision making and over economic resources is shared equitably, and each partner's work is given equal weight in the couple's life plans. Men in peer marriages choose to be peers with their wives because their marriage relationship is the primary one in their lives and they see their relationship with their wife as one with a lifelong best friend (Schwartz). "Post-gender couples" represent families in which husband and wife divide work equally without regard to gender and mothering is a conscious collaboration (Cowdery and Knudson-Martin; Risman and Johnson-Sumerford). Interactions between these couples appear to be guided by rules of fairness and sharing within egalitarian friendship where partners believe in gender equality (Cowdery and Knudson-Martin; Schwartz). These studies suggest that it is possible for wives to be treated equally when both individuals in a couple adhere to the notion of gender equality, showing us that gender does not have to be deterministic.

Research on feminist families, however, warrants further attention since the dynamics and consequences of participating in this type of family hold potential not only for wives to receive equitable treatment, but also for children to grow up with a sense of gender equality. For this reason, we include the children of feminist families in our study, and we define feminist families as those in which the parents identify with feminist principles and parent from feminist perspectives. Although there is often disagreement over exactly what feminism means, feminists generally take certain aspects of liberal feminism—the demand for equality, freedom of individual choice, and the recognition of the woman as an autonomous being—as their starting point (Evans). We, too, start with the definition of feminism as a movement directed at making women the social equals of men. We assume that this is the most familiar definition for many people. Hence, at a minimum, the families included in our study consistently express a commitment to promoting gender equality in raising their children (and between adults, if they are two-parent, heterosexual families).

While such a basic definition of feminism is useful as a starting point, we also understand that this definition by itself is a simplistic one. It does not include race, class, and heterosexism as well as other significant factors in discrimination, exploitation, and oppression. A primary component of our research with feminist families is an attempt to uncover whether these families, who parent from a sense of gender equality, understand the relation of sexism to other hierarchical arrangements and, if so, how they put this understanding into practice. In particular, we compare elements of feminist theory often associated with Third Wave feminism: the intersectionality of various "isms" with sexism and the refutation of the notion of hierarchy itself.

In our exploration of these notions of multiple oppressions and differences among women, together with the challenge to dualism and hierarchy that tends to be present with the recognition of diversity, we focused on the extent to which these families, who parent from a sense of gender equality, understand the relation of sexism to other forms of oppression and how they put this understanding into practice. Do these families, for example, foster recognition that oppressions can take different forms? Do they parent in non-hierarchical, nonauthoritarian ways? Are the children's concerns heard and thoughtfully considered in family decision making?

In asking these questions, we draw on the idea that the traditional family in our society has reflected the dualist values of hierarchy and coercive authoritarian control and that these hierarchical relationships are exemplified in both the parent–child relationship and husband–wife relationship (Cowdery and Knudson-Martin; Gunnoe, Hetherington, and Reiss). We also draw on the notion that universalizing an essential family form (i.e., the heterosexual, two-parent family) currently being promoted by "family values" advocates is both ominous and in conflict with feminist values. The "family values" advocates promote a two-parent, heterosexual family form to the exclusion of other families. They often emphasize the authoritarian family with strictly ascribed gender roles (where the husband is the "head of the household") and maintain that the decline of the intact two-parent family, or "fatherlessness," is responsible for our most pressing social problems (Coltrane and Adams; Gallagher). Conversely, feminists generally favor family pluralism (Mack-Canty and Wright). They allege that the structural disparity within the traditional gendered family creates an unjust institution, one that curtails the opportunities of girls and women. Feminists, then, are concerned that society recognizes the differences among families in a positive manner.

Our study highlights the specific practice of Third Wave feminism as articulated by members of the diversely structured families we interviewed. We consider the saliency of the topic, the family, to early Second Wave feminists who were primarily concerned with sexual equality. Then, we reconsider the family by applying Third Wave feminist considerations—we give attention to the notion of multiple oppressions, to diversity of the subject (the family), and to its historical situatedness. For example, we interview members of families who have chosen to constitute themselves in different ways: two-parent families, single-parent families, gay and lesbian families, and adoptive families. We look for an awareness of different kinds of oppression in their family practices. And we recognize that the male-headed, nuclear family is a historically specific form of familial arrangement.

Notes and transcriptions from a series of three in-depth interviews with twenty families provide the data for this study. All families included at least one child four years of age or older and living in the household. Initially, we identified a set of families, known to us through personal contacts, who we understood as identifying with and parenting from feminist principles.

Broadly defined, they were raising their children with a sense of gender equality. In addition, our interpretations were corroborated through participants' responses to questions that asked whether parents identified themselves as feminist, when they first began to identify as feminist, and how feminism shaped individual decisions about parenting (see the Appendix). We enlarged the sample by asking the first set of families we interviewed to identify other families who might fit the parameters of the study. No more than two referrals were taken from any individual source, and usually only one referral from any one source was included in the sample. Overall, slightly less than half of the families in the final sample were those originally identified by us. The rest of the sample was composed of families referred by the original sample.

This study covers a fairly wide range of family types. Of the twenty families we interviewed, twelve are two-parent nontraditional families—that is, they are not organized hierarchically by gender, nor are they necessarily heterosexual. In two of these families, the mother is the sole breadwinner and the father is the homemaker and in one, the parents are lesbian. Eight of the families are single-parent families in which all but one of the parents were formerly married to their child(ren)'s other parent. One of these parents is gay; the others are heterosexual single mothers. Two of the twenty families belong to racial/ethnic minority groups, three families are interracial, and fifteen are white. In terms of occupational status, seven of these families have a parent who is employed in professional occupations; in three families, one of the parents is a small business owner; in seven families, the parents are employed in nonprofessional jobs. The remaining three families are headed by single parents who are graduate students.

In interviewing these families, we wanted all family members to be actively involved in constructing the data about their lives. We also wanted to understand the families as a group, as well as the views of individual family members. Therefore, families in this study participated in a series of three face-to-face interviews. The first interview included all members of the household together and was usually conducted in the family's home. Family members as a group responded to questions about parenting ideology and practices, decision-making processes, typical family activities, and perceived differences between the family being interviewed and other families. This initial interview was followed by an interview with the parent most active in their children's lives at the time of the interview. Parents responded to questions about the ways in which they resolved parenting issues, including personal issues related to parenting and/or differences with other adult family members. The third interview took place with the oldest child living at home and was usually carried out in an environment that the respondent identified as being comfortable. Children responded to questions about perceived family differences, interactions with peers and parents, and their thoughts about their future interactions with children if they became parents.

We use a grounded theory approach, in which key themes and categories were allowed to emerge from the data (Charmaz), to analyze the interviews. Audiotapes of interviews were transcribed and coded with the help of a research assistant. Interviews from each family were then coded using concepts developed jointly by the authors through an initial reading of interviews from selected families. All subsequent coding involved one of the authors. In our analysis we use the rich textual data of the transcriptions to understand the ways in which the participant parents implement nonsexist parenting and the ways in which they go beyond nonsexist parenting, highlighting parenting practices that enable the children to become conscious of, and to challenge hierarchy and oppression more generally.

The traditional family in our society, as noted, has reflected hierarchal relations that take place in both the parent–child relationship and the husband–wife relationship (Cowdery and Knudson-Martin; Gunnoe, Hetherington, and Reiss). Further, the gendered structural disparity that exists within the traditional family creates a particularly unjust institution for girls and women. Our families challenge this idea. Indeed, we selected these families because the parents currently identify with feminist principles broadly defined; that is, they are raising their children with a sense of equality for women However, the identification with feminist principles occurred at different points for these parents. Some of them identified with feminism before they chose to parent; others came to feminist perspective through parenting. While the interaction between feminist ideology and parenting practice is complex and perhaps never complete, in this chapter we categorize families according to whether the families identified themselves as consciously deciding to parent from feminist perspectives before they began parenting (twelve families) or whether they discuss coming to feminist perspectives through the practice of their parenting (eight families) in order to determine how the timing of feminism and parenting might affect family interactions and values. This process allows us to compare differences between more ideological and pragmatic stances to parenting, as well as understand feminist parenting practices as a whole. We use examples from some of the parents' narrative to show how parents identify with principles of Third Wave feminism. Our conclusions are based on the frequency and consistency of the participants' discussion around various themes.

PARENTING THROUGH FEMINISM

We might expect lesbian and gay parents, whether two-parent or single-parent, to reinvent the family as a pluralistic phenomenon since they self-consciously build from the ground up a variety of family types that challenge the "family values" advocates' notion that families should be composed of a heterosexual couple. Deborah and Milee, a white middle-class lesbian couple with an adopted African American daughter, Chris, illustrate this process. Deborah and Milee met in a community living situation that was concerned with gender equality for the children and where members spent a lot of time discussing how little girls' traits were socially constructed. Deborah, already in the process of adopting Chris, had decided her child would not be hampered by any gender stereotypes that she could control. Milee liked Deborah's approach to parenting, and they spent hours discussing childrearing, which they still continue to do.

Deborah and Milee are particularly concerned with how to help Chris develop her sense of confidence. They have worked to acquaint Chris (now in grade school) with her racial heritage. Together, they celebrate numerous African American feast days. They do things for Chris such as braiding her hair in cornrows because Chris decided she would like to try this hair style as a way to identify both as a girl and an African American. Among other things, they have taught Chris "to hold her chin up and tell kids 'Black is good.'"

Brenda, an African American mother of teenaged Kristin, who chooses to parent as a feminist single mother, also challenges the "family values" advocates' notion of a universally ideal family form. Among these advocates is former senator Daniel Moynihan, who sided with those who see fatherlessness as the cause of most social problems by singling out "Black matriarchy" as the cause of the "disintegrating" Black family (Davis-Sowers). Our interaction with single-mother families in this study suggests that these families, including Brenda's, are encountering no unusual difficulty in parenting, with the exception of financial difficulties often experienced by single mothers (Ciabattari).

While Brenda feels that racist stereotypes generally make life harder for a black single mother than for her white counterparts, she also identifies benefits for single mothers in the black community:

> I have to do more than most white, single mothers have to do. But Kristin does have many women in her life who mother her. In that sense, I'm just her biological mother. Our friend Mary is what you'd call a radical feminist . . . she's in your face. It's been those "in your face" type

women in the black community who have also mothered Kristin. I would say Kristin's sensibilities and who she is are very woman-centered.

Brenda's feminist parenting, however, goes beyond simply challenging the nuclear family structure as normative. Brenda incorporates the term *inclusive communication* in describing her parenting style with her teenage daughter. Brenda explains that their communication pattern in decision making usually takes the form of a dialogue. She illustrates what typically occurs when they are shopping and disagree on appropriate fashion, admitting that they sometimes get rather loud. "But," she adds, "we're not really fussin', we're discussin' . . . Generally, we end up on the same side." Kristin concurs, "We agree about almost everything." Further questioning reveals that the "everything" includes nose-rings and tattoos—"yes on the nose-ring, no on the tattoos."

White, middle-class, heterosexual, professional families, however, can also choose to challenge norms of "family values" advocates. Tesha and Howard, who fit this profile, have an adopted African American son. They explain that they came into parenting expecting to be equal participants at all levels. Howard feels feminist parenting "means a sense of cooperativeness and egalitarianism so that no single person is making decisions that overrules someone else." In explaining how they attempt to carry out this approach, Tesha says,

> Usually, I do those things that are interesting to me. I can do creative kinds of things with Dan, because that's who I am. Howard tends to do the sports things with Dan. It does end up being almost stereotypical in this regard, but these are the things we each like to do. Regarding Dan's everyday material care, however, we have consciously worked that out and divided it up. For example, we take turns regarding who is going to put him to bed every night.

Both Tesha and Howard acknowledge that their interactions with Dan are often constrained by schedules, as well as influenced by individual interests. As their personal routines change, how they spend time with Dan also often changes. While Tesha, who is working on her doctorate, is going back to school every night, Howard, a teacher, does Dan's baths. Regardless of schedules, Howard and Dan bake cookies together every Saturday; they both like to eat cookies and this is another activity that helps to break down gender stereotypes.

Steve and Nancy, a white nonprofessional couple, have a girl and boy in grade school and have chosen alternative lifestyles that are more in keeping with their social and environmental concerns. For this family, feminist parenting appears to be an outgrowth of their general critique of patriarchy. Steve explains:

> I think we decided to parent from a sense of feminist values because we were so repulsed with the patriarchal society, which I feel is pretty oppressive to both women and men. Men are not allowed to show their feelings with their children very much . . . I think we're emphasizing the value of everyone being involved in the family, rather than just the mother . . . I think we started out in the beginning thinking that I would do at least as much as I could and be home as much as I could with the kids. I really wanted to be home with the kids.

Nancy adds: "But I also think it had something to do with us examining or beginning to examine our own childhoods and realizing there were serious inequities and confusions that arose in the way we were parented. And I think we really came up with a bunch of gender stuff that we didn't want to repeat."

Steve and Nancy explain that, in part, feminist parenting now means that whoever feels most strongly about an issue in their family has the most decision-making power at that time. Because of this, power shifts back and forth. About himself, Steve says, "When I feel like I'm dominating something, I either tend to get the message across and back off, or I realize that I'm dominating and back off. Then, Nancy takes the power and it shifts back and forth." Steve adds that "the children have a lot of say" in the way the family operates, especially in home schooling. Nancy concludes, "I think that so much depends on the sense of personal power that you feel you have at the moment. It's like, 'Well, I'm sure of this. This is how I feel.' For us, decision making just depends on who has the strongest personal investment."

Greg, a white divorced single gay father has joint custody of Sam (in high school) and Katherine (in grade school). He planned on parenting from a sense of equality between females and males before he and his former wife were married. That sense of equality between husband and wife has now been parlayed into one of general equality between parent and child. Greg provides the following insight into the process of dismantling adult privilege:

> I remember putting adults on a pedestal . . . But [for my kids] from the first grade on, they call their teachers by their first names. They've known so many of my friends (and I don't remember my dad having any friends) . . . they meet my friends and have fun with them just like they

do with me. So we've really broken a lot of barriers . . . that's important to me. That, to me, is a feminist value.

FEMINISMS THROUGH PARENTING

Of the twenty families in this study, parents in eight families come to feminism, in large part, through the practice of parenting. For these families, acts of parenting challenge the status quo and foster new ways of understanding gender relations. Families primarily discuss fostering gender equality between children or challenging traditional gender roles either for children or within the family. Parents sometimes mention fighting the sexism they had seen growing up. A few parents describe coming to feminism through education while parenting, and some parents also mention a focus on empowering children. For instance, professional couple Yvonne and Scott, while not explicitly feminist at first, have always been focused on empowerment through parenting, which included allowing their children to challenge gender roles. Yvonne explains,

> I think that one way that really kind of evolved was . . . to empower them as people and not really focus on gender equality or inequality or . . . anything like that, but we just wanted them to have choices. [So they weren't constrained by] certain gender roles. When Suzanne chooses her clothes at the store or whatever . . . When she was little I was thinking about challenging gender roles because I did go in the boys' section and choose things for her there because they were sturdier, you know.

Scott adds, "I didn't think 'we'll do it this way.' I just did it. I guess we [came to feminist parenting] through experience, really. That's the only way that we found out. [It] seems to work the best." And Yvonne concludes "It keeps them happy and it allows them to keep their power and then they don't act out so much."

Similarly, Sonya and Harrison came to feminism by letting their kids be individuals regardless of gender roles. Sonya owns her own small business and Harrison works part-time, sharing the care of Jade (in middle school) and Trevor (an infant). Sonya emphasizes this point by saying, "I never made a conscious decision about [feminist parenting] at all. [I just did] whatever seemed right. I think that mostly the kids are so individual . . . it's kind of whatever they want to do."

While the family initially only challenged gender norms for children, they have found that they now challenge a much broader range of power relations, including adult–child power relations. This shift appears to have occurred primarily through the practice of inclusive communication and child advocacy. Jade explains that her parents let her contribute ideas, "even if my ideas are way off base," and Sonya concurs that family members do always discuss options and decisions. Sonya also illustrates how child advocacy supports inclusive communication. She says, "I defend Jade's position constantly, saying to her father, 'You've got to let her grow through that.'" Jade's father, Harrison, adds, "Then if we have to go against Jade's wishes, we have good reasons for doing so and we explain them to her. While she may not be happy about having her wishes denied in these instances, she usually understands why."

Mary, too, found that parenting fostered feminism. A white, divorced, single mother, Mary's friendship with her children Diane (in high school) and Alicia (in junior high) and challenging roles in the family brought her to an understanding of feminism before her divorce. Studying feminism and thinking about how she wanted to raise kids differently changed her outlook on life. Of this transformation, Mary says:

> I think I always challenged the roles in the family in terms of the father and the mother having such separate kind of stereotypical roles. I think I grew up seeing that a little bit in my own family and with my own mother. And so as I felt more free to develop that, and I think the real jumping off point for me was when I went back to college and started studying feminist perspectives and took some women's studies classes and just began to really think about how I wanted to raise my kids differently, even though I had sort of a different perspective before. I though, "Wow! There are different ways of doing this." . . . And I think, too, becoming a single parent and moving, the girls and I together, it was kind of like we had to develop a whole new family system.

While many people would see a mother, especially a single mother, going to school and pursuing graduate work as being at the expense or neglect of the family, Mary and her children have quite the opposite perspective.

> I think our move and my undertaking graduate work really prompted the growth of my positive relationship with the girls. Diane and Alicia seemed to understand that we were in this endeavor together. We always

had to figure out how we were going to get through this on a day-to-day basis as it affected all our lives. We really grew together as a family while I was in school.

Mary explicitly links the inclusive communication practices in their household to feminist ideology. She describes this as a process of mutuality:

After my divorce, it was like we developed a new family system. It was difficult at first, but I found it had a real upside. We made more time for being together. My identity for a long time had been exclusively that of a caregiving mother and wife. I gave, all the time, which made me angry Now, I mentor them rather than playing servant. Our relationship is more mutual.

These parents, however, do not give any appearance of being the kind of parents who "let kids walk all over them," Mary's children, like other children in this study, appear to appreciate the trust their parents place in them and understand the responsibility it entails. Diane, Mary's older daughter, adds:

We talk about things a lot more now. Mom wants me to know a lot, which helps me with my decisions. Also, Mom instills values just by having a lot of discussions with us, letting us say what we think. This helps us to make decisions. My mom is like an advisor and this helps me more than if she told me exactly what to do.

INTERACTIONS WITH CHILDREN

While these feminist families generally talk a lot about values, they do not appear to have as many rules as other families. For example, the values actualized by Mary and her daughters as a family are not the structured kinds of requirements experienced by the daughters' friends. Mary's family actively practices the values of trust and responsibility, both of which are highly recognized values in our society. Mary explains that she gives the girls her cash card for grocery shopping. Alicia said her friends have more rules: "One girl in our class has a family with a lot of 'values', like they always have to sit at a nice table for a big dinner. We often just sit at the table or by the TV. We don't have big dinners too often, but we have big discussions. Other families hardly talk together, at least not when I'm there."

Challenging hierarchies and practicing democratic decision making in the family also appear to contribute to fostering a sense of empowerment in these children. In particular, the children in these families demonstrate the ability to negotiate and challenge both peers and parents on matters of principles and justice. The older children in this study often express both a readiness to accept diversity and a willingness to challenge oppression. These children seem to enjoy questioning some aspects of the dominant culture, and frequently gain peer support for their actions. For instance, Kristin, because she believes that people ought to show what they really look like, does not use makeup. Although girls at her school commonly use makeup, her friends have followed her lead and do not use it either.

Although many examples that these families offered illustrate aspects of personal power and responsibility for the kids, there are also situations when the children's negotiating power affects parents. Because these children are encouraged both to think for themselves and be aware of oppressions, our examples suggest that these children sometimes teach their parents a thing or two regarding "isms." Parents, even the most socially conscious, are products of their own historical situation and their children another. The children, who have been encouraged to perceive sexism, racism, and other oppressions, appear to be able to take this perception a step or two further than their parents, thus heightening their parents' awareness. In dialectal fashion, the parents can find themselves learning from their children. For instance, one family relayed how their younger son helped his parents realize they were still being somewhat sexist. Tom says:

It's fun to watch the children's reactions to sexism. Clair was given a coffee mug as a present. It was inscribed, "If men are god's gift to women, then god must like gag gifts." Liam, who is five, was hurt by this saying. He said, "I am a male, too." This provided us with a chance to explain to him that not all men are like that, but that a lot of men are. It was a good lesson for Clair and me to have to realize what we thought was funny was in reality another form of sex stereotyping.

Greg's son, too, seems to challenge gender distinctions (and the resulting sexism), beyond ways Greg would have envisioned. Greg relates the following incident involving Sam:

We were shopping for shorts and Sam had trouble picking out what he wanted. Tom, his friend who was with us, picked out a pair of shorts that said "Hanes for Her." Sam, much to my surprise, put them on. He liked them and he bought them. There's no way I would have done that, no matter how identical they were to a man's. I thought, "Me? At that age? I wouldn't have bought them and I wouldn't have worn them." But it makes absolutely no difference to him at all.

DISCUSSION

By definition, all the families interviewed for this study dispute the idea of male superiority. Moreover, all the families in this study challenge some type of hierarchal system such as: male privilege, racism, heterosexism, unnecessary adult authority, and universal family form. In exploring common themes, however, it appears that these feminist families go beyond nonsexist parenting to parenting that enables their children to become conscious of and to challenge hierarchy and oppression generally. Interrelated patterns emerge from our interviews with feminist families that challenge hierarchies, whether parenting through feminism or if they come to feminism through the practice of parenting. In these families, status is not based on sex, race, heterosexuality, or even adulthood in the sense that parents are not unequivocally the authority. All the families in this study practice some form of inclusive decision making, taking each member's concerns into account. If they are two-parent families, these families acknowledge and respect the level of expertise and investment of each parent. In addition, the parents routinely involve children in the decision-making process, and the children expect that their concerns will be given serious attentions (although not necessarily agreed to). It appears the children in these families can mature, more able to assume their right to reasonably question existing power arrangements in the larger society.

In this study, we observe feminist families who try to provide more than alternative gender role models for children. They consciously work to change accepted patterns of hierarchal authority in the family, including male privilege and unnecessary parental authority in decision making, thereby fostering the empowerment of all members of the family. It is arguable that, in so doing, these families help to undermine the traditional authoritarian family advocated by fundamental Christians. The single-parent families and the two-parent lesbian couple, by definition, contest the notion of a universal family form. Because these families constitute themselves in diverse arrangements, ones that seem to be proving viable, they also call into question the essentialist notions of family structure held by Christian fundamentalists.

We suggest that the connections the families in this study, as illustrated in the interviews, make between their concerns about oppression and their use of inclusive decision making characterize practices of Third Wave feminism. As discussed previously, feminists generally start with the notion of equality for women, but have different ideas about how this is best achieved. The fact that feminism is a constantly expanding theory adds to this complexity. The expanding nature, or wave, of feminist theory may be understood in terms of increasingly complex schema. While new information and ideas can sometimes be assimilated in a way that is compatible with existing understandings, beyond a certain point, a new and more complex framework must be accommodated. This framework, often now referred to as Third Wave feminism, is being shaped by the needs and experiences of diverse groups of women that challenge not just gender dualism and hierarchy, but dualisms and hierarchies in general.

We see the ideas about a more democratic family meshing with the broader approach of Third Wave feminism. Just as feminism, for the most part, has expanded its concern for oppression of women to a concern for oppression generally, the families in this study, by their practices, express (at least, implicitly, if not always explicitly) a concern not only for women's oppression, but for other oppressions such as racism, heterosexism, unnecessary adult authority, nondemocratic decision making, and universal family form. To some degree, each of these families seems to recognize the connections among oppressions and works to challenge hierarchy. We believe this endeavor is a move away from stratification generally, in addition to challenging patriarchal power relations. These families appear to characterize the way family life could be when authoritarian rule is replaced with shared responsibility and mutuality. We suggest these parenting practices coincide with Third Wave feminism.

APPENDIX

Family Group Questions

1. What do you like best about your family?
2. Do you parent from a feminist perspective? Why? When did you first identify as a feminist?
3. Tell me about parenting practices in your family. How does feminism affect these practices?
4. How are decisions made in your family? How do you think this differs from other families you know?

5. In what kinds of activities does your family participate as a family? With other families?

Parent Interview Questions

1. What difference has parenting made in your life? In your feminist views?
2. In what ways, if any, would you like to change your parenting practices? Why?
3. Who do you talk with about parenting? Are these discussions helpful to you? In what ways?
4. How do you and your (former) partner differ in your approach to parenting? How are differences usually resolved?

Child Interview Questions

1. What kinds of things do you like to do?
2. Would you tell me a little bit about your friends. What kinds of things do you usually agree on? Argue over? What do you do when you disagree?
3. Do you think that you will have children someday? What kinds of things would you like to do with your children? What kinds of rules do you think you will set as a parent?
4. Do you disagree with your parents sometimes? What kinds of things do you disagree about? What happens when you disagree about something?

REFERENCES

Charmaz, Kathy. *Constructing Grounded Theory, A Practical Guide Through Qualitative Analysis*. Thousand Oaks, CA: Sage Publications, 2006.

Ciabattari, Teresa. "Single Mother, Social Capital, and Work—Family Conflict." *Journal of Family Issues* 28 (2007): 34–60.

Coltrane, Scott, and Michelle Adams. "The Social Construction of the Divorce 'Problem': Morality, Child Victims, and the Politics of Gender." *Family Relations* 52 (2003): 363–372.

Coontz, Stephanie. *The Way We Never Were: American Families and the Nostalgia Trap*. New York: Basic Books, 1992.

Cowdery, Randi S., and Carmen. Knudson-Martin. "The Construction of Motherhood: Tasks, Relational Connection, and Gender Equality." *Journal of Family Relations* 54 (2005): 335–345.

Davis-Sowers, Regina Louise. "Salvaging Children's Lives: Understanding the Experiences of Black Aunts Who Serve as Kinship Care Providers within Black Families." Diss. Georgia State University, 2006.

Evans, Sara M. *Tidal Wave: How Women Changed America at Century's End.* New York: Free Press, 2003.

Gallagher, Maggie. *The Marriage Movement: A Statement of Principles.* New York: Institute for American Values, 2000.

Gunnoe, Marjorie Linder, Mavis E. Hetherington, and David Reiss. "Differential Impact of Fathers' Authoritarian Parenting on Early Adolescent Adjustment in Conservative Protestant versus Other Families." *Journal of Family Psychology* 20 (2006): 589–596.

Hook, Jennifer L. "Reconsidering the Division of Household Labor: Incorporating Volunteer Work and Informal Support." *Journal of Marriage and the Family* 66 (2004): 101–117.

Johnson, Miriam M. *Strong Mothers, Weak Wives.* Berkeley: University of California Press, 1988.

Mack-Canty, Colleen, and Sue Wright. "Feminist Family Values: Bridging Third Wave Feminism and Feminist Families." *Journal of Family Issues* 25 (2004): 851–880.

Okin, Susan Moller. *Justice, Gender and the Family.* New York: Basic Books, 1989.

Risman, Barbara, and Dannette Johnson-Sumerford. "Doing It Fairly: A Study of Postgender Marriages." *Journal of Marriage and the Family* 60 (1998): 23–40.

Schwartz, Pepper. *Peer Marriage.* New York: Free Press, 2003.

Stacey, Judith. "Toward Equal Regard for Marriages and Other Imperfect Intimate Relations." *Hofstra Law Review* 32 (2003): 331–348.

Zipp, John F., Ariane Prohaska, and Michell Bemiller. "Wives, Husbands, and Hidden Power in Marriage." *Journal of Family Issues* 25 (2004): 933–988.

CHAPTER NINE

Feminist Motherline

Embodied Knowledge/s of Feminist Mothering

FIONA JOY GREEN

When I was really young before I had any children—when I
thought, "do I want any children or not?"—I saw having children as making a contribution to society in that you're 'gonna
school them in a culture and an orientation. They were going
to be people who were maybe different or the same, but they
were going to have an impact. It wasn't neutral. It's the next
society, the next generation, and how you raise them is gonna
have a huge difference on what our future's like. For sure it's
political.
  —Tammy, forty-six-year-old mother of three children
                 aged eighteen, fifteen, and seven years

BETWEEN THE FALL OF 1995 and the summer of 1996, I interviewed sixteen
self-identified feminist mothers living in or close to Winnipeg, Manitoba,
about the realities of feminist mothering. Feminism is not only central to
their personal identity as women, it is essential to their philosophies for and
practices of parenting. For these women, feminist mothering is a conscious
political strategy they use to bring about social change in their lives and in
the lives of their children (Green 1999; 2001; 2004a; 2004b; 2005). Over the
past decade, I have had the good fortune to remain in touch with a number
of participants from the original study, and during the summer months of

161

2005 I conducted one-on-one interviews with ten of the original sixteen participants.[1]

This chapter addresses some of the preliminary findings from these more recent discussions with self-identified feminist mothers about their parenting. More specifically, I explore the challenges feminist mothers face, aspects of their feminist mothering they view as successful, and elements of their mothering that they may have done differently. I conclude with a call for more research into feminist mothering and the importance of a feminist motherline to carry the voices, wisdom, and wit of feminist mothers. A feminist motherline assists mothers in re/claiming their feminist mothering authority and grounds them in their knowledge and the knowledge of other feminist mothers. It also strengthens and provides, for some, a foundation for the ongoing political activism of feminist mothers. This longitudinal study draws on the experiences, knowledge/s, and theorizing of feminist mothers over a ten-year period, thus enriching and enhancing our understanding of feminism and feminist mothering.

SELF-IDENTIFIED FEMINIST MOTHERS

All of the mothers participating in the 2005 study identify themselves as feminist and are temporarily able-bodied birth mothers between the ages of forty-four and fifty-eight years.[2] Two women are also mothers of adopted children, with one additionally being the social mother to four adult children of a former male partner. Since the initial interviews in the mid-1990s, one mother has birthed a third child, now aged seven years, and another has recently adopted an infant, making her a mother of four. The twenty-six children of the ten mothers range in age from sixteen months to thirty-six years. Two women have one child, four women have two children, two women have three children, one woman has four children, and one woman has six children. Eight women identify as heterosexual and two as lesbian. Seven women are single, five are separated or divorced, and three are married or living in common law relationships.

The ethnic ancestry of the group is varied. One woman is African and one is Jewish. Two women have Columbian/European heritage, two are of Jewish/European decent, and four have mixed European lineage. All mothers have some postsecondary education, and are either self-employed or employed by others. Two women identify themselves as poor, while the other eight see themselves as middle class.

THE CONTINUAL CHALLENGES OF MOTHERING

Throughout our conversations, all mothers note how hard it is to parent and are critical of the lack of social acknowledgment about the realities of mothering. These issues were of concern to each feminist mother the first time we spoke about the complexities of mothering almost ten years ago. Today, they critique the mythical standards of motherhood and the social neglect of the real isolation many mothers experience. They all identify the general lack of social support for mothers and recognize the lack of support for feminist mothers, in particular. Four of the ten women are particularly vocal about the need to expose the challenging conditions associated with the hard work of raising children and call for greater support from feminism.

LACK OF SOCIAL ACKNOWLEDGMENT AND SUPPORT FOR MOTHERS

Tammy, a common-law wife and mother who has two teenaged children, an eighteen-year-old daughter and fifteen-year-old son, as well as a seven-year-old son, speaks candidly about negative social attitudes toward mothers and her perception that there is a general lack of social investment in mothers and in children:

> Everybody treats you like an idiot when you're a mother. But structurally, and more important I think, is the whole business of it's not only unpaid labour; it's the hardest job that you could possibly do. And there's not the supports that are needed; not just economically, but in terms of information, respite, supportive systems for information. There's lots that should be done to help mothers, I think. And, you know, the whole "It takes a village to raise a child"; the whole idea that it's somehow an individual family's, and usually the woman's, responsibility to raise her kids is just weird. They're not MINE, you know. They're just the next generation and they could be anybody's kids, really. This is the next generation and I don't understand NOT investing in it.

Tammy's frustration is tangible during the interview and sits just below the surface of our conversation. The lack of respect she has been shown over the years as a mother, as well as the attitude that mothers are solely responsible for raising and caring for children, is central to Tammy's critique of the inadequate, and often nonexistent, support—whether economic, respite, or information—for mothers.

Kim, a forty-five-year-old married mother of two boys, aged eleven and thirteen, agrees with Tammy's analysis and notes how she personally craves honesty about the realities of childrearing and mothering. She tells me:

> What I would say is to validate just how hard it is, how isolating it is. Nobody talks like that about mothering. Like, "Ya! They drive you nuts." And, "Ya! It is hard." And kind of validating that part because there's all this pressure on you to be a great mother all the time and that nothing should bother you and that your kids should come first and there's still all those pressures there.

As Adrienne Rich notes in *Of Woman Born* (1986), the mothers I spoke with attest to their deep love for and commitment to their children, while also speaking frankly about the frustrations, tensions, and harsh realties of mothering. They spoke about the complex and sometimes seemingly contradictory feelings experienced as mothers toward their child/ren during our initial interviews, and again during our most recent conversations. According to these feminist mothers, this element of mothering must be exposed and validated as typical and ordinary, especially if the work of mothering is to be understood and mothers and children supported.

Beverly, a fifty-two-year-old mother of two adult daughters, aged twenty-five and twenty-eight, who has been in a lesbian partnership for the past five years, is well aware of the pressures that Kim, Tammy, and the other mothers mention. Beverly shares her experience of feeling isolated, misunderstood, and disrespected when she was a mother of young children, as well as her insights into the complex position of being a feminist mother:

> I've always sensed that my friends and colleagues who were feminist, who had no children, valued my work in the workplace way more than my work as the mother. So there's that friction there, and it's real and tangible. And particularly for those feminist moms who choose to stay at home for a few years and raise the children without societal supports like day-care and that kind of thing.
>
> It's a tough one because I think what we're doing, what the feminist movement has done, is to kind of judge women in relationship to men's achievements. And while we applaud men when they get involved with childreading, there's an expectation that still, you know, childrearing is

women's work and you're gonna do that if you're a good mom. If you're a super mom, you're gonna do that on top of, you know, your education and your work, your paid work. And I think it puts an enormous amount of pressure on feminist mothers that doesn't necessarily have to be there.

Not only are there social pressures on "good mothers" (Green 2005) who are expected to be doing "it all," feminist mothers experience additional expectations or pressure to be competent and capable women from feminists who don't have children. Beverly is not the only one to experience this pressure or to express this opinion.

Paula, a self-employed, single, heterosexual mother of three children, aged thirteen, seventeen, and twenty, agrees with Beverly and other feminist mothers who are critical of the lack of support they have experienced from feminism and other feminists. Paula, who lives with her children in a women's housing co-op, reflects on the isolation and lack of support she has experienced, particularly from feminism:

> As a mother, I didn't feel supported by feminism. In fact, I felt ghettoized by my motherhood. When the kids were really small, I found it really tough—like every day was really hard for me to get through. I felt very isolated, particularly, I think, being a feminist mother. I didn't want to hang out at the playground; it gives me the willies still. I don't want to hang out with other people who are happy being isolated or not being able to participate fully. What helped me most was bringing my children into my life in other ways; so, bringing them to meetings, organizing, combining parenting with the things that I was already doing. And sometimes I was doing that in the face of opposition. Like my first workplace gave me a hassle; didn't want me bringing my baby there. But other places, she was welcome. So, I looked for opportunities where I could incorporate parenting into my life, and they weren't that easy to find. I think we need to adapt society more to tolerate children.

Paula finds that mothering has become easier in the past year, now that two of her children have become teenagers and one is a young adult. Yet there are times when she is still unsure of her mothering, as her motherwork has shifted in focus to providing appropriate emotional and physical support for each of her unique children without creating dependency.[3] In striving to provide balance to the fluidity of their ever-changing needs, Paula feels as if she is constantly "navigating" the tension between supporting her children's needs and encouraging their independence rather than dependency. She still finds herself not always knowing when she has given enough support to her children.

Like the other mothers in the study, Paula has a small, yet committed, support system. She finds strength and understanding for her current work as a feminist mother from close friends and the women and children living in the housing co-op. For Paula, collective action with feminists is an effective strategy for social change. She tells me, "When I think about women being liberated I think women have been brought into the patriarchal cage."[4] Feminists and mothers need to "learn to work together" in order to dismantle and get out of the patriarchal cage. Living in a feminist co-op is a step toward this end for Paula.

The ten feminist mothers in this study long for, and work toward, acknowledging and validating the systemic challenges and difficulties facing all mothers. They believe the perpetual myths about mothering and the constant and complex social barriers that undermine their motherwork need to be uncovered and eradicated. For these women, feminist mothering is an essential strategy for contributing to positive political social change. Through contesting notions of motherhood and practices of mothering, by engaging in honest and sometimes challenging relationships with their children, as well as raising children to be critical thinkers who are able to articulate and challenge perspectives that do not necessarily confer with the status quo, feminist mothers believe they are continuing, and reaping the benefits of, the political activist work they began a decade or more ago as mothers. They believe, with the support and assistance of feminists, the feminist work of mothering can be successfully done. As May, the mother of two adult daughters notes: "It is hopefully true that the strategy of feminist mothering can bring about social change because it just takes one person to start something. It is a political act, because the personal is political, that's the thing."

ASPECTS OF FEMINIST MOTHERING
THAT HAVE GONE WELL

In our conversations about their feminist mothering over the past decade, I asked participants to reflect upon aspects of their parenting they thought had gone well. Participants in the initial study told me they valued relationships with their children that are not intimidating or domineering and that they were committed to work toward relating to their children in ways that are not based on the use or abuse of their authority and power as adults and mothers

(Green 2005: 93; Green 1999: 103). Upon reflection, many of the women in the smaller, more recent research group thought they had succeeded in this aspect of their mothering. Rather than exercise power over children, they strived for relationships based on respect, responsibility, and accountability. They encouraged their children to think critically about their own and their mother's ideas. They also acknowledged the experiences and knowledge of their children and encouraged them to talk about their own understandings and experiences with them in respectful dialogue.

HONEST COMMUNICATION THROUGH TRUSTING RELATIONSHIPS

Carol, a fifty-eight-year-old heterosexual, single mother of her biological nineteen-year-old son, an adoptive mother of her twenty-four-year-old niece, and the social mother to four adult children of a previous male partner, told me that "the talking, with everything out in the open" is what has gone well with her parenting.

I met with Carol one afternoon in late August at her home, where she was having some minor renovations done in her basement. We sat together in her living room drinking iced tea while repairs were being done downstairs and her teen-aged son slept upstairs after working a late shift. Eager to talk, Carol started our conversation by saying, "I just wanted to tell you this one thing 'cause the whole premise is feminist and this happened because of their feminist upbringing."

Carol anxiously relayed an alarming incident that occurred seven years before, when her adopted daughter, then aged seventeen, told Carol that the man Carol had been dating for four years, and living with for some time in their home, had initiated a sexual relationship with her by secretly giving her money and writing her a note. Carol credits her feminist mothering practice of talking directly with her children since they were very young—especially about issues of safety and inappropriate behavior—with her daughter's ability to tell Carol about the situation as quickly as she did and without shame. They had participated together in many open and frank talks about inappropriate behavior, with Carol often telling her children, "If anything happens, you tell Mum, especially if they say, 'don't tell.'"

Carol believes practicing honest and open communication and having trusting relationships with her children ensured that her daughter "trusted me enough to say something the first time she felt uncomfortable about the way my boyfriend took a run at her." The practice of not keeping secrets meant that as soon as Carol learned about the incident she confronted the man about his behavior and told him to "pack his things and get out," which he immediately did. According to Carol, "He's gone, that man, never to be seen again. It was just one minute he was there and one minute he was not."

The effects of the situation have been very hard on Carol, who sought six years of counseling to deal with feeling responsible and guilty for what happened. She has only recently been able to forgive herself for putting her children in a vulnerable situation. Carol told me, "I am just now able to poke by nose out 'cause that really devastated me." She feels "like a statistic instead of someone who has nobly marched on" and while she wasn't sure "feminism helps you choose men, it certainly helps your children tell."

Carol believes her feminism—which values good communication, openness and honesty, even when it is painful—ensured her daughter's ability to both analyze what was going on and instantly confide in Carol. Trust is essential to good communication and respectful relationships. Carol unequivocally accepts what her daughter said; she doesn't question or doubt her daughter's experience or knowledge. Knowing her mother believes her, without hesitation and without dispute, demonstrates the depth of the relationship Carol and her daughter share. The strength of their communication and their solid relationship, Carol believes, is underpinned by strong feminist principles of trust and respect.

May, the forty-nine-year-old, divorced mother of two daughters, aged twenty-two and twenty-four, believes the most rewarding aspect of being a feminist mother is the way she and her adult children can "talk, and share, and have a kind of real understanding of one another." May told me; "I always imagined what kind of conversations would happen with my children when they became older, when we could really talk, and I am not disappointed. They are beginning to understand the role of a woman, the role of a mother. When they look at themselves and the world there's so much we can talk about. And we do."

May and her recently married, eldest daughter are building on their long history of talking and confiding in one another—a practice May has shared with both of her daughters and the sisters have shared with each other. At present, May and her firstborn are speaking about "some of the social structures that influence the roles of women and wife," roles that May's daughter had not understood in the same way before her marriage. In fact, it is May's daughter who is introducing topics specific to married relationships during their conversations. Lately, she has wanted to talk about "equality in relationships," including "the division of domestic labour, and the role of money and the ways in which it can be used as a way of gaining more power in relationships."

While May has always encouraged her daughters to be "free in their thinking and to always question things, like racism, they heard outside [the family]," her daughters are currently coming to understand, through their own adult experiences and their honest discussions with their each other and their mother, "how society is structured, and how it influences women to become the way we are." Without the solid base of communication and the long established practice of speaking with each other over the years, May believes she and her daughters would not be able to talk as openly and as freely as they do about their lives today. For May, this is a dream come true.

AUTONOMY AND SELF-GOVERNANCE

Shar, a fifty-eight-year-old retired teacher, values communication and fosters respectful relationships with her four children, her two grandchildren, and the dozen children she cares for in her home-based childcare. According to Shar, her work as a mother, teacher, grandmother, and childcare provider has always encompassed lessons about how to create respectful relationships because "it's something that is really not taught; parents take it for granted and teachers don't teach it." Shar tries to instill good communication skills and respect in the daily interpersonal interactions she and the children in her care engage in. She does this by ensuring that she, and all of the children, acknowledge each other when they speak. For Shar, "that's part of the respect thing; trying to teach them to respect the other person that they're with and that you have to respond to the person you're with when they speak."

Self-governance and self-respect coincide with effective and respectful communication. Children in Shar's care quickly learn to ask for what they need and want, and that physical force is not an acceptable way to do so. Shar tells me, "On the one hand I am gentle to the extreme, but on the other hand, very clear about what I want and what I don't want." One of the rules in Shar's home is, "You don't put your hands on somebody else's body unless you have their permission." Rather than saying, "don't hit them," Shar uses loving examples such as, "If you want to hug somebody, you ask them if they would like a hug." When children bump into each other too hard—as children are apt to do at times—Shar will ask them if it was an accident. She instructs the children to immediately say, "I'm sorry, are you OK?" When children don't want to apologize, Shar will role model for them by putting her arms around both children and saying, "Oh, we're so sorry that this happened. What were you doing before you had this accident?"

By highlighting the fun and personal connection children shared before the clash/crash, Shar reminds them that they are friends and not enemies. Central to Shar's teachings is a willingness to accept that people are "flawed individuals and you don't dismiss them just because of their flaws or because of their gender or because of their mistakes." She believes it takes a long time for people to learn that "this other walking set of bones and skin is like them." And because Shar is patient in "teaching them to be really gentle" with each other and with themselves, the end result is children learn to engage in respectful relationships with Shar and with each other.

Shar has seen evidence of this lesson in the older children she has cared for over the past fifteen years in her childcare, as well as in her own three thirty-something-year-old children, who, she believes, are well-adjusted autonomous people doing meaningful work they enjoy. Shar tells me that her thirty-one-year-old daughter, the youngest of her adult children, "has always been assertive in her relationships with men," often telling them directly, "I don't like that, don't do that." Shar believes that her daughter learned very early on to be assertive because she learned to respect herself and "to take for granted her right to ask for the same in return."

Shar shares an example of her daughter's assertiveness based on self-respect, stating, "In fact, before she would have sexual relationships with anyone, she would tell them that they'd have to go to the doctor and get a certificate clearing them of any AIDS or HIV." Shar believes her children are "much more assertive" than she was at their age, and possibly even now, because as children they learned they have the right to be treated with respect. Helping children develop into autonomous individuals who are respectful of others, and are competent and confident in self-governance, are positive outcomes of Shar's feminist mothering.

Deb, the forty-three-year-old single, heterosexual mother of a sixteen-year-old son, tells me about the way she and her son communicate, in particular when they have differing opinions. Throughout her mothering, Deb has always acknowledged that her son "has his own path and his own experience." She has also been open about her "standpoint feminism," which is one way she is able to identify for him where she is coming from. At times, discussions between Deb and her teenaged son become heated because, as she says, "When two intelligent people really go at it, the swords are out (laughter)."[5]

During these exchanges, Deb is vigilant in ensuring that the interactions are respectful. In particular, she and her son are watchful for condescending or other negative behavior; "We talk about when we feel the power shift in the room and when we feel disrespected. While we aren't always able to mediate those things in the moment, we do come back to a whole process that we are both engaged in." Deb notes it's "bloody amazing" that they are able to have contested discussions in which her son "won't let go of his power," where she "doesn't lose hers," and where they come to an understanding that while they may not agree, they continue to respect each other.

Not only is open and respectful communication between mothers and their children an aspect of feminist mothering that is valued and has been successful, so is thinking critically about the world and one's place within it.

CRITICAL ANALYSIS

Jody, the forty-three-year-old separated mother of nine-year-old daughter and an eleven-year-old son, believes she has done well teaching her children to think critically and to challenge ideas they are uncertain of. Jody understands that once children enter the school system, they are introduced to multiple ideas and perspectives that may not coincide with those of their parents. She is aware her control and influence in the lives of her children decrease when they are in school and she must "let go of that and realize all you can do is give a little bit of direction to what they hear."

Jody shares a self-described "good story" with me to illustrate this understanding and the success of her feminist teaching as a mother:

> My daughter came to me one day, but she said—before she even started—"Mom, would you be offended if I told you a joke about a native person?" That's what she said to me. And I went, "What? Is this a joke?" is what I said. She proceeded to tell me an extremely racist joke that she had heard on the bus, from some kids. And I said, "Yes, that offends me very much." But the fact that she even had that consciousness to think this might offend, I thought, "That's right. Oh my god! Something did get through!" (Laughter). And then we had a big discussion about it; about what this joke said and how would she feel if it had been HER culture that was put in this place and what did that really mean when they said those things. I mean, I was horrified, HORRIFIED that this joke is out there. But, at the same time, she had the sense to think there's something wrong with this. I'm like, "Wow!"

Clearly, Jody's daughter had learned from previous discussions with her mother that placing people at the brunt of so-called jokes is hurtful and offensive. Like Carol's daughter, Jody's daughter trusted her mother would be open to her questions and, in this case, helps her further understand how and why a joke was racist. Together through their discussion, Jody was able to honestly discuss the hurtful consequences of racism with her daughter and provide her with a deeper understanding beyond simply sensing there was something wrong with what she had heard. It also gave Jody the occasion to validate her daughter's "sense that something was wrong" and offer her the chance to engage in a critical analysis of the situation.

Ten years ago, each woman I interviewed spoke about the significance of introducing her child/ren to a feminist analysis of the world (Green 1999; 2001; 2004a; 2004b; 2005). All of the mothers I revisited reconfirmed their commitment to parenting from this standpoint and believe their children (are learning to) view and understand that the world is constructed in ways that privilege some people over others. Feminist mothers believe they have successfully developed relationships with their children that foster closeness and the sharing of ideas through respectful and honest communication. While these topics of discussion can, at times, be controversial and painful, they nevertheless cultivate space in which mothers and children openly and honestly discuss various attitudes, beliefs, and ideas. Being forthright about each other's ideas, and the ideas of others, continues to work well for feminist mothers.

While the women I spoke with are proud of elements of their parenting, they also identified some aspects of their mothering that they might do differently if they had another chance to do so.

WHAT FEMINIST MOTHERS WOULD DO DIFFERENTLY

I asked each woman if she would do anything differently as a mother, now that she has the 20/20 hindsight of the past ten—or more—years of parenting. Several mothers told me they would tweak the limitations, rights, and conditions of behavior they set for and engage in with their children. In particular, they spoke of the need to balance providing more guidance for their children with respecting their children's autonomy and self-governance.

Provide More Guidance

Tammy, the forty-six-year-old, heterosexual, common-law mother of three children, aged seven, fifteen, and eighteen, realizes she can be "negotiated out" of the limitations she sets. She believes that this has been detrimental to her daughter who is "a very strong personality" and "a bit of a powerhouse." As a younger mother, Tammy thought that when "you showed somebody

respect, they would reciprocate by understanding that things were nego-
tiable." Since then, she has discovered this strategy has not been good for her
eldest child because "she pushed and pushed and now she's a person who feels
that that's one way of getting, of achieving, what she wants, by pushing."
While Tammy believes negotiating worked well with her other two children,
in retrospect she thinks she shouldn't have negotiated as much as she did with
her eldest daughter, saying, "With her personality, it was a misjudgment."

Willow, a forty-five-year-old single lesbian mother of an eighteen-year-
old daughter, reflected on feeling uncertain about decisions she made as a
young mother:

> There were certain things I was unsure about. I didn't know how far to
> push my authority or how much I had a right to it. But I'm much more
> sure about where you're allowed to make your own decisions and where
> you're not, much more sure. When you're authoritarian, it doesn't mean
> that you're abusive. That means you're authoritative, you're confident,
> you're absolutely clear about what's needed here and you make sure that
> the child trusts you to make the right decision for them. So, it's a leader-
> ship issue, that's all. When do you set limits and when do you not. I
> think I'm more clear about that than I used to be.

Willow has been able to put this assessment into practice with the children
she cares for in the home-based childcare she has been operating for the past
three years. She tells me, "I think I am a better mother now than I was eighteen years ago. And I think the parents who are paying me to do this are getting the benefit of that. I think I'm more honed at it in some ways. I love my
little boys, and I've got lots of them. And I'm parenting them to love themselves unshakably and to know who they are."

Like Tammy, Willow notes she has learned her "expectations are really
tethered heavily to the circumstances particular to the child." She has also
discovered that consistency is essential to good parenting, stating: "I'm here
every day, and I am consistent in my parenting of them. So they know what
to expect and they know what's going on here, and they know who I am."

Willow thinks she is "probably more authoritarian now" than she was
when her daughter was young, and suggests if she had been more sure of
herself as a younger mother, her daughter "may have benefited from greater
clarity because she didn't always make the right decisions." Today, Willow
believes she is much more clear about decisions she makes in her life, especially those as a parent to her own daughter and to the children in her home
care where she encourages them to be true to themselves.

WHERE TO GO FROM HERE:
DEVELOPING A FEMINIST MOTHERLINE

Reflecting upon the experiences revealed by feminist mothers through the course of these and the previous interviews, I am struck by the need to continue sharing and recording feminist motherline stories to ensure that the difficult, yet rewarding work of feminist mothering remains a communal and political endeavor.[6]

A feminist motherline acknowledges the many struggles that accompany the embodied experiences and knowledge/s of feminist mothering. It provides space and a place for feminist mothers to record and pass on their own life-cycle perspectives of feminist mothering and to connect with those of other feminist mothers. Additionally, a motherline ensures that feminist mothers have a connection with a worldview that is centered and draws on feminism's crucial-gender based analysis of the world—including parenting. It also promises a legacy of feminist mothering and motherwork for others.

Motherline stories contain invaluable lessons and memories of feminist mothering, as well as support for mothers. The authenticity and authority that Willow and Tammy continue to search for, and are able to practice at times, is likely to be solidified when they are consciously connected with their own path and the path of other feminist mothers through a feminist motherline.

I admire and respect the feminist mothers who have allowed me to get to know them a little bit over the past ten years. In sharing their experiences, knowledge/s, and wisdom with me, and with others, they are engaging in the practice of "cultural bearing" (O'Reilly 37); the act of passing on important life lessons regarding the realities of feminist mothering that challenge the myths around mothering and provide models of feminist mothering that honor social activism through the personal self-governance of mothers and children alike. This is a courageous act and one that needs to be supported and repeated, time and time again. Through developing a feminist motherline, with feminist mothers being the cultural bearers of feminism in their daily lives, empowerment for mothers and children will surely follow.

NOTES

1. For the second round of interviews in 2005, I contacted as many of the original sixteen participants involved in the 1996 study as possible by telephone or e-mail, and asked each woman if she would be interested in speaking about her

experiences of feminist mothering during the ten years since our previous interview. Eleven women agreed; I was unable to reach four of the original participants (two had left the province) and, sadly, one woman died of cancer a number of years ago. At the time of publication, one interview was pending. Using Grounded Theory (see Dick; Glaser), I draw on common experiences and reflections arising from these most recent interviews.

2. I originally located participants by canvassing groups, organizations, and facilities supportive of feminists and mothers. I also placed announcements in local feminist newspapers and on bulletin boards in a number of women's organizations and health clinics asking for interested women who identified as feminist mothers to contact me. I interviewed sixteen participants over a period of two years about the realities of feminist mothering. See Green 2001 for further discussion on the research methods and results of the initial research.

3. For an excellent discussion on the concept and practice of motherwork, see "A Politics of the Heart" by Andrea O'Reilly (26–35).

4. See Marilyn Frye's *The Politics of Reality* for further discussion on the patriarchal cage.

5. For further discussion on Feminist Standpoint theory, see Dorothy Smith.

6. I am thankful to Andrea O'Reilly's discussion of motherline in her opening chapter of *Toni Morrison and Motherhood* (11–12), which proposes and explores Toni Morrison's maternal theory in her seven novels.

REFERENCES

Dick, Bob. *Grounded Theory: A Thumbnail Sketch.* [On line] 2005. http://www.scu.edu.au/schools/gcm/ar/arp/grounded.html. Accessed 4/13/2006.

Frye, Marilyn. *The Politics of Reality: Essays in Feminist Theory.* Trumansburg, NY: Crossing Press, 1983.

Glaser, Barney. *Doing Grounded Theory: Issues and Discussions.* Mill Valley, CA: Sociology Press, 1998.

Green, Fiona Joy. "Feminist Mothering: Attending to Social Gender Inequality by Challenging the Institution of Motherhood and Raising Children to be Critical Agents of Social Change." *Socialist Studies* 1.1 (2005): 83–99.

———. "Feminist Mothers: Successfully Negotiating the Tension between Motherhood as 'Institution' and 'Experience.'" *Mother Outlaws: Theories and Practices of Empowered Mothering.* Ed. Andrea O'Reilly. Toronto: Women's Press, 2004(a). 31–42.

———. "Feminist Mothers: Successfully Negotiating the Tension between Motherhood as 'Institution' and 'Experience.'" *Motherhood to Mothering: The*

Legacy of Adrienne Rich's Of Woman Born. Ed. Andrea O'Reilly. Albany: SUNY Press, 2004(b). 125–136.

————. "What's Love Got to Do With It?: A Personal Reflection on the Role of Maternal Love in Feminist Teaching." *Journal for the Association for Research on Mothering* 5.2 (2003): 47–56.

————. *Living Feminism: Pedagogy and Praxis in Mothering.* Unpublished PhD dissertation. University of Manitoba Interdisciplinary Studies. 2001.

————. "Living Feminism through Mothering." *Journal of the Association for Research on Mothering* 1.1 (1999): 99–104.

O'Reilly, Andrea. *Toni Morrison and Motherhood: A Politics of the Heart.* Albany: SUNY Press, 2004.

Rich, Adrienne. *Of Woman Born: Motherhood as Experience and Institution.* London: Virgo Press, 1986.

Smith, Dorothy. "Women's Perspectives as a Radical Critique of Sociology." *Feminism and Methodology.* Ed. Sandra Harding. Milton Keynes, Buckinghamshire: Open University Press, 1987. 84–96.

CHAPTER TEN

(Un)usual Suspects

Mothers, Masculinities, Monstrosities

SARAH TRIMBLE

> In this dirty-minded world, she thought, you are either some-
> body's wife or somebody's whore—or fast on your way to
> becoming one or the other. If you don't fit either category, then
> everyone tries to make you think there is something wrong
> with you. But, she thought, there is nothing wrong with me.
> —John Irving, *The World According to Garp*

CONSIDER THE OPENING LINE of John Irving's 1978 novel, *The World According to Garp*: "Garp's mother, Jenny Fields, was arrested in Boston in 1942 for
wounding a man in a movie theatre" (1). Thus begins Irving's insightful,
darkly comic story about a feminist negotiating the various claims made upon
her, and about her bastard son's ceaseless efforts to outline a worldview that is
distinctly his own. With this first line, we are introduced to the son, his
mother, and her vexed relationship to the law; it is this triad with which I am
concerned, and which I intend to explore through a theoretical framework
organized by considerations of space. The movie theater incident with which
the novel begins—wherein Jenny, a nurse, slashes a man with a scalpel to stop
his unwanted advances—highlights how relations of power are distributed
spatially; rules and norms are operational within bounded "zones" such that
those who cannot or will not submit to the rules of engagement are forced,
metaphorically and literally, to the periphery. Irving's first paragraph tells us

that "[i]n the movie theatre she had to move three times, but each time the soldier moved closer to her until she was sitting against the musty wall, her view of the newsreel almost blocked by some silly colonnade, and she resolved she would not get up and move again" (1). The soldier manifests a connection between male privilege and state power, and Jenny's refusal to capitulate to his implicit demands pushes her to the limits of this particular public space; with her back against the wall, it becomes clear that if she is willing to be neither "somebody's wife" nor "somebody's whore," then she is monstrously deviant—a "mad nurse!" or "crazed slasher!" (10)—in other words, an outlaw. The birth of her illegitimate son only exacerbates this marginality. As a mother outlaw, Jenny's negotiation of the fringes of patriarchal space—and of its prescribed versions of motherhood—sweeps her son up in a process of what Patricia Hill Collins, in a different context, calls "fashion[ing] an independent standpoint" (qtd. in O'Reilly 129) on masculinity, one that will eventually allow him to articulate a version of masculinity with/through the healing practices of maternal activism.

I would like to deviate from Irving's text for a moment to examine more closely the outlaw and the contours of her terrain—in this case, a space at the limits of patriarchal motherhood from which the latter may be threatened with unnerving otherness. Following Adrienne Rich's groundbreaking distinction between mothering as practice and motherhood as patriarchal institution, feminist scholars and activists have been urgently outlining a practice—or set of practices—organized around this figure of the outlaw. For, in order to realize the potentialities of empowered and/or feminist mothering,[1] Rich tantalizingly suggests that women must become "outlaws from the institution of motherhood" (qtd. in O'Reilly 11). The patriarchal institution of motherhood identified by Rich is a set of prescriptive ideologies and sociopolitical policies outlining the "good mother"; it is an organizing principle whose axioms depend for their authority on a regular situation or frame of reference to which they apply—for "[t]here is no rule that is applicable to chaos" (Agamben 16). In other words, Rich's motherhood, like all disciplinary apparatuses, defines for itself a bounded territory in which its organizational and evaluative principles operate. It creates and defines this territory through ongoing decisions with respect to who or what does not "pass," who or what constitutes the outlaw against whom the law will cohere.

Borrowing and recontextualizing some of the insights of Italian philosopher Giorgio Agamben, it can be said that the relationship between the rule and the exception—between the law and the outlaw—is one of abandonment. The rule withdraws from, thus abandons, the exception so that the latter is literally "taken outside" and becomes a form of exteriority through which the rule establishes itself as such (Agamben 18). The ideal of the "good mother" is produced through motherhood's abandonment of a myriad of "bad mothers" and their associated practices, through a discourse establishing critical distance between good and bad, inside and out.[2] These theoretical insights allow us to consider the tense relationship between patriarchal motherhood and mother outlaws. The legitimacy of the former guarantees itself through its withdrawal from the latter; or, in other words, the patriarchal institution of motherhood has validity only in a space—an "inside"—created and defined by the *ban* on "bad mothers." Included via their exclusion, mother outlaws continuously threaten patriarchal motherhood from the very boundaries through which it localizes and orders itself; the outlaws are repudiated, but dangerously integral to the system. That being said, the structure of the exception explains why, as many feminist scholars have already pointed out, those who are outlawed are not simply free to pursue any and all kinds of mothering; for "[w]hat has been banned is delivered over to its own separateness and, at the same time, consigned to the mercy of the one who abandons it—at once excluded and included, removed and at the same time captured" (Agamben 110). Mother outlaws are nonetheless constrained by the institution of motherhood, engaged in fraught negotiations along the frontiers of this officially sanctioned site.

Motherhood as institution is what Gilles Deleuze and Félix Guattari would call a territorializing assemblage—an amalgam of discourses, behaviors, and practices that bites into the myriad of female/feminine possibilities, imperiously organizing and grouping them in order to declare some combinations "legitimate" and others not. It selects, extracts, and combines elements from the range of what Rich called "female potentialities" (O'Reilly 13) and channels them into "appropriate" modes of action and intelligible formations, abandoning others to its own chaotic fringes. By outlawing certain (groupings of) potentialities, the patriarchal institution of motherhood constitutes itself as a site of regulation and containment. As Andrea O'Reilly has posited, the ideology of the "good mother" shifts to keep up with the needs of social (re)organization (38), ensuring that women's time, energy, and capital are organized in such a way that their capacities for disruptive empowerment are disciplined and the status quo upheld—that is, children are raised to be good little (gendered) citizen-consumers. Indeed, it is striking that what O'Reilly identifies as "intensive mothering"—an ideology of care whose standards are impossible for any woman to meet, guaranteeing that her efforts are anxiously and relentlessly directed in specifically predictable ways—emerges in the West alongside "women's increased social and economic independence: increased labor participation, entry into traditionally male areas of work, rise in female-initiated divorces, growth in female-headed households, and improved education" (O'Reilly 43). Intensive mothering is a practice sanctioned by the institution of motherhood at a particular sociohistorical juncture; as Western women unleash more of their (especially public) potentialities and engage in what Deleuze and Guattari would call becomings of all kinds, patriarchal motherhood (re)colonizes their energies and efforts under the renewed rubric of the "good mother." Rich's institutional motherhood is an apparatus of capture.

Jenny Fields, however, is not a good mother. "In her autobiography, Jenny wrote: 'I wanted a job and I wanted to live alone. That made me a sexual suspect. Then I wanted a baby, but I didn't want to have to share my body or my life to have one. That made me a sexual suspect, too'" (Irving 15). In a willful act of what Nicole Pietsch, following Patrick Hopkins, has called "gender treachery" (Pietsch 68), Jenny Fields impregnates herself via a single, well-planned encounter with a mortally wounded ball turret gunner under her care: Technical Sergeant Garp, whose mind has been shattered by a sliver of shrapnel. In "Un/titled: Constructions of Illegitimate Motherhood as Gender Insurrection," Pietsch outlines the ways in which the unmarried pregnant woman, whose body signals a "gross and public departure from 'good' woman status" (Vance qtd. in Pietsch 69), is conceptualized as a lawbreaker. Amid war and postwar anxieties around social reorganization and race/gender insubordination, Jenny Fields chooses single motherhood and enters the ranks of those who are considered "agents" of social unrest (Pietsch 65); "she is seen as mutinous, a rebel who knows the boundaries of female sexual propriety and maternity and actively violates them" (Pietsch 68). Moreover, Jenny does not demonstrate the remorse appropriate to a fallen woman; her pregnancy and subsequent birthing process, the physical manifestations of her transgression, do not have the requisite disciplinary effect. Against the wishes of her family, who would keep her hidden in their estate, Jenny takes a job running the infirmary at the all-boys Steering School where, it is noticed, she is rather arrogant for a woman in her situation; "Jenny Fields appeared to be proud of an illegitimate child. Nothing to hang her head about, perhaps; however, she might show a *little* humility" (Irving 35). Jenny is not diminished by her illegitimate status, and demonstrates this by not confining herself to the private and the secret.

When her child is born, Jenny does not question her entitlement to participate in his life, a decision implicitly contradicting the patriarchal narrative of mother–son separation, which enforces a disconnect that enables hegemonic masculinity—the ostensibly healthy and natural, authentically "male" mode of living—to emerge. By insisting on maintaining a close relationship with her son, the story goes, a mother stunts and warps the boy's growth into manhood; the boy will be s/mothered and the properly masculine subject aborted. In *Rocking the Cradle*, O'Reilly examines feminist contestations of the separation narrative through counter-readings of the myth of Achilles and Thetis;

> Thetis, according to the myth, dipped her son Achilles into the river Styx to render him immortal. However, fearing that he might be lost to the river, she held onto him by his ankle. Achilles, as the story goes, remains mortal and vulnerable to harm. Thetis would forever be blamed for her son's fatal flaw, his Achilles heel. (161)

The patriarchal moral of the story is that mothers must "let go" or risk leaving their own fatal mark on their sons' development; too-close involvement with his mother will keep the boy from fulfilling the imperatives of masculinity and transcending to the universal subject position to which he is entitled. However, as O'Reilly relates, feminists are revisiting the myth of Achilles and positing that "the holding place of vulnerability [. . .] was the thing that kept him *human and real*. In fact, we consider it *Thetis' finest gift* to her son" (qtd. in O'Reilly 161, emphasis in original). Amid the male-dominated, upper-class snobbery of the Steering School, Jenny Fields pays deliberate and conscious attention to maintaining a zone of proximity in which the lives of mother and son coexist.

At the school, before Garp is old enough to be enrolled in classes himself, Jenny sits in on every class *both* to educate herself *and* to discern which ones are useful and engaging and which ones superfluous to her son's future education; "she was screening the Steering School for her son. When Garp was old enough to attend, she'd be able to give him lots of advice—she'd know the deadweights in every department, those courses that meandered and those that sang" (Irving 37). Jenny not only assumes that her insights will be valuable to her son, but also remains unconcerned that her presence in her son's future, completely homosocial, learning spaces might be construed as transgressing a variety of boundaries. Garp may be enrolled in an all-boys school, but his mother will live there with him, pre-attend his classes, tend to his wounds, and even—when he complains that he is unable to decide on a sport for himself—sign him up for a sport of her choosing. Indeed, stumbling accidentally into the warmth of the contained and padded wrestling room—which, she notes, allows for closeness and safety "[d]espite the apparent violence of [the] sport"—Jenny chooses her son's activity through the eyes of a mother and nurse (Irving 84–85).[3]

Remarkably, Irving succinctly frames Jenny's refusal of the separation narrative through a harrowing scene that resonates with the myth of Thetis and Achilles. Full of both mischief and good intentions, the five-year-old Garp ascends to the roof of the school infirmary where he promptly slips, one leg breaking through the rain gutter and dangling in midair. When Jenny finally locates her missing son, she climbs out onto the fourth-floor fire escape and takes a firm grip on his calf from below, unsure of how to disentangle him from the weakened gutter. By this time, the Dean and an army of "men"—his name for his decidedly boyish students—have piled mattresses below in preparation for "the ultimate emergency" (Irving 49); but when the gutter finally gives way, Jenny maintains her hold on her son, knocking them both back onto the fire escape platform while a piece of the gutter and a dead pigeon plummet toward the Dean. Echoing Thetis's fearful grip on her son's ankle, Irving's narrative notes that "[a]n elaborate bruise, in the near-perfect form of [Jenny's] fingerprints, would be on his calf for a week" (49). The mattresses, the Dean, and the army of boys are all waiting to receive Garp, for better or for worse, into their midst—but Jenny Fields is tenacious. Lunging to catch the falling boy, Dean Bodger comes up with the dead pigeon; later in life, his memories of the moment confused, Bodger will tell the story of the night he caught young Garp falling from the roof of the infirmary. Jenny maintains her hold, and the well-meaning army below is left grasping at shadows; she steadfastly refuses to relinquish her son to the masculine world that surrounds them, symbolically challenging what O'Reilly refers to as "the son's community of identification, the male peer group" (167).

At the margins of patriarchal culture, outlawed mothers are busily engaging in mothering practices that challenge the dogmas of institutional motherhood; also operating in these marginal spaces are a proliferation of masculinit*ies* that have been foreclosed upon by hegemonic masculinity's relentless efforts to shore up its territory, so to speak. These are, among other qualifiers, racialized, queered, dis/abled, and feminized masculinities that have been compulsively disavowed by patriarchal cultures. A spatialized theoretical framework brings these overlapping marginalities to light. For, a mother outlaw who refuses to disconnect from her son raises him from a standpoint at the fringes of dominant culture, where the latter's stranglehold on both feminine *and* masculine potentialities is weakened (though certainly not absent); abandoned by the rule, which locates its space of operation *via* this withdrawal, the exceptions are simultaneously given over to themselves and strictly monitored—"removed and at the same time captured" (Agamben 110). This double mechanism defines marginality and has led to the paradox identified by a number of feminist thinkers who note that, despite their persistent and passionate efforts to subvert patriarchy and its norms, feminist mothers often fear alienating their sons from the very culture that they themselves reject (O'Reilly 151).

At the all-male Steering School, Garp's masculinity is de-formed along axes of difference that correspond to his mother's refusals of class and, indirectly, race privilege. The daughter of the "footwear king of New England" and "a former Boston Weeks" (Irving 35), Jenny Fields was raised within an extremely wealthy family. But Jenny insisted on working and, more disturbingly, "she wore her nurse's uniform when she could have dressed in something smarter" (36); Nurse Fields asserts her self-appointed identity, wearing the uniform throughout her life as if to ceaselessly articulate her/self with her public role as healer, a point to which I will return. In this way, and according to school policy, Garp is admitted to Steering as the son of an employee—not quite a "faculty brat" (34), but close. His class difference intersects with racialized differences, manifesting itself against the "[a]lmost albino-like, almost translucent-skinned" Percy children with whom he plays as a child—and with whom his mother is "at war" (Irving 58). Garp recalls, "[f]or my mother, I think, it was a class war, which she later said all wars were" (63). Indeed, pondering Garp's unknown father, Stewart Percy, who spent the war in the Pacific, emphatically decides that he must have been Japanese. "He was looking," Irving writes, "at Garp's shining brown eyes, at their color and at their shape, and he seemed to convince himself of something, because he nodded austerely and said to his foolish blond Midge, 'Jap'" (62). By embracing her anomalous self and separating from her rich, white, paternalist family, Jenny unleashes possibilities to pursue and choices to make; Garp's school life, where he is situated at the fringes of the upper-class, white, masculine Steering School, then echoes his mother's familial marginality.

It is from this standpoint at the periphery that Garp pieces together a view of hegemonic masculinity and its *officially recognized* outlaws—the abusers, rapists, and other criminals who violently manifest masculinity's disowned imperatives. At first, looking to the center and keenly fearful of his proximity to dominant modes of masculinity, Garp unwittingly allows this "center" to determine the shape of the margins to which he feels he belongs. With this space as his point of reference, the frontiers proper to the outlaw become peopled with criminals and "monsters," and Garp learns to fear his own becoming-monster.[4] From this point of view, masculinity is a dangerous, violent, oppressive force that he imagines encroaching on him and claiming him—his own monstrous, uncanny double. There is one powerful scene in particular that is organized along these lines. An older Garp, married with a son, is jogging through a neighborhood park when he comes upon a young girl, naked, and clearly having just been viciously sexually assaulted; the girl is terrified of Garp and of Garp's beard. In the midst of this swarm of emotions—the girl's terror, Garp's anguish and shock—the latter finds himself crying in desperation, horrified at his own inability to find a way to differentiate himself from her attacker (Irving 199). In the confusion, two policemen on horseback assume that Garp is the culprit; standing over her in only his running shorts, he is the unwitting, naked embodiment of patriarchal culture's effect on girl children. When the young girl is eventually able to indicate that the man who assaulted her had a beard, but also a mustache, Garp tears through the park looking for him—and finds him emerging from a public washroom, having just shaved off the facial hair that would make him identifiable to a child's eyes. From this point on, Garp associates beards and mustaches—the signifiers of adult masculinity—with the monstrosity from which he desperately seeks to distance himself.[5] Years later, following an uncomfortable run-in with the girl from the park in which she recognizes him via his beard, the narrative focuses through Garp's reflections on his own facial hair.

> He saw her several times after this meeting, but she never recognized him again because he shaved off his beard. "Why don't you grow another beard?" Helen occasionally asked him. "Or at least a mustache." But whenever Garp encountered the molested girl, and escaped unrecognized, he was convinced he should remain clean-shaven. (208–209)

Clearly, Garp does not imagine himself as the hero who nabbed the child molester, but rather as a man implicated in a culture in which girl children are systematically wounded. In a perverse repetition of the Mustache Kid's method of remaining undetected, Garp feels that his hairless face enables him, like a criminal, to "escape unrecognized" from the girl in the park. Through Garp, Irving wonders if "[p]erhaps rape's offensiveness to Garp was that it was an act that disgusted him with himself [. . .]. He never felt like raping anyone; but rape, Garp thought, made men feel guilt by association" (209). Indeed, when Garp's wife, Helen, becomes pregnant again, he finds himself hoping that the child will be a boy. Wondering at this, he thinks of the girl in the park, of women with whom he had sex as a younger man, and, sadly, of the eighteen-year-old babysitter with whom he has just committed adultery. "Garp," Irving writes, "didn't want a daughter because of *men*. Because of *bad* men, certainly; but even, he thought, because of men like *me*" (212). Garp's intense looking-in prompts him to understand his own sociocultural coordinates in relation to the oppressive masculinity at the center; he exists at the fringes, aligned, he imagines, with masculinity's other monstrous deviants. It seems to me that this is what it means to be both expelled and captured by the rule. Garp is both *apart* from and *a part* of the hegemonic masculinity that conditions his experience of life at the fringes.

Thus, unable as yet to (re)imagine and (re)articulate his own marginality, Garp's acute awareness of the dangers that confront children in his culture has a paternalistic edge to it; his feelings of proximity to *bad* men push him in the opposite direction so that he becomes obsessed with vigilance, with being the neighborhood guardian. On foot, he chases speeding cars to warn the drivers to slow down, fearing that they will hit one of his kids. When his eldest son, Duncan, goes to a friend's house to spend the night, Garp's concern for the child focalizes around the friend's mother, whom he judges to be a less than adequate caretaker. When, unable to sleep, he jogs over to "check on Duncan" in the wee hours of the morning and opts to bring his son home—Duncan still asleep, wrapped in his sleeping bag—Garp is stopped by the police and becomes aware that he appears as a "furtive, half-naked kidnapper sneaking away with his bright bundle of stolen goods and stolen looks—and a stolen child" (Irving 294). The narrative suggests that, insofar as Garp's compulsive vigilance is a *reactionary attempt* to differentiate himself from the rapists and kidnappers who endanger children, the vigilante and the molester are too closely related; in the world according to Garp, the former bleeds horrifyingly into the latter.[6] Even when one of the policemen recognizes Garp as "the one who grabbed that molester in that park"—just when a heroic image of Garp might emerge to eclipse the tinge of criminality hanging over the scene—the officer continues, "And what was it you did [for a living]? [. . .] I mean, there was something funny, wasn't there?" (Irvin 298). What is "funny" about Garp is that he is a writer and a stay-at-home Dad. In this passage from paternalistic vigilante to criminal night-stalker to queered masculine outlaw, Irving traces a complex negotiation of hegemonic masculinity and the marginal positions that it opens up and recontains.

At this point, my thoughts require a slight detour in order to return to and elaborate on Deleuze and Guattari's notion of becoming. Becomings have nothing to do with teleologies, evolutions, and coherence; they are effected by "unnatural participation" (Deleuze and Guattari 240), the coming-together of heterogeneous elements in a zone of proximity such that each infects, contaminates, the other toward the production of something new—something different and unexpected. Territorial assemblages—the institution of motherhood, the nuclear family, the state, and so on—strive to conserve themselves by *arresting* becoming, regulating and curbing its spontaneity so that children grown into adults; boys into men/fathers/sovereigns and girls into women/wives/subjects. These assemblages require stable forms and predictable, governable subjects to maintain the relations of power that structure them. The margins of a territorial assemblage, the frontiers peopled by outlaws negotiating an indeterminate point between order and chaos (motherhood and mothering), constitute a zone of proximity.[7] It is here that a child might engage in a becoming-animal, that a man might be swept up in a becoming-woman, that a "good" mother might embrace a becoming-outlaw. It is for this reason that the periphery and those moving within/through it are simultaneously abandoned and compulsively policed. The margins are a kind of threshold—a frontier between chaos and order—attesting to the dangerous potentialities of passage.

What locks Garp into the self-destructive, vigilante-monster cycle is his insistence, like his mother before him, on acting from what Toni Morrison has referred to as "a spiritually dangerous position of being self-sufficient" (qtd. in O'Reilly 139). Garp is a solitary figure, a self-appointed watchdog guarding against the outlawed variations on a (masculine) theme that capture his imagination; he looks "in," wary of the center, rather than shaping a standpoint through alliances with outlaws radically *un*like himself. In his aloneness, he does not see the horizons of possibility opened up by "unnatural participation"—the masculini*ties* that might proliferate if his point of refer-ence is not hegemonic masculinity, but the overlap between his own (produc-tively) *failing* masculinity and Jenny's outlawed mothering practices. Long before Garp is troubled by the "case[s] of mistaken identity" (Irving 299) that transform him from vigilante to criminal, his mother seems to have become aware of the perils of self-sufficiency. In her autobiography, *A Sexual Suspect*, Jenny Fields makes public her illegitimate motherhood, her method of con-ception, and all other details of her life, inadvertently becoming a feminist figurehead. Shortly after the publication of her book, Jenny inherits the Dog's Head Harbor estate—a giant home by the New England sea that becomes a site of pilgrimage for wounded women. In this unexpected fashion, Jenny dis-covers a community of outlaws—refugees from patriarchal culture on whom she will (re)focus her nursing skills in what I am arguing is a form of the "maternal activism" referred to in Andrea O'Reilly's work.

In "A Politics of the Heart," O'Reilly explores four components of mothering outlined by Sara Ruddick, and which she rearticulates through the fictions of Toni Morrison: "preservation, nurturance, cultural bearing, and healing" (131). It is this last on which I would like to focus in order to conclude my reading of *The World According to Garp*. Through her considera-tion of the African American mothering practices elaborated on by Morri-son, O'Reilly outlines Morrison's emphatic concern with the recovery and protection of the *self*, that kernel of "me-ness that [. . .] is central to well-being" (O'Reilly 145). This sense of irreducible selfhood is integral to a child who will be bombarded throughout his or her life with any combination of the eroding forces of racism, sexism, classism, homophobia (etc.); and, O'Reilly insists, it can be imparted to a child by motherwork or *restored to an adult* by the healing practices of maternal activism (145). The healing of adults is a profoundly political and social practice (O'Reilly 134), and one of the public faces of feminist mothering. It is to this practice that Jenny Fields dedicates the rest of her life, and *re*dedicates her family's estate by the sea. The house at Dog's Head Harbor becomes a refuge for wounded women— and it is to this location that Garp and his broken family retreat after a chain of events that begins with adultery (both Garp's and Helen's) and ends in a car crash that kills their youngest son, Walt. Here, Garp finally confronts the dangers of the solitary life of a vigilante, and begins a (new) relationship to his mother's healing practices.

When Jenny Fields is eventually assassinated by, importantly, a lone gunman while she speaks at a rally in support of a female candidate for the New Hampshire gubernatorial election, Garp is swept up in what Deleuze and Guattari would call a becoming-woman—a process of de-forming and rearticulating his masculinity through a series of alliances organized around his mother's activism. Having disguised himself in drag in order to attend New York's "first feminist funeral" (Irving 494)—an act enabled by his already profound connection to Jenny's transsexual friend and admirer, Roberta Muldoon—Garp is found out and forced to flee, maintaining his drag persona on board the plane that will take him home. Forced like his mother to safeguard his space, Garp evicts a predatory man from the seat beside him, freeing it up for the girl with whom he will effect his most important alliance, the "original" Ellen James, now a teenager.[8] Orphaned by a car accident, Ellen had been on her way to stay at Dog's Head Harbor when Jenny was assassinated, and had gone instead to the funeral in New York so that her path might intersect with Garp's. It is in this encounter, in this instantaneous alliance with the girl, that Garp's becoming-woman is most clear; knowing what his mother would have done in such a situation, Garp tells Ellen, "'[w]ell, you have a family *now*' [. . .]; he held her hand and winced to hear himself make such an offer. He heard the echo of his mother's voice, her old soap-opera role: The Adventures of Good Nurse" (Irving 509). Through this complicated, humorous, and poignant process of becoming, Garp begins to disentangle his masculinity from the dominant models (and their shadows) that he has negotiated thus far; instead, he begins to articulate masculinity with healing, an "unnatural participation" made possible by a community still held together by Jenny Fields—the absent center.

On his return from New York, Garp discovers "that Jenny, as if to plague her son, had designated *him* to be the executor of her last wishes for her fabulous loot and the mansion for wounded women at Dog's Head Harbor" (Irving 527). Always wry and cynical, Garp complains to Roberta that his mother "was out to get [him]," only to have his friend reply, "[o]r she was out to make you *think* [. . .]. What a good mother she was!" (527). Thus, in memory of his mother—and working with a Board of Trustees assembled by Roberta—Garp establishes the Fields Foundation, which provides women with grants and a temporary residence through which to pursue their arts, their recoveries, or their birthing processes. Thrust on him by his mother, this exercise in feminist thinking reorients Garp's masculinity, redirecting the energies he had previously devoted to paternalistic vigilance toward healing practices and community-building. As many feminist thinkers, including Sara Ruddick, have already considered, the political implications of this shift are many; for instance, it is useful to consider Garp's solitary vigilantism as a mode of masculinity that is expressed in political schemes structured around unilateral preemptive strikes. The "benevolent" vigilante is always already morphing into a looming, criminal threat that devastates those whom he or it purports to protect. *The World According to Garp* underlines that the healing practices associated with maternal activism gesture to a different kind of politics, an acting in from the margins that may intervene in the endless processes of strike/counterstrike that perpetuate today's bleakly familiar political narrative.

NOTES

This essay is dedicated to Gail Trimble, my very own Jenny Fields, with gratitude.

1. See Andrea O'Reilly's foreword to *Rocking the Cradle* for a useful discussion of the theoretical distinction between empowered and feminist mothering.

2. I have tried to avoid asserting rigid distinctions between inside and outside, order and chaos, and so on; rather, I intend for these terms to gesture to a series of relations and passages that speak to the positions and movements of the outlaw.

3. It is notable that the 1982 film version of *The World According to Garp* (starring Robin Williams as Garp and Glenn Close in a remarkable performance as Jenny Fields) alters the sequence of events through which Garp comes to the sport of wrestling. In the film, Garp chooses wrestling *against Jenny's wishes*, and despite her protestations. This is one of a number of moments in which the film

enforces a somewhat simplistic separation between mother and son—one that is refused by the nuances of Irving's novel.

4. At this point, I am mobilizing the conservative connotations of "monster" and "monstrous" in order to underscore that Garp's view of de-formed masculinities is limited to negative possibilities. I hope to show, by the end of this chapter, that "becoming-monster" can—indeed *should*—also be associated with resistance to the dominant culture, for it is the latter that defines the monster as "evil" and outsider.

5. It is worth noting that the young rapist becomes known in Garp's mind as "the Mustache Kid" (Irving 207–208).

6. That the molester and vigilante are the obverse of one another—two sides of a patriarchal coin—becomes clear when Garp writes a blatantly autobiographical short story about his car-chasing habits called "Vigilance." In it, he describes "himself" as having a mustache (Irving 323).

7. Becoming is intimately linked to discourses organized around frontiers and the outlaws who negotiate them, and can be usefully illustrated via "classic" pop culture motifs. For example, in traditional Western films depicting the frontier as a space of intersection of "cowboys" and "Indians," there is most often a becoming-native of the (cowboy) hero that is central to the narrative—a becoming that is usually recontained by the film's closure, in which the hero rejoins "civilization" in a symbolic way (e.g., he gets married). Similarly, science fiction narratives often delimit a "frontier" in space, wherein human heroes are swept up in becomings-alien that are signaled through shifts in worldview, emotional capacity, or physical ability. In *A Thousand Plateaus*, Deleuze and Guattari outline a cluster of "kinds" of becomings loosely ranged from becomings-woman to becomings-animal to becomings-imperceptible, all of which have to do with the productive interactions of unlike elements and the possibilities that unfold from these encounters. For Deleuze and Guattari, all becomings must pass through a becoming-woman; for insofar as becoming indicates the transgression of formal boundaries, it is immediately implicated in that zone of dangerous excess that feminists have noted is associated with femininity. Predicated on the disruption of dominant forms, becomings are always already feminizing moves.

8. The story of Ellen James and the Ellen Jamesians is an important narrative thread in *The World According to Garp*; however, to do it justice would require an essay in itself. Roughly sketched, Ellen is a girl who was raped at age eleven and had her tongue cut out by the perpetrators so that she wouldn't be able to identify them. The Ellen Jamesians are women who, on hearing this story, had their own tongues surgically removed in what they perceived to be an act of solidarity or protest, and many of whom congregate around Jenny Fields at Dog's Head Harbor. The Ellen Jamesians enrage Garp, who eventually writes an essay damning them for their "self-mutilation" and arguing that these acts only do further harm to the real Ellen James (an argument with which the latter agrees). Even

after many of the Ellen Jamesians no longer identify as such, a few radical, mute women attempt to assassinate Garp, the undeserving son of the brilliant Jenny Fields. In the end, one such woman succeeds. Irving's dark, strangely comic comment on extremism is underscored by parallel assassinations: Jenny shot by a disgruntled hunter, and Garp shot by an enraged Ellen Jamesian.

REFERENCES

Agamben, Giorgio. *Homo Sacer: Sovereign Power and Bare Life.* Trans. Daniel Heller-Roazen. Stanford: Stanford University Press, 1995.

Deleuze, Gilles, and Félix Guattari. *A Thousand Plateaus: Capitalism and Schizophrenia.* Trans. Brian Massumi. Minneapolis and London: University of Minnesota Press, 1987.

Irving, John. *The World According to Garp.* 1978. New York: Ballantine Books, 1998.

O'Reilly, Andrea. *Rocking the Cradle: Thoughts on Motherhood, Feminism, and the Possibility of Empowered Mothering.* Toronto: Demeter Press, 2006.

Pietsch, Nicole. "Un/titled: Constructions of Illegitimate Motherhood as Gender Insurrection." *Mother Matters: Motherhood as Discourse and Practice, Essays from the Journal of the Association for Research on Mothering.* Ed. Andrea O'Reilly. Toronto: Association for Research on Mothering, 2004. 65–78.

CHAPTER ELEVEN

"That Is What Feminism Is—The Acting and Living and Not Just the Told"

Modeling and Mentoring Feminism

ANDREA O'REILLY

THE SUBJECT OF feminist or empowered mothering more generally, as noted in the introduction, has largely been ignored by feminist scholars on motherhood. Only two books have been published solely on the topic of feminist mothering: *Mother Journeys: Feminists Write About Mothering* (1994) and Tuula Gordon's *Feminist Mothers* (1990), books now nearly twenty years old. In response to the lack of scholarship on empowered mothering I developed two volumes on this subject matter: *From Motherhood to Mothering: The Legacy of Adrienne Rich's* Of Woman Born and *Mother Outlaws: Theories and Practices of Empowered Mothering.* Surprisingly, in the forty plus chapters included in these two collections, only a handful look specifically at the topic of feminist mothering. This omission, as I note in the introduction, puzzled me. Feminist mothering is an evident example of empowered mothering and so provides a promising alternative to the oppressive institution of patriarchal motherhood, first theorized by Adrienne Rich and critiqued by subsequent motherhood scholars. So why is the subject of feminist mothering so marginal to feminist scholarship on motherhood, a scholarship committed to imagining and implementing other, less oppressive ways to mother? While I still remain unsure on the answers, I believe that this absence is due, at least in part, to our inability to define what we mean, or more particularly what we w*ant or expect to achieve* in, through, and from feminist mothering. Is the concern of feminist mothering antisexist childrearing, or the empowerment of mothers? Or is it perhaps a combination? In order to define and develop a theory of feminist mothering we must, I believe, begin with such questions. In this chapter, I seek to answer these questions by way of a conversation with my two teen daughters on their perceptions and experiences of being raised by feminist mothering.

FROM MOTHERHOOD TO MOTHERING

Adrienne Rich in *Of Woman Born*, as I note in the introduction and explored at length in my edited volume *From Motherhood to Mothering*, defined motherhood as a patriarchal institution that is oppressive to women. She argued that this institution must be abolished so that the "*potential* relationship of woman to her powers of reproduction, and to children" could be realized (13, emphasis in original). In other words, while motherhood, as an institution, is a male-defined site of oppression, women's own experiences of mothering could nonetheless be a source of power if they were experienced outside of motherhood. The goal then for feminist mothers was to move from motherhood to mothering, or, more specifically, to mother against motherhood. While Rich's distinction between motherhood and mothering and her call for a feminist mothering apart from patriarchal motherhood have been employed and developed by feminist theorists, what seems to have gone missing in this use of Rich is the radical impetus and implications of her vision.

Feminist mothering, in Rich's view, must first and primarily be concerned with the empowerment of mothers. For Rich, the central reason for feminist mothering was to free mothers from patriarchal motherhood. In contrast, the current literature on feminist mothering is concerned with antisexist childrearing, particularly raising empowered daughters and relational sons with little attention paid to the mother herself or the condition under which she mothers. The focus of this literature is the children and how to better their socialization with little attention to how motherhood needs to be changed so as to make mothering better for women. While Rich was evidently interested in antisexist childrearing, as shown in her two chapters on mothers and daughters and mothers and sons, the overarching purpose of *Of Woman Born* was to abolish patriarchal motherhood so that women could achieve an empowering, or more specifically, a feminist experience of mothering. This mother-centered—and I believe far more radical—vision has become lost in our current preoccupation with antisexist childrearing. Moreover, having made the oppression of mothers in patriarchal motherhood tangential to their goal of antisexist childrearing, feminist theorists now find themselves in the difficult, nay impossible, situation, of trying to achieve feminist mothering without first having abolished patriarchal motherhood.

Rich's concern was mothers and dismantling patriarchal motherhood so as to make mothering less oppressive for mothers. However, she also realized that the achievement of antisexist childrearing also depended on the abolition of patriarchal motherhood. Mothers cannot effect changes in childrearing in an institution in which they have no power as in the case with patriarchal motherhood. Antisexist childrearing depends on motherhood itself being changed; it must become, to use Rich's terminology, mothering. In other words, only when mothering becomes a site, role, and identity of power for women is feminist childrearing made possible. In dismantling patriarchal motherhood, you invest mothers with the needed agency and authority to affect the desired feminist childrearing. Only then does antisexist childrearing become possible.

A challenge to traditional gender socialization is, of course, integral to any theory and practice of feminist mothering. However, I argue, as Rich did thirty years ago, that the empowerment of the mother must be the primary aim of feminist mothering if it is to function as a truly transformative theory and practice. To fully and completely liberate children from traditional childrearing, mothers must first seek to liberate themselves from traditional motherhood; they must, to use Rich's terminology, mother against motherhood. By way of a conversation with my two daughters—Erin (eighteen) and Casey (sixteen)—this chapter will explore the interface between the empowerment of mothers and antisexist childrearing, and Rich's argument that the latter depends on the former. More specifically, I will argue that, for mothers to mentor feminism for their daughters, they must model it in themselves.

MOTHER AND DAUGHTERS: "AS DAUGHTERS WE NEED MOTHERS WHO WANT THEIR OWN FREEDOM AND OURS"

The early literature on mothers and daughters, notably the writings of Adrienne Rich, Judith Arcana, and Jesse Bernard, recognized this connection between mentoring and modeling. As I discuss in my article "Mothering against Motherhood and the Possibility of Empowered Maternity for Mothers and Their Children," these writers argue that that mother–daughter connection empowers the daughter *if and only if* the mother with whom the daughter is identifying is herself empowered. "What do mean by the nurture of daughters? What is it we wish we had, or could have, as daughters; could give as mothers," asks Rich:

> Deeply and primally we need trust and tenderness; surely this will always be true of every human being, but women growing into a world so hostile to us need a very profound kind of loving in order to learn to love ourselves. But this loving is not simply the old, institutionalized, sacrificial, "mother-love" which men have demanded; we want courageous mothering. The most notable fact that culture imprints on women is the sense of our limits. The most important thing one woman can do for another is to illuminate and expand her sense of actual possibilities. For a mother, this means more than contending with reductive images of females in children's books, movies, television, the schoolroom. It means that the mother herself is trying to expand the limits of her life. To *refuse to be a victim*: and then to go on from there. (246, emphasis in original)

Similarly, Sociologist Jesse Bernard wrote to her daughter: "For your sake as well as mine, I must not allow you to absorb me completely. I must learn to live my own life independently in order to be a better mother to you" (272). Judith Arcana in her book on mothers and daughters wrote: "We must live as if our dreams have been realized. We cannot simply prepare other, younger daughters for strength, pride, courage, beauty. It is worse than useless to tell young women and girls that we have done and been wrong, that we have chosen ill, that we hope they will be more lucky" (33). What daughters need, therefore, in Rich's words:

> [are] mothers who want their own freedom and ours [. . . .] The quality of the mother's life—however, embattled and unprotected—is her primary bequest to her daughter, because a woman who can believe in herself, who is a fighter, and who continues to struggle to create livable space around her, is demonstrating to her daughter that these possibilities exist. (247)

Whether it is termed courageous mothering, as Rich describes it, or empowered or feminist mothering, this practice of mothering calls for the empowerment of daughters *and* mothers, and recognizes that the former is only possible with the latter. As Judith Arcana (1979) concludes: "If we want girls to grow into free women, brave and strong, we must be those women ourselves" (33).

As a mother of two feminist daughters, I read all the feminist literature on mothers and daughters and increasingly became intrigued by the connection made in the scholarship between modeling and mentoring feminism. I am the mother of three children, a son Jesse, twenty-one, and two daughters Erin, eighteen, and Casey, sixteen. I had my children quite young, between the ages of twenty-three and twenty-eight, when I was an undergraduate and later a graduate student. I write this chapter as a forty-four-year old heterosexual woman of Irish/Scottish/English descent who has been in a common-law relationship with the children's father for twenty-three years. While I was raised middle-class, my partner and I raised the children as penniless full-time students. Now, as a tenured professor and my partner an adjunct professor, we are upper middle class (though still paying off our own student loans and funding the education of two children who live away from home).

I am a mother, a feminist, and a feminist mother. My daughters Erin and Casey are radical 'out' Third Wave feminists: Erin has been so forever and Casey in the last two to three years. The question that brings me to this chapter is, how did my daughters become feminists, or, more specifically, what is the relationship between my feminist mothering and their becoming feminists? The feminist mothering of my son is not explored in this chapter, but not because I do not think it is important. Rather, I believe that the feminist mothering of a son *is* different from that of a daughter and the space allowed in this chapter does not permit me to examine both well.[1] What I am interested in exploring is not my feminist mothering per se but my *daughters' perceptions and experiences of being raised by feminist mothering.* In particular, I want to examine in the context of our lived lives as a feminist mother and feminist daughters the argument made by Rich and other early writers, that feminist mothering must first be concerned with the abolition of patriarchal motherhood so as to empower mothers. Only then is feminist childrearing made possible. In other words, how did my identity as a feminist and my work of feminist mothering give rise to the feminism of my daughters? How did they become feminist: was it through antisexist childrearing, that is, raising empowered daughters, as is the focus of more contemporary writers, or was it through my being a feminist, or more specifically a mother who sought to mother against the institution of patriarchal motherhood and practice feminist mothering? Was it my challenge to patriarchal motherhood that afforded me the agency and authority to impart my feminism to my daughters, and to practice antisexist childrearing? I will return to these questions after a summary of my daughters' observations.

FEMINISM: 'A SATURATED REALITY'

The comments of Erin and Casey are drawn from an eighty-minute taped discussion. This informal discussion took place as we sat on the floor of Casey's bedroom. I asked a general question and then asked them to take turns answering. I instructed them to answer the questions honestly. And while I do agree that an interview between a parent and child can never be fully candid, I believe that our interview was as honest as one could be, as my daughters and I enjoy a intimate and very open relationship.

I opened the interview with a general question: How would you define a feminist mother; what does she do or not do, what is feminist mothering? Erin commented: "A feminist mother quietly incorporates feminism into your life. And it is not like feminism is a separate thing, it is the makeup of the world that you live in because everything that you do is textured by feminism and the entire way that you grow to see the world is being shaped for you through a feminist perspective . . . so things like the absence of teen magazines lying around the house or books written by women piling up in front of you that you could read at your leisure. I would say a feminist mother makes feminism something that is a normal part of your life." Casey commented: "I remember when I was in grade eight, this girl came up to me and said, 'Your mom is a feminist, eh?' She was so confused and concerned as to why my mom was a feminist or what feminism even was. But in some way or another every mother incorporates feminism as basic survival because girls *need* feminism, whether it is called feminism or not, to survive. It is absolutely essential to the survival of girls."

When they were asked for specific examples of feminist mothering from their own childhood Erin and Casey mentioned examples of antisexist childrearing. Casey remembers in grade three not listening to the Spice Girls or playing with Barbies as her friends did, and being made fun of for wearing sweatpants by her fashion-conscious friends. Erin also remembered when she was in grade five and received a Barbie doll and "understanding in some vague way that it was a symbol of patriarchy." Both commented on how all their friends received plastic makeup sets in elementary school while they did not. Erin also said that, while she did play with girl toys as she grew up, there was, she explained, "more variety; the toys were more geared to my personality and not my gender, for example I collected coins . . . that is a dorky thing for a girl to do." Casey remembers not knowing how to put on makeup or nail polish like the other girls who were taught this: "I remember not knowing how to do this . . . I never got those lectures on [beauty and hygiene]. I didn't start wearing makeup until grade eight. I am now glad that I [never learned like the other girls] because now I can do whatever the fuck I want with it." When I mentioned to them that I did wear makeup and wore fashionable clothing, Erin remarked: "You were a femme feminist, but you didn't force it on us. Being a girl didn't mean that . . . it could mean what we wanted it to mean." "Other mothers," Erin went on to say, "want her daughter to exist successfully in patriarchy, so the daughter has to be feminine. You had different hopes for us, different than that." Erin also noted that I might have worn fashionable clothing, "but then you walked off to work and talked about issues to me . . . what I noticed about you was not that you were or were not fashionable . . . but that you were constantly expressing your mind."

Significantly, even these examples of antisexist childrearing also bespeak learning feminism by way of it being modeled to them. When I asked them about their earliest memory of being raised by a feminist mother, Erin said: "You worked. Work was a normal part of your life, the same as Dad's, if not more so. It didn't seem weird that you went out to work. When kids of stay-at-home moms came to our house they saw not a fresh batch of muffins but a brand new batch of graded essays." Casey, too, remarked that she was proud that her mom worked, though she was teased by others because of it. Wanting to understand more on modeling feminism, I asked them about how they perceived the relationship of me and their father growing up. They both agreed that in some ways our relationship was traditional. When they were young, the discipline was done by their father, but they both emphasized that they were still not like other families. "You both cooked dinner . . . and he was always the one doing the dishes." Also "dad had really long hair. That was weird among my friends. I have seen dad cry, most people don't." Speaking on how opposite-sex relationships are structured by traditional gender roles, Erin commented that while that was there, "you never took it . . . you were always a bitch . . . and would fight back. [The idea] that he was the 'man' would only go so far . . . you would scream and yell and say 'Excuse me, I don't think so." We saw it [traditional roles] happen, but we also saw that if it does happen the woman can say no . . . I will do it my way."

When asked how the general feminist belief that patriarchy is wrong and that women should be equal to men was conveyed to them, Erin commented: "It was in everything we did and around us. I was a girl and I knew that boys would think they were better than me and I knew they weren't." The message, Erin continued, "was that it was great to be a girl. A lot of girl pride given to me. Books. Goddess worship was a big thing. You always said, thank the goddess. Just the idea that a woman could be worshiped like that. Around the house there were goddesses everywhere. You also talked about being a mother. This sense of pride of being a woman was in the things you said, things that were up on the wall, subtle ways, in books, comments. It saturated our existence." Casey agreed: "It was constantly everywhere. Saturated feminism as you say. When I was little, I ignored it as I wanted to be a 'normal' girl." Yet Casey goes on to say that when she was in kindergarten, a boy wouldn't stop bothering her, so she warned him to stop or she would cut open his finger. He said that she wouldn't fight back because she was a girl. Casey: "I said 'Wanna bet?' . . . so I did."

Speaking of their own experience of coming to feminism, Erin said: "I was always a freak. I couldn't avoid it because it was so saturated. I didn't realize that I was doing feminist things, it was just the way I acted. I was a loud girl. If I had something to say, I said it. Feminism did make it harder for me growing up because it made me different, but it was so worth it in the end. I came out the other side of all that. I am my own person. The girls I grew up with are still playing all those games. Still trapped in that world . . . still don't say what they think." Casey commented: "I feel the same way. Worth it in the end, though going through it was hard, particularly in elementary school. I was always a freak. I couldn't be pretty. I just failed. I didn't know how to dress 'normally.' As you grow older you come to appreciate it more. I live in this world without being swallowed up."

Central to their understanding of feminist mothering was "being allowed to express myself" and being supported in this. Erin talked about how when she stopped shaving her armpits, "mom was okay with it. Other girls are told it is disgusting and unclean and their mother wouldn't let them." Both Erin and Casey emphasized the development of critical thinking. Casey remarked: "I always had arguments with dad on music and movies. I never sat and accepted things that are supposed to be accepted. They gave us access to information to make our own opinions. Just because you have strong opinions doesn't mean that I would have your own opinions...because we grew up in this household that was possible." Erin explained that the difference was that they were "treated like people instead of being treated like children. Other parents just say *no*, and while we got that to a degree, I would argue. Say what I wanted to say; not told to shut up just because you are a kid." Erin commented further: "People think if you are raised in a feminist setting ideas are put in your head. In our family we were encouraged to think for ourselves . . . that was the big thing . . . encouraged to think about things. Even if you disagreed we would argue it to the end. We were encouraged to think for ourselves . . . critically to come up with our own opinions despite the fact that the world is trying to shove other ideas down your throat."

At the conclusion of the interview I explained the research questions of this chapter and asked them to speak directly to two sets of questions. The first: How is feminism learned—is it modeled or taught? I explained Rich's argument that more important than feminist childrearing is the mother's seeking to achieve in her own life what she wishes for her daughters. In response, Erin commented: "That is what I mean when I said our reality was totally saturated with it. It was shown, not just told (though we were told as well). I agree with you, definitely 100 percent. If it has just been talked about, it would not have been the reality that it was. Feminism was the world I lived in because of the fact that you were a feminist in what you did and acted. I mean I remember you going out with your friends . . . and me saying 'I want you to stay home and be a good mother and baby me' and you saying mothers need to go out, too. This is what feminism is: the acting and living...not just the told. Feminism was expressed to us in the way you lived your life. And the way you set things up . . . we saw it everywhere. That is how it became our reality. Instead of something we talked about, it was what everything was." Casey remarked: "When I was young I was resentful that my mom wasn't home making me cookies. I am now glad you worked and was not home baking cookies." On the related topic that there is the assumption that a feminist mother is selfish while a good mother selfless and that the former puts her career first and the latter her kids, Erin said: "Anybody who said you put your career first would be a liar . . . no way in hell you put your career first. You were an involved mother . . . and you had a career. What is so amazing is that you were so involved with kids and did a career." She went to explain: "When I was little, there were times that I said 'Come play with me' and you said 'I have to do this' . . . It was not a big deal. Around enough . . . Times that you weren't, I never felt neglected. I never ever felt that way. I think it is a demonizing idea that they put out against women who work and decide to be a mother. It is completely possible to do it . . . you did both very well."

I also asked them to reflect on another common assumption in some feminist writings on the mother–daughter relationship: namely, that mothers represent to the daughter patriarchal oppression and hence the daughter must turn against the mother to become a 'free' woman. Adrienne Rich termed this sentiment matrophobia: "The fear not of one's mother or motherhood but of becoming one's mother" (235). In response, Erin said: "Never felt your life was inhibited . . . you got what you wanted . . . had three kids, still managed to suck fun out of life." "In this you were a role model to me," Erin continued, "you have your cake and eat it too. [The belief] is that a woman is not allowed to be a mother and get a Ph.D. . . . and you always did it all . . . that is inspiring to me. I knew that I could have it all . . . which I do." Speaking specifically on what impact, if any, being raised by a feminist mother has made on whether they plan to be mothers, Erin concluded: "You definitely made motherhood something I want to do . . . I know it is a lot of work, but you have shown that it is possible to be a mother and have your own life."

DISCUSSION

From this commentary it is evident that my daughters perceived and experienced their upbringing as antisexist childrearing and that they understood their childhood in this way. They both mentioned several times that we didn't 'girl' them in their upbringing (Casey spoke of how fishing, playing with frogs, and getting dirty in the mud were a normal part of her childhood). They also commented on how they did not experience the 'normal' sexist feminization of daughters (they didn't play with Barbies, wear makeup, or listen to the Spice Girls). Both of them emphasized the importance of being offered alternative—empowered—examples and images of womanhood (feminist books/music, goddess figures, etc.). But equally my daughters spoke about how they learned feminism directly from the way I lived my life. This came up far more than I had anticipated. What they remember about me is "working, standing up to traditional gender roles and always talking about issues." They saw me living a life outside of motherhood. As Erin remarked: "You had a long relationship with dad, work, friends, partying. You did everything: you never had a shitty nonlife." My daughters, in watching me live my life, learned that feminism was possible, doable, and normal. And, as important, they learned that motherhood does not, should not, shut down other dimensions of a woman's life: work, sexuality, friendship, activism, leisure, and so forth. Listening over and over to my daughters' voices as I transcribed the interview, I finally 'got' Rich's insight at a deeply personal level. To paraphrase Rich: The quality of my life—however embattled and unprotected it may have been—was my primary bequest to my daughters because in believing in myself, in fighting, in struggling to create livable space around me, I demonstrated to Erin and Casey that these possibilities exist. Feminist mothering of girls is not about choosing blue over pink, or trucks over dolls but about *living*, to use the title of Marilyn Waring's work, *as if women counted*. And, more specifically, in the context of motherhood, feminist mothering demonstrates to our daughters that women have a selfhood outside of motherhood and possess power within motherhood.

CONCLUSION

This story is evidently that of myself and my two daughters. What I learned in interviewing my daughters is not generalizable to all women. Moreover, the routes by which daughters come to feminism are many and varied: feminist mothering is just one of many. However, what I take from this narrative, and what I believe may be of use to others who likewise seek to imagine and achieve feminist mothering, is that the future we wish for our daughters must be struggled for today in our *own daily lives.* We must be the changes that we seek. Would my daughters have become feminists in patriarchal motherhood? The interview findings suggest that this would not have been possible, or not to the degree that I, as a feminist mother, would wish. In patriarchal motherhood, feminism would not have become the "the saturated reality" of my daughters' upbringing. I certainly could not have lived and modeled a feminist life in patriarchal motherhood; nor would I have had the agency and authority to impart feminist childrearing to my daughters. I believe that what our daughters need most from us is not self-sacrifice or selflessness, as preached in patriarchal motherhood, but selfhood and, yes, a healthy dose of *selfishness.* For a mother who insists on "a life of her own" tutors her daughter that she, too, is deserving of the same. Or to conclude with Erin's words: "What you have shown us is that it is possible to be a mother and have your own life." That is the lesson that we, as mothers, must impart to our daughters by living it ourselves.

NOTES

1. Please see my article and edited book for a discussion of feminist mothering of sons: "A Mom and Her Son: Thoughts on Feminist Mothering." *Journal of the Association for Research on Mothering* 2.1 (Spring/Summer 2000): 179–193; *Mothers and Sons: Feminism, Masculinity and the Struggle to Raise our Sons.* New York: Routledge, 2001.

REFERENCES

Arcana, Judith. *Our Mother's Daughters.* Berkeley: Shameless Hussy Press, 1979.

Bernard, Jesse. "Letter to Her Daughter." *Between Ourselves: Letters Between Mothers and Daughters.* Ed. Karen Payne. Boston: Houghton Mifflin, 1983. 271–72.

Gordon, Tuula. *Feminist Mothers*. New York: New York University Press, 1990.

O'Reilly, Andrea. "A Mom and Her Son: Thoughts on Feminist Mothering." *Journal of the Association for Research on Mothering* 2.1 (Spring/Summer 2000): 179–193.

———. *Mothers and Sons: Feminism, Masculinity and the Struggle to Raise Our Sons*. New York: Routledge, 2001.

———. *From Motherhood to Mothering: The Legacy of Adrienne Rich's Of Woman Born*. Albany: SUNY Press, 2004.

———. *Mother Outlaws: Theories and Practices of Empowered Mothering*. Toronto: Women's Press, 2004.

———. "'We Were Conspirators, Outlaws from the Institution of Motherhood': Mothering against Motherhood and the Possibility of Empowered Maternity for Mothers and Their Children." *From Motherhood to Mothering: The Legacy of Adrienne Rich's* Of Woman Born. Ed. Andrea O'Reilly. Albany: SUNY Press, 2004.

Reddy, Maureen, Martha Roth, and Amy Sheldon, Eds. *Mother Journeys: Feminists Write about Mothering*. Minneapolis: Spinsters Ink, 1994.

Rich, Adrienne. *Of Woman Born: Motherhood as Experience and Institution*. New York: W.W. Norton, 1986.

Waring, Marilyn. *If Women Counted: A New Feminist Economics*. San Francisco: Harper & Row, 1988.

PART FOUR

Activism

CHAPTER TWELVE

Rocking the Boat

Feminism and the Ideological Grounding of the Twenty-First Century Mothers' Movement

JUDITH STADTMAN TUCKER

> Patriarchy was not simply a means of privileging men. It was
> also a means of ensuring an adequate supply of care.
> —Nancy Folbre, *The Invisible Heart:*
> *Economics and Family Values*

IN EARLY 2006, I was invited to speak at an informal gathering of socially
conscious mothers about what I call the "motherhood problem"—the combination of cultural factors, social trends, and policy shortfalls that makes
mothers and other caregivers disproportionately vulnerable to economic insecurity and the daily work of mothering harder than it has to be. The organizers advised me that this particular group of mothers—and others who
attended similar "Mother Talks"[1]—realize that the deck of gender, work, and
family is not stacked in their favor and wanted to know what to do about it.
Yet when it comes to striking up a conversation about the politics of motherhood, there's a clear consensus among activists and the general public that
mothers today really don't want to talk about feminism.

Perhaps I should mention I consider it my duty to talk about motherhood and feminism as often as possible. I'm convinced that we can't give up
the fight for women's rights until women's equality in every aspect of social
life is fully compatible with women's reproductive potential and desires.

Moreover, I find it difficult to explain the precipitous decline of agency, autonomy, and opportunity that women experience when they become mothers without resorting to a feminist analysis of gender and power. However, as I've learned from eight years as an organizer and advocate for mothers' and caregivers' rights, the impression that the typical American mom is indifferent to the feminist project is not unfounded.[2]

Mothers on the ground are unequivocal in their support for women's equality in and outside the workplace, but tend to eye feminism with suspicion. Specifically, there's a common—and not entirely unwarranted—perception that the priorities of Second Wave activists were not family-friendly, and that abandoning the notion that marriage and motherhood can be legitimate components of a woman's identity and self-fulfillment is a prerequisite for induction into the feminist sisterhood (Umansky 16–17). Observations that this formulation sounds more like Phyllis Schlafly than Betty Friedan are met with polite disinterest. Like the majority of their peers, the present generation of middle-class mothers has absorbed—and actively participates in—a popular, quasifeminist discourse regarding women, work, and family that confuses freedom of choice with freedom from oppression (Hirshman 16–18; Peskowitz 98–99). Today, activists and organizations intent on mobilizing mothers for political action face the challenge of problematizing the institution of motherhood without alluding to the patriarchy.

Despite their ambivalence about feminism as a cause, there are encouraging signs that a critical mass of mothers are ready to act for change. For example, a 2004 survey of mothers' attitudes found that 90 percent of American mothers believe the United States can do a better job of meeting the needs of mothers and families (Erickson and Aird 5). This is not surprising, since a recent international comparison of key health and social indicators found that, among wealthy Western nations, the United States is the worst place to be a mother.[3] Whether they view the emerging "mothers' movement" as a response to the disconnect between workplace norms and family needs or as a continuation of the long struggle for women's equal rights, a growing number of women in their primary childbearing and childrearing years support the idea of a broad-based grassroots social movement to improve the status of mothers.[4]

In the past five years, several U.S. organizations that originally confined their scope to support and parenting education for mothers—including Mothers & More and the National Association of Mothers Centers—have refined their mission statements and programs to include advocacy and direct action on selected policy issues (Stadtman Tucker 189–194). The National Organization for Women recently renewed its commitment to advancing mothers' and caregivers' economic rights with a comprehensive policy agenda and widely publicized call to action (Pettine and Stadtman Tucker). New groups and organizations have also entered the fray. In May 2006, MoveOn cofounder Joan Blades[5] and author/activist Kristin Rowe-Finkbeiner launched MomsRising.org to facilitate one-click activism by and for mothers and generate support for the policy solutions highlighted in their book, *The Motherhood Manifesto*. (In a commentary for a popular progressive news service, historian Ruth Rosen praised Blades and Rowe-Finkbeiner for prescribing "such essential changes as paid parental leave, flexible working conditions, after-school programs, universal health care, excellent, affordable and accessible child care and realistic living wages" without ever using "the F-word.")

The outlines of the emerging mothers' movement are also visible in the growth of a sophisticated, independent media that disseminates critical ideas and information. The alternative mothers' media attract significant readership with magazines, 'zines, Web sites, and blogs investigating the politics, experience, and practice of motherhood from a clear-eyed, unsentimental, and often feminist perspective.[6]

Proponents of the new mothers' movement are quite clear about what they want. They want mothers to have better lives with less role strain and better options for combining work and family. They want respect and recognition for the social and economic value of mothers' work—both paid employment and the unpaid care work mothers do at home. They want flexible workplaces, and equal pay for equal work. They want public policies that respond to the needs of dual-earner couples and single-parent women, they want reasonable protection from economic hardships mothers may incur due to their maternal status, and they want men to take a more active role in childrearing and domestic life (Stadtman Tucker 187–194). There is less consistency among advocates about why change is necessary. Is the goal to improve the lives of women or to better the lives of children?

SOCIAL MOVEMENTS AS STORYTELLING

Successful social movements depend on a number of factors—not the least of which are opportunity and timing—but the most important factor is the ability to establish a resilient and compelling change narrative. You could say the role of revolutionaries is to expose the fractures and fallacies of the existing order and provide the blueprint for a suitable replacement. The most effective change narratives provide a map to a specific destination—that is, they identify a social problem and who or what is harmed by it, propose a realistic way to fix it, and provide an attractive vision of social life once the problem is removed. Change narratives also transform the chosen cause into a "worthy" cause by defining the targeted social conditions as immoral, unjust, inhumane, or otherwise in violation of a culture's core values (Lakoff 3–19).

A successful change narrative has to reach people where they live, so it must contain enough obvious or shared truths to be resonant and memorable. Very often, this requires developing a script and themes using familiar language and concepts to validate new ideals and describe new possibilities. The best change narratives are *persuasive*, *provocative*, and *evocative*—they help people think differently about what they hear, feel, and know (Gardner 69–89).

I've introduced the analogy of social movements as storytelling because I believe the reason the twenty-first century mothers' movement has yet to make a lasting impression on the public mind is not because the motherhood problem is inconsequential, or that mothers are resigned to the inequity of current conditions, but because its leaders are struggling to construct an effective change narrative out of common language and moral concepts that fail to serve the movement's radical intent (Wilkinson).

Naming the problem is fairly easy—thirty years of feminist-informed research on demographic, economic, and social trends provides ample evidence that despite legal guarantees of equal opportunity, North American women are still getting the short end of the stick and are further disadvantaged by maternity. In terms of a coherent agenda for policy reform, solutions are close at hand. We know from time-tested European models that a combination of caregiver supports, working time regulations, and job-and-earnings protections enable maternal employment, reduce the gender wage gap, decrease maternal and child poverty, improve health outcomes for women and children, and, when gender equity is a social priority, increase men's participation in caregiving and household labor (Crittenden 2001: 239–250; Jacobs and Gerson 169–192). What's sorely missing from the U.S. mothers' movement is a stable, ideological framework for social activism and a workable vision for a future society in which maternity and women's equality go hand-in-hand without exacerbating the commodification of intimate life (Fraser 226–227).

Since straight-up feminism is viewed as a nonstarter for mobilizing today's mothers, advocates for change resort to blending and weaving several strands of political philosophy to articulate and justify their objectives. A range of humanistic and socialistic theories contributes to the ideological grounding of the twenty-first century mothers' movement, but the predominant influences are liberal feminism, maternalism, and feminist care theory (Hewett 36–40).

Liberal feminism is commonly associated with the political objectives of the "mainstream" element of the mid-twentieth century women's movement. Although definitions vary, here I use the term to denote feminist theory and activism concerned with expanding women's individual and constitutional rights, especially the right to reproductive self-determination and equal access to higher education and leadership opportunities. Liberal feminism offers a rich vocabulary of rights, responsibilities, justice, equity, empowerment, and identity, and is fundamental to the articulation of mothers' entitlement to selfhood within and beyond the bounds of the maternal role. (This principle is vividly expressed in the "Core Beliefs" statement of the support and advocacy organization Mothers & More, which leads with the proclamation, "A mother is more than any single role she plays. . . . She is entitled to fully explore and develop her identity as she chooses: as a woman, a citizen, a parent or an employee.")

Liberal feminism qualifies mothers as equal citizens in an ideally egalitarian society, and legitimates the perception of the negative economic and occupational consequences of motherhood as disproportionate and discriminatory. Leading advocates frequently refer to the mothers' movement as "the unfinished business" of feminism,[7] but do not necessarily conceptualize the mothers' movement as a feminist movement (Hewett 35).

"Maternalism" typically refers to the ideological underpinnings of middle-class women's social activism during the American Progressive Era (1890–1920). Working parallel to the women's suffrage movement, maternalist organizers invoked the rhetoric of "social housekeeping" to enlist married homemakers in a variety of grassroots campaigns. Their efforts were extremely successful, resulting in the enactment of an array of federal legislation and social programs to protect vulnerable women from exploitation or destitution and promote children's health and education.[8]

Maternalism provides a language of morality and compassion and emphasizes the importance of maternal well-being for the health and safety of children. Maternalist advocates tend to idealize the power of maternal love to transform the future of children and society, and praise maternal selflessness, strength, and stamina as heroic qualities. Maternalism contrasts the humane values of "the mother world" with the heartless values of "the money world" (The Mothers' Council, "Call to a Motherhood Movement"), and supplies a logic for championing mothers' care work as a precious resource that must be supported, honored, and accommodated by private entities and the state.

Although contemporary maternalist organizers may define their goals as feminist, their published rhetoric and political strategies routinely reinforce

gender difference, especially the belief that women are "naturally" or intu-
itively more empathic, less violence prone, and more sensitive to human needs
than males.[9] Although the language and moral logic of maternalism threads
its way through the public statements of a number of groups associated with
the emerging mothers' movement, the most undiluted example appears in the
Motherhood Project's "Call to a Motherhood Movement," which exhorts "all
mothers" to "a renewed sense of purpose, passion, and power in the work of
mothering. . . . We call for a motherhood movement to ensure the dignity and
well-being of children."

NEGOTIATING CONFLICTING IDEALS

From a practical perspective, a key variable is whether the divergent frameworks of liberal feminism and maternalism resist or conform to the dominant
ideology of motherhood. The dominant ideology of motherhood is a complex
and contested topic in feminist scholarship (Glenn 1–26), but for the sake of
brevity, I offer this shorthand version: *The belief that children's optimal growth
and development are directly and exclusively related to the quality and quantity of
maternal care they receive, and caring mothers always put children's needs ahead of
their own.* Traditionally, feminists have attacked the dominant ideology of
motherhood as part of a system of oppression, while maternalists contend
that mothers' learned or natural orientation toward preserving life and fostering human development is the source of their special wisdom and power
(Plumez 1).

Challenging the dominant ideology of motherhood is an attractive alternative to movement organizers due to a growing awareness in popular culture
that the idealization of "intensive," selfless mothering detracts from the lived
experience of motherhood, relieves fathers of equal domestic responsibility,
and constrains mothers' personal freedom and employment options. (A suc-
cinct example of this discourse appeared in a February 2005 cover story for
Newsweek magazine, adapted from Judith Warner's *Perfect Madness: Motherhood in the Age of Anxiety.*) But movement leaders are justifiably reticent about
rocking the boat too much. Dismantling the dominant ideology of motherhood—and the imbalance of power it protects—is a risky and complicated
project, and one that is bound to encounter political resistance. For advocates
invested in upending the meaning of motherhood, winning support for their
cause depends on the ability to find—and effectively transmit to the dominant culture—a new and better way to acknowledge the centrality of care-

giving to good societies and the intrinsic value of mothering to individual women and children.

For organizers seeking reform rather than revolution, rowing with the current has definite appeal. Frameworks that conform to the dominant ideology of motherhood are regarded as nonalienating to the target audience and support a plea for better treatment of mothers without posing an immediate threat to the status quo (which, given the present political climate in North America, is considered a strategic advantage). The dominant ideology of motherhood also provides accessible and emotionally immediate language to describe the value of mothering to women, children, and society, and portrays motherhood itself as empowering rather than problematic—as exemplified by the dubious axiom, "Motherhood is the most important job in the world." (Whereas a feminist critique might suggest that if motherhood really was the most important job in the word, only a handful of women would be allowed to do it.)

The prevailing approach of today's mothers' advocates is to negotiate the movement's practical and political conflicts with the dominant ideology of motherhood by blending the feminist perspective of rights and equality with the maternalist morality of putting children and families first. Rather than transcending the political limitations of either frame, this exercise produces a mixed message. The incorporation of maternalist thinking into feminist-informed change narratives becomes especially murky when left-leaning organizers envision the mothers' movement as a unity movement. As Joan Blades of MomsRising remarked in a 2006 interview, "I think when you focus on what's best for kids you see that your goals are the same . . . ultimately conservatives are going to hook up with us because it's the right thing to do" (Burliegh). For their part, conservative women's groups dismiss the policy proposals of progressive activists as "asking for special treatment" at the tax-payers' expense, and counter that "government subsidized parenting" is not a "core American value" (Monaghan). More typically, proponents of the contemporary mothers' movement argue that bias against mothers in the workplace is wrong—not because discriminatory treatment based on a person's sex and reproductive status is illegal, morally offensive, harming to society, and just plain unfair, but because workers should not be penalized for making family life a priority.

The strategic combination of liberal feminist and maternalist frameworks does satisfy some of the requirements for developing an accessible and compelling change narrative. This method does not, however, create a story line that challenges the deeper ideological wellsprings feeding the motherhood problem: the myth of individual autonomy, the cultural construction of gender difference, and the delusion that, in a good society, the worlds of work and family can be functionally and emotionally separated and governed by opposing values. "As the mothers' movement grows, it will in effect articulate an understanding of motherhood, whether or not it does so consciously," observes Patrice DiQuinzio. "But without conscious consideration of its self-definition, goals, strategies, and tactics, the movement risks reconsolidating ideas about motherhood that have proven to be exclusionary and often not especially empowering in the past" (57).

DREAMING BEYOND DICHOTOMY

A third—and, I believe, more promising—framework for creating an effective change narrative for the twenty-first century mothers' movement is a feminist ethic of care. Most advocacy groups sample from a care ethic in their political construction of "mothers' issues," but always in combination with the ideological push–pull of liberal feminism and maternalism (Stadtman Tucker 188–189).

As with maternalism, feminist care ethic—particularly as articulated by Joan Tronto in *Moral Boundaries* (1994) and economist Nancy Folbre in *The Invisible Heart* (2001)—designates caring for others as an essential social function. But rather than valorizing maternal sensitivity and altruism as a vital resource, feminist care ethic aims to liberate caregiving from its peripheral status as women's work and reposition it as a primary human activity. To that end, Tronto defines "caring" as "*everything that we do to maintain, continue and repair our 'world' so that we can live in it as well as possible*," a world that includes "our bodies, our selves, and our environment, all of which we seek to interweave in a complex, life-sustaining web" (103, emphasis in original).

For proponents of the contemporary mothers' movement, grounding the agenda for change in an ethic of care opens up the possibility of developing a gender-neutral approach to social policy (as required by liberal feminism) without discounting the unique qualities and intimacy of the mother-child bond, and an opportunity to expand the language of care as a public good beyond the maternalist paradigm. Care ethic also provides a basis for understanding caregiving as class of work—*care work*—and characterizes maternal care as a deliberate practice arising from a discreet cognitive process rather than an instinctive female response. The ethic of care suggests that the public concept of obligation can and should be reconfigured so that caring for children and dependent adults is allocated as a broad social responsibility rather than isolated as the principal duty of women and other marginalized workers. Finally, by identifying *interdependence*—rather than *independence*—as the normal, healthy and ideal human state, care ethic challenges the proposition that complete self-sufficiency is possible, or even desirable, in a habitable society (Folbre 22–25).

From the perspective of crafting a persuasive, provocative, and evocative change narrative, the care frame offers mothers' advocates fresh language and ideas that relate work–family conflict and the stress of contemporary mother-hood to the cultural and economic devaluation of care. Thinking and talking about what life for men, women, and children might look like in a society that measures its success by how well people are able to care for each other and the world they share may have greater appeal to the average mom or dad than demands to dismantle the patriarchy. Yet the feminist ethic of care calls for nothing less than a radical refashioning of the dominant moral order. In the process of creating a caring society, the patriarchy as we know it would be badly damaged, if not utterly undone. As Tronto notes,

> In our present culture there is a great ideological advantage to gain from keeping care from coming into focus. By not noticing how pervasive and central care is to human life, those who are in positions of power and privilege can continue to ignore and degrade the activities of care and those who give care. To call attention to care is to raise questions about the adequacy of care in our society. Such an inquiry will lead to a pro-found rethinking of moral and political life. (111)

There is fourth ideological framework—fully compatible with an ethic of care—that I believe will be crucial to achieving the full potential of the new mothers' movement. The *reproductive justice* frame, which developed in the context of the women of color reproductive health movement, prescribes an end to the exploitation and oppression of women's reproductive power (both biological and social) with an articulation of women's rights that fuses the demand for reproductive autonomy with the concepts of human rights and social justice. Recognizing the guarantee of "choice" as an unstable and inade-quate platform for women's right to reproductive self-determination—espe-cially for poor women, women of color, and women in marginalized communities—reproductive justice supports "the complete physical, mental, spiritual, political, economic, and social well-being of women and girls," and will be achieved when all mothers, nonmothers, and future mothers have "the economic, social and political power and resources to make healthy decisions about our bodies, sexuality and reproduction for ourselves, our families and our communities in all areas of our lives" (Shen).

By acknowledging every woman's right to bear children (as well her right *not* to bear children) and the inequities and environmental conditions that conflict with maternal and child well-being, reproductive justice requires optimal social conditions for childbearing and childrearing for *all* women, not just an elite few. By addressing the multiple intersectionalities of race, class, age, ethnicity, sexuality, and ability in women's social exclusion, the reproductive justice framework has tremendous potential to inject the necessary complexities of diversity, big picture social justice, and reproductive rights into the ideological architecture of the contemporary mothers' movement.

I offer this analysis to suggest how to begin a productive discussion about the political framing of the twenty-first century mothers' movement, not to predict where it will end. The subtle dimensions and moving parts of the theories and philosophies informing the ideological grounding of the movement are too varied to acknowledge in a brief overview. Sorting out the politics of motherhood is a little like tumbling down Alice's rabbit hole—one encounters all sorts of fascinating things along the way, but there's a nagging feeling we may never get to the bottom.

I've tried to touch on how and why long-standing conflicts in feminism are related to the impetus of the mothers' movement, and how the movement's objectives are articulated by its leaders and perceived by its intended constituency. At present, the practice of mingling the incompatible frameworks of liberal feminism and maternalism with the occasional dash of care ethic produces uneven results and, I fear, remains unconvincing to the public at large. But given the power of social movements to both *create* meaning and *change* meaning through the process of narrative, in time the mothers' movement may realize its radical potential and have a profound impact on the common understanding of moral action, social justice, and women's rights.

NOTES

1. The "Mother Talk" project (http://www.mother-talk.com) provides virtual and real-world literary salons to bring mothers together with writers who address the complexity of contemporary motherhood in their work. The project was founded by authors Andrea Buchanan (*Mother Shock: Loving Every (Other) Minute of It*) and Miriam Peskowitz (*The Truth Behind the Mommy Wars*).

2. In a 2001 survey, 83 percent of American women reported that "being a mother" was "very important" to their sense of personal identity, while only 21

percent reported that "being a feminist" was "very important." Of over 2,000 women surveyed, only 9 percent agreed the term *feminist* has completely positive connotations (Center for Gender Equality, *Progress and Perils: How Gender Issues Unite and Divide Women, Part One*).

3. Among wealthy nations, only Japan ranked lower than the United States due to a lower score on women's health and political participation (Save the Children Foundation, "2006 Mother's Index Rankings").

4. For example, when the National Association of Mothers Centers launched the Mothers Ought to Have Equal Rights (MOTHERS) initiative in 2002, approximately 3,000 supporters joined the mailing list in the first year. When the MomsRising project launched in May 2006, 30,000 supporters signed on in the first week (personal correspondence with Ann Crittenden and Kristin Rowe-Finkbeiner).

5. MoveOn (http://www.moveon.org) is a U.S. internet-based nonprofit organization with over three million registered members. The group has raised millions of dollars for progressive political candidates and causes.

6. These outlets include the print 'zine *Hip Mama* (launched in 1993) and Web site HipMama.com, launched in 1996 (http://www.hipmama.com); *Salon's* "Mothers Who Think" (1997–2000); *Mamaphonic* (http://www.mamaphonic. com), launched in 1998; *Brain, Child Magazine,* first published in March 2000; *Literary Mama* (http://www.literarymama.com), *The Mothers Movement Online* (http://www.mothersmovement.org), and *Mommy, Too! Magazine,* a full-feature Web-based magazine for mothers of color (http://www.mommytoo.com), all launched in 2003; *MojoMom* (http:www.mojomom.com), founded in 2004; *mamazine* (http://www.mamazine.com) launched in 2005; and hundreds of well-written, well-read blogs exploring the motherhood problem.

7. For example, Ann Crittenden writes, "I believe that this is the big unfinished business of the women's movement" (in Blades and Rowe-Finkbeiner's *The Motherhood Manifesto* 4).

8. For in-depth analysis and overviews of maternalist activism, see Molly Ladd-Taylor, *Mother-Work: Women, Welfare and the State, 1890–1930* (Chicago: University of Illinois Press, 1991); Robyn Muncy, *Creating a Female Dominion in American Reform 1890–1935* (New York: Oxford University Press, 1991); and Theda Skocpol, "Foundations for a Maternalist Welfare State?" in *Protecting Soldiers and Mothers: The Political Origins of Social Policy in the United States,* (Cambridge: Belknap Press, 1995).

9. An example is the antiwar group CodePink, whose founder's call to action describes women as "the guardians of life" and states: "We call on mothers, grandmothers, sisters, and daughters, on workers, students, teachers, healers, artists, writers, singers, poets and every ordinary outraged woman willing to be outrageous for peace. . . . Because of our responsibility to the next generation, because of our own love for our families and communities and this country that we are a

part of, we understand the love of a mother in Iraq for her children, and the driving desire of that child for life."

REFERENCES

Blades, Joan, and Kristin Rowe-Finkbeiner. *The Motherhood Manifesto: What America's Moms Want—and What To Do About It.* New York: Nation Books, 2006.

Buchanan, Andrea J. *Mother Shock: Loving Every (Other) Minute of It.* Emeryville, CA: Seal Press, 2003.

Burleigh, Nina. "The Maternal Is Political." *Salon* 23 May 2006. Accessed 25 May 2006: http://www.salon.com/mwt/feature/2006/05/23/mothers_movement/.

CODEPINK Women for Peace. *CODEPINK Call to Action.* ND. Accessed 20 February 2007: http://www.codepink4peace.org/article.php?id=49.

Crittenden, Ann. *The Price of Motherhood.* New York: Metropolitan Book, 2001.

———. "Why the Most Important Job in the World Is Still the Least Valued" [sidebar]. *The Motherhood Manifesto.* Eds. Joan Blades and Kristin Rowe-Finkbeiner. New York: Nation Books, 2006. 4.

DiQuinzio, Patrice. "The Politics of the Mothers' Movement in the United States: Possibilities and Pitfalls." *Mothering and Feminism: Journal of the Association for Research of Mothering* 8.1,2 (2006): 55–71.

Erickson, Martha Farrell, and Enola G. Aird. "Motherhood Survey Annotated Questionnaire." *The Motherhood Study: Fresh Insights on Mothers' Attitudes and Concerns.* New York: Institute for American Values, 2005. (Separate appendix.) Accessed 23 September 2006: http://www.motherhoodproject.org/wpcontent/themes/mothe2/pdfs/annotatedquestionnaire.pdf.

Folbre, Nancy. *The Invisible Heart: Economics and Family Values.* New York: New Press, 2001.

Fraser, Nancy. "Gender Equity and the Welfare State: A Postindustrial Thought Experiment." *Democracy and Difference: Contesting the Boundaries of the Political.* Ed. Selaya Benhabib. Princeton: Princeton Univ. Press, 1996. 218–241.

Gardner, Howard. *Changing Minds: The Art and Science of Changing Our Own and Other People's Minds.* Boston: Harvard Business School Press, 2004.

Glenn, Evelyn Nakano. "The Social Construction of Mothering." *Mothering: Ideology, Experience and Agency.* Ed. Evelyn Nakano Glenn, Grace Chang, and Linda Rennie Forcey. New York: Routledge, 1994. 1–29.

Hewett, Heather. "Talkin' Bout a Revolution: Building a Mothers' Movement in the Third Wave." *Mothering and Feminism: Journal of the Association for Research of Mothering* 8.1,2 (2006): 34–54.

Hirshman, Linda R. *Get To Work: A Manifesto for Women of the World*. New York: Viking, 2006.

Jacobs, Jerry A., and Kathleen Gerson. *The Time Divide: Work, Family and Gender Inequality*. Cambridge: Harvard University Press, 2004.

Lakoff, George. *Moral Politics: How Liberals and Conservatives Think*. 2nd ed. Chicago: Chicago University Press, 2002.

Monaghan, Kate. "Mother's Group Wants 'Progressive' Family Solutions." *Cybercast News Service* June 15, 2006. Accessed 30 August 2006: http://www.cnsnews.com/Culture/archive/200606/CUL20060615a.html.

Mothers' Council. *Call to a Motherhood Movement*. The Motherhood Project, Institute for American Values 2002. Accessed 23 Sept 2006: http://www.motherhoodproject.org/wp-content/themes/mothe2/pdfs/call.pdf>

Mothers & More. *Mission Statement & Core Beliefs*. Accessed 23 September 2006: http://www.mothersandmore.org/AboutUs/mission.shtml.

Peskowitz, Miriam. *The Truth Behind the Mommy Wars: Who Decides What Makes a Good Mother*. Emeryville, CA: Seal Press, 2005.

Pettine, Laurie, and Judith Stadtman Tucker. "Mothers and Caregivers Economic Rights Campaign Gains Momentum." *NOW National Times*. Summer 2006: 3.

Plumez, Jacqueline Hornor. *Mother Power: Discover the Difference That Women Have Made All Over the World*. Naperville, IL: Sourcebooks, 2002.

Princeton Survey Research Associates. *Progress and Perils: How Gender Issues Unite and Divide Women, Part One*. Center for Gender Equality: October 2001. Accessed 20 February 2007: http://www.advancewomen.org/files/File/PDFs/PartOne.pdf.

Rosen, Ruth. "The Care Crisis." *AlterNet* 11 May 2006. Accessed 12 May 2006: http://www.alternet.org/workplace/35686/.

Save the Children Foundation. "2006 Mother's Index Rankings." *State of the World's Mothers 2006: Saving the Lives of Mothers and Newborns*. May 2006. Accessed 20 February 2007: http://www.savethechildren.org/publications/mothers/2006/SOWM_2006_final.pdf.

Shen, Eveline. *Reproductive Justice: Toward a Comprehensive Movement. Center for American Progress*. 20 January 2006. Accessed 20 February 2007: http://www.americanprogress.org/issues/2006/01/b1363945.html.

Stadtman Tucker, Judith. "Care as a Cause: Framing the Twenty-First-Century Mothers' Movement." *Socializing Care: Feminist Ethics and Public Issues*. Eds. Maurice Hamington and Dorothy C. Miller. Lanham, MD: Rowman & Littlefield, 2006. 183–203.

Tronto, Joan C. *Moral Boundaries: A Political Argument for an Ethic of Care*. New York: Routledge, 1994.

Umansky, Lauri. *Motherhood Reconceived: Feminism and the Legacy of the Sixties.* New York: New York University Press, 1996.

Warner, Judith. "Mommy Madness." *Newsweek.* February 21, 2005. 42–49.

———. *Perfect Madness: Motherhood in the Age of Anxiety.* New York: Penguin Books, 2005.

Wilkinson, Stephanie. "Say You Want a Revolution: Why the Mothers' Movement Hasn't Happened Yet." *Brain, Child Magazine* Fall 2005: 33–43.

CHAPTER THIRTEEN

Women Staging Coups through Mothering

Depictions in Hispanic Contemporary Literature

GISELA NORAT

IN THE HISPANIC WORLD we can find a variety of ways in which women stage coups against patriarchal systems that oppress them. Contemporary Hispanic literature is filled with examples of women engaged in brave and unexpected or uncommon acts that effect change in their life, community, or country. While most female rebellions go unnoticed and undocumented because they lack political impact, the one orchestrated by the Mothers of Plaza de Mayo in the then-dictatorial Argentina of the 1970s and 1980s made news around the world, politicized the institution of motherhood, and challenged a repressive military regime.[1] Maternity had been the Argentine women's sole motivator and their only ammunition. This was revolutionary in Latin America. Their story, literally a female-organized coup that flexed maternal power to bring about social change, sets the parameter here for reading other manifestations of feminist mothering recorded in contemporary Latina and Latin American literature.[2] Other mother-centered initiatives discussed here, for example, include Chilean Isabel Allende, who breaks with mainstream literary tradition by narrating *Paula* from the perspective of a mother grieving a dying daughter. Mexican-American Cherríe Moraga undermines heterosexual dictates and journals her experience of pregnancy and childbirth as a lesbian mother. And, increasingly, Latina fiction writers portray daughters who, turning the tables on tradition, attempt to socialize their mothers in feminist ways.

PUBLIC SUBVERSION: MOTHERS OF PLAZA DE MAYO

A feminist agenda—broadly defined as a plan of action that promotes political, economic and social equality between men and women—was inconceivable to the mothers and grandmothers who first gathered in Buenos Aires' main square, the Plaza de Mayo, across from the Government House, the Casa Rosada, to protest the disappearance of their daughters, sons, and grandchildren after the military coup in 1976. Among the missing figured many student activists, labor leaders, and anyone who had advocated for social and economic improvements for the working-class poor. Life for women of this sector revolved around tending to family and home.[3] Among the general population in 1970s Latin America, the term *feminist* connoted women who spurned tradition, bashed men, acted like men, or maybe even wanted to be men, but in any case their demands for equality had to do with upper-class women.[4] John King notes the scant attention the feminist movement received in the late 1960s in Argentina and how, given the political instability in the country in the 1970s, "most intellectuals and young people were drawn more to theories of social revolution than to sexual revolution. . . . The appropriation of Evita [Perón] was that of a proto-revolutionary rather than a proto-feminist" (King 17). Women's organizations, which existed and were striving for social awareness of women's issues and rights, were severely crippled by the coup and its violent aftermath.[5]

With large numbers of Argentine citizens dead, detained, and disappeared, mothers and grandmothers set out in search of information about loved ones. Irene, the protagonist of Marta Traba's novel, *Mothers and Shadows*, captures the general state of affairs regarding the missing, in this case a friend's daughter: "No one, anywhere . . . in any office, would admit to having seen her or known her or filed her name or imprisoned her or interrogated her: no one had ever set eyes on her, she never went through the door of any police station . . . they never entered her name on any list" (74).[6] For state authorities, the missing were subversives and terrorists who were to be treated as if they did not exist or had never been born. One key mother character in the novel makes numerous, but fruitless, inquiries at police stations and government offices. As in real life, women in *Mothers and Shadows* then begin approaching each other and, out of a common experience of suffering, the

Association of Mothers of Plaza de Mayo is born.[7] Unlike men, women felt less intimidated by the repressive regime since in Argentine popular opinion they were doing no less than patriarchal society expected of mothers in their situation. Hence, the public denunciation of government-orchestrated disappearances was, from the beginning, an almost exclusive female platform.

Feminist concerns—associated in Latin America with self-centered notions of personal gain at the expense of family obligations—were far from the minds of those anguished women who spent their energies making the rounds of government institutions, tackling household duties and the survival of those at home, battling depression and the stigma that came with having a missing relative. Not surprisingly, despite success in organizing and attaining international recognition for their cause, Latin American mothers in the Southern Cone—Argentina, Chile, and Uruguay—did not conceive of their endeavors or their associations as feminist. In an attempt to call attention to their demands, the Argentine mothers, probably unbeknownst to them, used tactics employed by suffragettes in both England and the United States at the turn of the twentieth century, among them: posters, banners, marches, chanting, civil disobedience, chainings to government buildings, and hunger strikes. En masse, the Argentine mothers personified to the world a bereaved Demeter searching for the kidnapped Persephone, snatched away and kept detained by the dictator/patriarch in his underworld, the Hades described by those Latin American sons and daughters who disappeared and made it out of prison alive (Hirsch 5).

In a quandary as to how to handle female protestors in a culture that sanctifies motherhood, the Argentine police first forbade public congregation and made the women move around the plaza, an imperative that inspired the idea for the weekly march circling the square. Later authorities discouraged the mothers with ridicule, arrests, jailings, beatings, and even disappearance. If one considers that feminism as a social theory and political movement is primarily informed and motivated by the experiences of women and promotes women's rights, interests, and issues, then these Latin American women acted as feminists.[8] Publicly accusing a repressive regime of wrongdoing is nothing short of subversive. Forgoing a feminist label they would have rejected for themselves, nevertheless, their fundamental struggle against the government involved a mother's inalienable right to her children, a claim that reverberates back to the Declaration of Sentiments prepared by Elizabeth Cady Stanton in what would initiate Women's Suffrage in the United States.[9]

In the course of their campaign to denounce human rights violations, Latin American mothers became conduits for reaffirming the value of life and the female reproductive body took on a political (and paradoxically a feminist) voice against institutions of power.[10] Mothers of Plaza de Mayo, as well as the Chilean "arpilleristas," circulated incredible stories of repression that fed a 1980s boom in women's writing in the region and created an opening in literature to legitimize a mother's perspective and often a feminist one at that.[11] It makes sense that from a punitive system of government—that paid lip service to the importance of the family while in some sectors of its population threatened its very survival and the core of women's identity—feminist writings proliferated to record aspects of Latin American life needing radical change. "Feminist mothering," no longer an absolute oxymoron, became an important partnership that proffered a coup d'état to the literary establishment and facilitated women's insertion in its mainstream.

Traba's *Mothers and Shadows* is one example of the explicit partnership between feminism and motherhood in a novel that spans the Southern Cone during the period of repressive regimes that swept the region. In the novel, Irene is a middle-class actress and divorced mother. Although these roles allow her to narrate from various perspectives, Traba's predominant use of a mother's point of view is significant because it is rare in Latin American and women's literature in general. In her study of women autobiographers, feminist scholar Shirley Nelson Garner confirms that "literature has not provided us with enough stories written from the mother's point of view to encourage us to write from this perspective. The absence of these stories leaves us with the special burden of creating our own forms and language for telling them, as well as suggests that they are not interesting or not the proper subject of literature" (87).

Irene's maternal point of view in Traba's novel reflects the voice Latin American women felt most comfortable using when broaching political issues of life-and-death magnitude. Traba, an art critic by profession, employed multiple perspectives in the novel that suggest options available to women. Both Irene's divorce and self-supporting career, albeit somewhat disreputable for decent women in a strict patriarchy, liberated her from the traditional marriage bond and all the restrictions it entails. The protagonist's lifestyle alone is subversive within the Argentine society of the time. Dissident, too, is Irene's willingness to entertain in her apartment in Montevideo a young female acquaintance seeking refuge after being tortured and released from jail. Risking her own welfare to nurture someone else's distressed child emphasizes Irene's core identity as mother and blurs career accomplishments. Out of fear for her own son with whom she has lost contact during his university studies in Santiago, Chile, Irene admits the primacy of motherhood: "I knew no one could free me from the sensation of failure, of having made a mistake, which always seemed to mar my major state triumphs" (Traba 83). Irene needs to nurture the young woman visitor in whom she recognizes her own son who may have "disappeared" in Chile. All the while in Buenos Aires her good friend Elena is experiencing the same tragedy with her detained daughter. Traba captures in the novel a society in which women, left without children or partners, or even supportive kin, empower each other on the common ground of motherhood. Unlike Irene, her friend Elena is from the upper class and has enjoyed a fairy tale life until her daughter's arrest and disappearance. While marching with the mothers of Plaza de Mayo, Elena's social class does not matter, only that she is a mater dolorosa; she is one more grieving mother multiplied by hundreds of voices demanding in unison their children's return.

In keeping with the centrality of motherhood in the novel, Traba inscribed the physiology of maternity in the text. For instance, Elena's symptoms—lack of appetite, nausea, vomiting, and depression—after moving into her daughter's studio to await her return (literally with the hope of a rebirth, given the threat of death) suggest a pregnant female body (Traba 81). Elena's physical transformation during the rally also evokes symptoms of pregnancy and birthing. "I wish I could forget," says Irene of her friend, "that twisted face, that gaping, howling mouth and, even worse, her skin, that delicate skin of hers, discolored with purple blotches" (Traba 90). Irene recounts how at the time of the mothers' march the plaza empties of passersby as if people went out of their way to avoid witnessing pain too great to describe (Traba 87). In the midst of the demonstration Irene herself experiences extreme distress, "as if someone was trying to rip my insides out," a violent yanking reminiscent of childbirth (Traba 88–89). During the short, but intensive, period of the rally, Irene depicts the transformation of the public square into one massive gut-wrenching howl with women holding, swaying, and rocking photographs back and forth. One "woman was holding a passport photograph in the palm of her hand, shielding it as if it were an egg she'd just that minute hatched" (Traba 88–89). Again, Traba uses birth images to capture the mothers' public display of hope and grief at a time when they fear their children's death. From this "zone of pain," women collaborated to mother, support, and empower each other while continuing the effort to locate their children and undermine the regimes' cover up of the hideous crime called "disappearance."[12] Now recorded as history, Argentine women organized as mothers to stage a public coup that demanded attention and accountability by government authorities.

FEMINIST AND LITERARY (FORE)MOTHER:
ISABEL ALLENDE IN *PAULA*

Isabel Allende also publicly shares the pain of a mother struggling to keep alive the hope that her child may live, despite the threat of a premature death. Recalling the posters of the missing displayed by mothers during the political marches at the Plaza de Mayo, the photograph of Allende's daughter has circulated widely on the cover of the book titled after her.[13] Paula, too, was snatched early from her mother's life and hence Allende gives written testimony to a mother's love. The mothers of Plaza de Mayo compiled lists of the missing and rallied in a public square against a regime's disregard for human life. Allende writes as her only weapon to keep herself sane: "My soul is choking in sand . . . I plunge into these pages in an irrational attempt to overcome my terror. I think that perhaps if I give form to this devastation I shall be able to help you, and myself and that the meticulous exercise of writing can be our salvation" (*Paula* 9).

Alone with her anguish, Allende inscribes her protest of loss in a narrative that only insinuates the medical malpractice that led to Paula's brain damage and eventual demise. The author has alluded in an interview that whether dealing with the military (as did the mothers of the disappeared) or the medical establishment, responsibility for harm to loved ones falls on the heads of powerful men shielded from accountability for wrongdoing by a patriarchal network of protection ("Listen" 407). A mother stands little chance of winning justice for her child's death, but the protest must be voiced and recorded nevertheless. This is a feminist posture.

In her first nonfiction book, *Paula*, Allende takes the reader through the year she spent at the bedside of her comatose twenty-eight-year-old daughter afflicted with porphyria, a rare hereditary enzyme deficiency that is nonlife threatening if treated correctly. Fearing that Paula would have some memory loss after recovery, Allende began to write a letter as a way of refreshing her daughter's recollection of family life. But when the state of coma continued and "faced with the overwhelming need to rescue her daughter from the possibility of death, Allende recalls, narrates, or reconstructs those events in her past that project her as Isabel the brave, Isabel the daring, Isabel the rebel, Isabel the risk-taker" (Levine, "Defying" 30). In other words, she draws strength from her past and writes in order to cope with despair. Hence the letters, later turned memoir, make up a tour de force inventory of the author's life and recount, on the one hand, the uniqueness of one Latin American mother and her feminist views, while on the other Allende universalizes motherhood's worst nightmare.

Readers familiar with Latin American literature find in *Paula* a rare combination of mother-narrated feminism in action and a traditional mother caught in devastating maternal angst, a duality consistent with Allende's early married life when she espoused the public life of a hippie (complete with granny dresses, a car "painted like a shower curtain," and the "reputation of a feminist") while at home she honored "the formulas for eternal domestic bliss" (*Paula* 145). Given the absence of a mother-narrated tradition in Western literature as noted previously, Allende's book, filtered through the lens of motherhood, constitutes a literary coup d'état in the mainstream market in which the author holds a strong position. *Paula* is revolutionary in the same way it, too, suggests the mothering/feminist oxymoron discussed earlier. While the circumstance and motive for writing the book are in keeping with a mother's conventional caregiving role, the author's feminist revelations clash with expectations of motherhood within Hispanic tradition. When compared to the portrait presented of a pious, practicing Catholic, and conservative Paula, the doings of her self-searching feminist mother flip the generational relationship on its head. But unlike the Argentine mothers who acted in feminist ways without consciousness of it, in an interview Allende makes self-labeling clear: "I have to be a feminist. I am aware of my gender; I am aware of the fact that being born a woman is a handicap in most parts of the world" ("Writing" 359). Both for its feminist and mother-narrated perspective, *Paula* respectively challenges family and literary norms.

We learn in *Paula* that the author's early awareness of gender bias at age five (when she was expected to sit up straight and keep her knees together like a lady as she learned to knit, all the while her brothers played in the garden) develops into feminist convictions that seem extravagant and even scandalous to Chilean sobriety (*Paula* 142). Allende's willingness to shock everyone insinuates that she did not mother her children according to the model imposed on her as a child and as expected within her social class. In consonance with this assumption, Allende rejects the myth of matriarchy in Chile as a "fallacy" turned "dogma" (*Paula* 140). Worth quoting here at length, she debunks the popular Chilean credence:

If women have influence, it is only—and then only sometimes—within their home. Men control all the political and economic power, the culture and customs; they proclaim the laws and apply them as they wish, and when social pressures and the legal apparatus are not sufficient to subdue the most rebellious women, the Church steps in with its incontestable patriarchal seal. (*Paula* 140)

Attributing some of the blame on mothers, while at the same time enlight-
ening them, Allende calls for reform: "What is unforgivable, though, is that it is
women who perpetuate and reinforce the system, continuing to raise arrogant
sons and servile daughters. If they would agree to revise the standards, they
could end machismo in one generation" (*Paula* 140). Allende looks to the poor
class at the crux of the explanation for the myth of matriarchy in Chile, but her
observations apply to a way of life across Latin American territories and her
comments about women mostly pertain to mothers—namely, adherence to
"marianismo" or the code of conduct ascribed to the Virgin Mary:[14]

> The men come and go, but the women stay put; they are trees rooted in
> solid ground. Around them revolve their own children and others they
> have taken in; they care for the aged, the ill, the unfortunate—they are
> the axis of the community. In all social classes except the most privi-
> leged, abnegation and hard work are considered the supreme female
> virtue; a spirit of sacrifice is a question of honor; the more one suffers
> for family, the prouder one feels. Women are used to thinking of their
> mate as a foolish child whose every serious fault, from drunkenness to
> domestic violence, they forgive . . . *because he's a man.* (*Paula* 140)

Such cultural insights and authorial commentaries throughout the book,
along with numerous accounts of personal rebellion (including episodes of
extramarital experiences, one where she takes off with a lover to live abroad
without her children; her playing the part of chorus girl, which to her family's
embarrassment aired on television; writing for the first feminist magazine in
Santiago, which published articles on then "unutterable subjects" such as contraceptives, divorce, abortion, and suicide; and providing refuge in her home
to marginal people and aid to the politically prosecuted at great personal risk)
draw a portrait of a subversive woman, a feminist in a provincial Chilean capital of the 1960s, and all of which, given our focus here on feminist mothering,[15] lead the reader to surmise that Allende was an extraordinary model in
the upbringing and identity formation of her children. In making all this
public, Allende may or may not have intentionally presented to a wide Latin
American readership alternate ways of being for women and mothers. At
times willing to unmask body and soul, Allende anchors the memoir in
motherhood and thus successfully renders a literary coup by vesting a
mother's voice with narrative authority.

Would the literary establishment have welcomed *Paula* enthusiastically if
it and not *House of the Spirits* had been Allende's first incursion into book
publishing? Would the meditations of an anguished mother have caught the

attention of the reading public, no matter how universal the nature of the crisis? Indeed it may have been fate that it was not Allende's first book because Western and certainly Latin American literature needed someone to open the way for mother narratives. In this regard, Allende's literary coup turns her into literary foremother—literally mother first, then writer—from whose notoriety other women writers can go on to build a legacy of mother-centered writings. A mother's perspective rings clear when the author fuses cultural and biological production and speaks about literary creation in terms of human reproduction: "It often happens that I don't even know that I am pregnant with another story. And only time and silence allow me to feel the child moving inside—and the voices begin to speak" ("I Remember" 448). The word choice contains a deliberate message at the heart of the "literary coup through mothering" theorized in this chapter. This perhaps unwitting but significant contribution to women writers everywhere is truly in keeping with the spirit of Paula, the daughter, and *Paula* the book, each a creation spawned of the author's foremost identity as mother.

Leaving no doubt about what's supreme in her life, when posed with the question of what she would present as her greatest achievement, Allende responds with one word: "Motherhood." "Not a book?" her interviewer urges. "No, that's not important in the larger scheme of things," Allende elaborates. "People may not read or remember me in a few years. But the memories of my children and my grandchildren, and my love for them, is (sic) what is important for me and how I define myself as a person. It is what justifies my existence" ("I Remember" 461). When Allende started writing *Paula*, her "only goal was to survive; that is the only time that [she has] written something without thinking of a reader" ("Writing" 363). The decision to publish the book after Paula's death as a show of camaraderie with the suffering of humanity, and especially for those who, lacking a cathartic outlet, must cope with the devastating loss of a child, evinces a caregiving act of love true to Allende's calling as a mother first, and fulfills her destiny as a feminist writer second ("Mother's Letter" 401; "I Remember" 448).

FEMINIST, LESBIAN, AND CHICANA MOTHERING: CHERRÍE MORAGA'S *WAITING IN THE WINGS: PORTRAIT OF A QUEER MOTHERHOOD*

Cherríe Moraga's journal-like book is also about a child's life-and-death crisis and of a mother's personal introspection and painful journey. Perhaps, too, because of this mother's lack of control over the survival of her child, like

Allende, Moraga recalls in her writing the power of the dream and spiritual worlds as a way of summoning answers and interpreting the unknown. As central to the book as are the intimacies of conception, pregnancy, birth, the battle to keep her premature son alive and all the mothering that pulled him through to life, health, and growth, pivotal, too, are the journal entries in which Moraga shares her outlook as a lesbian. For example, she reveals that she "had maintained the rigid conviction that lesbians . . . weren't really women. We were women-lovers, a kind of third sex, and definitely not men. Having babies was something 'real' women did—not butches, not girls who knew they were queer since grade school. We were *defenders* of women and children, children we could never fully call our own" (*Waiting* 20). This last statement, which suggests a feminist (woman-centered) and masculine (butch) self-image, leaves a gap that in the process of Moraga's narration will evolve to incorporate her new identity as a biological mother.

Attempting to conceive at age forty seemed a logical milestone for Moraga who describes: mothering a lover's son only to lose him after the breakup of the adults' relationship; mothering young Latina lesbians in her workshops; mothering women hurt by "the rape, the incest, the battering, the betrayals, the alcoholism, the orphanhood"; mothering her own mother whose refrain—"*Men (and women) come and go. All you really got are your children*"—the author takes to heart (*Waiting* 19–21).[16] Moraga surely must have approached her previous mothering stints from a feminist perspective and specifically that of a lesbian rejecting patriarchal dictates. Her conviction to circumvent the norm for "family" by conceiving a child by artificial insemination facilitated by a gay friend and in cohabitation with her lover attests to Moraga's need for creating her own blood kin. This permanent and irrevocable motherhood has more to do with her Chicana than her sexual identity.[17]

Alfredo Mirandé and Evangelina Enríquez have documented the characteristics and importance of the family within the Chicano community, a culture that "places more emphasis on *la familia*," a structure that, unlike its Anglo counterpart, "includes immediate family and extended relatives"; sometimes a few generations may live together under one roof to provide economic and emotional support to each other (106–108). Although universal, the basic family functions of procreation and socialization that permit the transmission of the culture and value of the group commonly become essential and clan-like in groups somehow marginalized by a dominant culture (Mirandé 96–97).

Moraga grew up in a large extended Chicano family that included the concept of *compadrazgo*, a system whereby close "friends are initiated into the family as they become godparents to one's children" and despite their lack of consanguine relations the *comadre* or *compadre* gains a place of honor and will be counted on as a blood relative in time of family crisis (Mirandé 107). Although Moraga's search for self took her "beyond the confines of heterosexual family ties," she has stated that "the need for familia, the knowledge of familia, the capacity to create familia remained and has always informed my relationships and my work as an artist, cultural activist, and teacher" (*Waiting* 17–18). As the following quote reveals, Moraga's sense of family is profoundly rooted in a Mexican, rather than a lesbian, identity:

> I've always experienced my lesbianism as radically different from most white gays and lesbians. For that reason, I have never been a strong proponent of lesbian marriages (although I've officiated at a few), nor particularly passionate about the domestic partnership campaigns for which my white middle-class gay counterparts continue to rigorously fight. No, I've always longed for something cross-generational, something extended . . . something Mexican and familial but without all the cultural constraints. (*Waiting* 18)

The book's essence then—a woman's call to motherhood—has more to do with the inner yearnings of Moraga the Chicana than Moraga the lesbian.

Nonetheless, within the patriarchal Chicano family, Moraga, as lesbian and mother, experiences marginalization differently from her heterosexual Chicana kin. "There are days when I am afraid of life hurting us, the homophobia, the racism," Moraga writes in an entry, "When I hear of my brother . . . asking my sister, 'Was it artificial insemination or did she just get together with some guy?' the harshness in his tone chills me. Is it anger? Fear? What he wants to know is: Who is the father? Where is the man in the picture? The chasm I would have to transverse to have my brother understand who I am is too daunting" (*Waiting* 37). Other judgmental inquiries come from outside the family and are more confrontational, as an incident at the hospital security desk when mother and partner sign in after hours to secure a pass to visit their preemie son:

> "Only immediate family," the young man tells us . . . [referring to her partner Ella]. The same old ritual, the same harassment night after night. Then he can't help himself, and a grin begins to crack the professional façade. "You say you're both the moms!" He eyes his buddies, his co-workers, and the street gang begins to form around us. Oh, they're gonna milk this one for all it's worth. They are very bored. "I didn't know two women could have a baby together." (*Waiting* 75)

"Don't fuck with me tonight, boys," Moraga thinks to herself, and the security guards become the brunt of an explosive answer, her demeanor that of an exhausted and worried mother being detained from seeing her very sick child (*Waiting* 75). A threat to this primordial bond would turn any mother into a raging feminist, a madwoman spilling forth ages-old and boundless anger against men who use their power to deprive women of their children, denying them the right to mother. This is a commonplace experience for lesbian mothers who have lost custody of their children to ex-husbands.[18] Moraga's choice to conceive through artificial insemination guards her from male usurpation of the child and from the scrutiny that comes with adoption.

One lesbian mother who opted for foreign adoption comments on the legal process during which she chose to withhold her sexual identity and keep silent about the existence of a parenting partner:

> While we read daily of mistreated and abused children, children left unattended, given cocaine, starved and locked in rooms by people whose decision to parent never had to pass through the layers of bureaucratic approval, fingerprinting and paperwork we have faced, I was required to convince half a dozen state agencies, the governments of three countries, and the Family Court of a large city, that my home is a fit place to raise a child. I needed letters and affidavits certifying my moral character, my financial assets, and my ability to love a child. (Bruckner 36)

This woman's self-inflicted repression and silencing of her true identity in order to be allowed the chance to be a mother speak of personal sacrifice characteristic of motherhood and of the stifling nature of patriarchy for nonconformists. Her keeping quiet about her sexuality is common among Latinas. "To be a lesbian means to be forever measuring the impact of our truth on other people," points out Chilean writer Mariana Romo-Carmona (xxiv). Fear of losing custody of a child or child support, alienating family and friends, losing a job, or being harmed by an ex-husband may push lesbians to live in anonymity and keep silent about their experiences, hence the importance of publications such as *Waiting in the Wings: Portrait of a Queer Motherhood*.

Rare for its multilayered—feminist, lesbian, maternal—focus, Moraga's book helps fill a twofold dearth of mother-narrated writing and Latina lesbian narratives.[19] In *The Mother/Daughter Plot*, Marianne Hirsch concentrates on "texts of women writers who write within [an] Euro-American patriarchal context of discourses and representation and, more specifically, within a sex-gender system which . . . identifies writing as masculine and insists on the incompatibility of creativity and procreativity" (Hirsch 8). As feminist critics have pointed out, often "female plots . . . attempt to subvert the constraint of dominant patterns by means of various 'emancipatory strategies'" that must be recognized as a writing of "resistance, revision and emancipation" (Hirsch 8). Whether the masculine attributes that Moraga has admitted are socially assigned or self-imposed, the lesbian may be freer to write in emancipatory ways and thus challenge mainstream literary attitudes with nonorthodox topics and discourse. Moraga presents a different kind of "family romance," a nonheterosexual familial structure, one outright not acceptable in the social reality of most members of either Latino and Anglo communities (Hirsch 9).

If true enough for heterosexual women, it must also be so for lesbians that "feminist mothering involves coming up against social expectations for how to be a mother that lack appropriateness, truth, or even meaning for women. Each woman is left with the potentially creative task of resisting and transforming the socially dominant ideas of motherhood in order to fashion her own truth of the experience" (Reddy, Roth, and Sheldon 313–314). For a woman, a feminist perspective involves self-awareness about what it means to be "female" within one's particular community. And if a feminist is someone who shows resistance to cultural constraints that limit women's freedom, can a lesbian not be a feminist?

In *Paula*, Allende tells of a life often at odds with her surroundings, her pushing the limits of Chilean society toward "emancipatory strategies," and in interviews she has voiced feeling much like a foreigner in the United States, which is why she identifies with the writing of minority women.[20] Gloria Anzaldúa, a Texas-born lesbian Chicana of Indian ancestry, recognized that like outsiders the mestiza and nonheterosexual women occupy the margins of Anglo society and hence their struggle is a feminist one (Anzaldúa 84). Cherríe Moraga, as lesbian Chicana, shares Anzaldúa's experience of Anglo/Latino "borderlands," a term that conceptualizes a minority space and subculture in which its inhabitants both espouse and reject certain aspects of two cultures, one nationally dominant and the other usually ancestral.

Latina lesbians who admit a bicultural identity also perceive themselves judged as double outcasts: "In our countries and communities of origin, many of us are seen as foreigners because we speak another language and have developed some different cultural ways. As lesbians, we are also foreigners. Our sexuality and lifestyle are regarded as abnormal, and most people would prefer that we did not exist" (Romo-Carmona xxii). Moraga's decision to birth a child turned into another type of journey with new "borders," in which the lesbian mother meets with frustrations and restrictions largely outside her Chicano family. Her women kin prove a great source of support. "I knew as I held my lover's and my sister's hand in the grip of labor that this was what I understood as hogar, sustenance; that this is how a woman should always give birth, surrounded by women," Moraga writes, "And how lucky I was to be a lesbian, to have it all—mother, sister, lover—that family of women to see me into motherhood" (*Waiting* 54).

Still, biological reproduction and lesbianism—a contradiction in terms for some—can produce adverse reactions within the queer community as well as a woman's own family. At a time when a lesbian mother needs support from close friends or kin, she may struggle to defend and define herself within the new chosen role. One Latina lesbian who decided to take her pregnancy to term admits her ignorance about conception and goes on to tell of her eventual estrangement from her gay friends who consider motherhood a treasonous act.[21] For this woman, "feminist mothering" her biological daughter meant battling with heterosexual as well as homosexual constraints in a community where both straights and gays questioned her morals, standards, and beliefs, and for that reason took issue with her ability and right to mother a child (Ramos 205).

Moraga's writing on queer motherhood leaves an imprint in the world. Both text and child are self-expressions, both a body created for posterity, both a reflection of this feminist, lesbian, Chicana, mother and writer with a particular interest in representing the powerless and voiceless in society. She relishes the idea of instilling in her son the dignity of his "rich copper-rose color" (99) because her "colored boy" (97) has changed her and her writing, enriched both and challenged both: "I will never write the same. . . . With the appearance of Rafael in my life, I can never return to the writer I once was. Not because of the time constraints, which are awesome, but because my soul is never completely empty in the same way" (*Waiting* 95). Moraga makes clear that mothering informs her craft as much as her feminist convictions imbue her writing about the intimacies of the lesbian maternal body. Besides making a powerful contribution to a much needed corpus of mother-centered writing by Latinas, *Waiting in the Wings: Portrait of a Queer Motherhood* deals its own subversive coup with a literary incursion that undermines patriarchal norms and makes the voice of a Chicana lesbian mother available to dominant and minority cultures alike.

LATINA DAUGHTERS SOCIALIZING THEIR MOTHERS IN FEMINIST WAYS

The women highlighted so far stand out as exceptional in their respective countries and communities. They challenge patriarchal dictates openly as individuals or as part of a group and show their commitment to motherhood in native cultures plagued by the excesses and abuses of men. Latina fiction regularly features the theme of women's powerlessness. Daughters typically narrate to reject oppression and inject female resistance into the family, a stance that often leads to leaving home. The dearth of mother-narrated writing among Latinas makes sense in light of Garner's findings that a mother's immigrant status, one common trait among the minority women autobiographers that she studied, situates her "outside the dominant culture" (86). Since in real life the mothers of many Latina writers are immigrants or somehow marginal in mainstream society, it follows that in their fiction daughters tend to *write/right* the mother's story along with their own (Davies 56; emphasis added). Precisely because most Latinas grow up as witnesses to a mother's lack of power, a daughter's writings often expose, condemn, and redress the inequities of a patriarchal social order, hence the need to "write" their mother's and grandmother's stories for them, as well as to set those stories "right" or symbolically grant them due "rights."

For many Latinas who have endured alongside mothers and grandmothers subjugation from male kin, it is difficult to narrate from a mother's perspective, a voice traditionally deprived of authority. What better example of a patriarch's negation of a mother's rights than in Judith Ortiz Cofer's novel *The Line of the Sun* in which the despotic Juan Santacruz gives away his youngest child to his American employer and his barren wife. Symbolically, in the novel the protest of the child's biological Puerto Rican mother is not heard. She remains silent, nameless and unseen, secluded in her room where her other children attend to her, mother her, and worry about the unknown illness that causes "Mamá" prolonged bleeding and weakness. Given a culture that permits a patriarch's travesties to routinely strip mothers of their voice, rights, and dignity, it is no wonder that Hispanic women's literature lacks a tradition of mother-narrated works.

In narrating the oppression of their elders, the younger generation of Latinas presents a feminist posture, one in which they may be the ones to mother or instruct female kin. In this role they introduce possibilities for changing traditions that stifle women's autonomy. The daughter/narrator of Judith Ortiz Cofer's *The Meaning of Consuelo* tells the story of her Puerto Rican family, all the while rejecting the role of her suffering mother who is loyal to an unfaithful husband because that is what a decent woman in her society should do for the sake of the children. Although the mother has followed every gender code expected of her, she is no happier for it. Consuelo's decision to leave Puerto Rico after high school graduation and settle in mainland United States suggests that her generation of English-speaking young women is not willing to endure their mothers' fate on the island. For them, abandoning their birth family is a viable option for escaping a tradition that traps women in oppressive marriages.

In contemporary literature, education as a path to women's liberation serves Latina daughters as a ticket out of oppressive homes. However, obstacles abound. In the play *Simply María or the American Dream*, by Josefina López, when the father prohibits his daughter from accepting a four-year college scholarship, Carmen, the mother, makes a plea more to persuade her daughter's conformity than to coax her husband into granting María's wishes:

> Carmen: Ricardo, why don't you even let her try, ¿por favor? . . . María don't cry. Don't be angry at us either, and try to understand us. ¡M'ija! We are doing this for you. We don't want you to get hurt. You want too much; that's not realistic. You are a Mexican woman, and that's that. You can't change that. You are different from other women. Try to accept that. Women need to get married, (sic) they are no good without men. (130)

Like Consuelo in Ortiz Cofer's novel, María has been a model child and daughter, but shows the insight to reject those constraints of her native culture that render her mother powerless. In choosing education over the traditional role designated to females in her native culture, María provides an example for social change within her home and community. Increasingly, Latina writers portray daughter/protagonists who are conscious of their feminist stance vis-à-vis a family and community that judge them negatively or spurn them altogether. Yet the desire to avoid repetition of the mother's life is worth the risk of rejection and, in doing so, Latina daughters put themselves forth as models for other females in the immediate household or ethnic group.

In another play, *Shadow of a Man*, by Cherríe Moraga, the older daughter, Leticia, a college student, not only acts as mother to her battered mother, but takes on the role of outspoken Chicana feminist. When the mother laments her daughter's nonchalant relinquishing of her virginity, Leticia comments: "I was tired of carrying it around . . . that weight of being a woman with a prize. Walking around with that special secret, that valuable commodity, waiting for some lucky guy to put his name on it. I wanted it to be worthless, Mamá. Don't you see? Not for me to be worthless, but to know that my worth had nothing to do with it" (45). The implication for feminist mothering, once college-educated Latinas become mothers themselves, must be read between the lines.

The Dominican-born but American-educated sisters in Julia Alvarez's *How the García Girls Lost Their Accent* also model most immediately for their mother and for women kin back on the island the possibility of a feminist posture. "Back in their adolescent days during summer visits, the four girls used to shock their Island cousins with stories of their escapades in the States" (7). Among them, the sisters have destabilized the parents' sense of cultural tradition and propriety with misdemeanors that include going out unchaperoned, smoking marihuana, traveling alone, having lovers, and, once married, getting divorced. Exile in the United States had begun to transform the mother also: "She did not want to go back to the old country where, de la Torre or not, she was only a wife and a mother (and a failed one at that, since she had never provided the required son). Better an independent nobody than a high-class houseslave" (144). As one daughter observes about her mother's changing attitude, although not condoning unconventionality, apparently her elder had softened about patriarchal dictates and adopted a feminist perspective: "Recently, she had begun spreading her wings, taking adult courses in real estate and international economics and business management, dreaming of a bigger-than-family-size life for herself. She still did lip service to the old ways, while herself nibbling away at forbidden fruit" (116). Raising four daughters in the United States during the 1960s push for women's liberation certainly marks this mother.

When it comes to daughters changing mothers' attitudes or socializing them, in *Memory Mambo* Cuban-American Achy Obejas presents one mother who, once widowed, embraces her rebellious daughter's feminist ways and the illegitimate child she births:

> Suddenly, Tía Celia shone with pride about her daughter, the previously problematic child who had often embarrassed her. . . . And her crazy independence, her sexuality and vigor, all these became medals of honor. To hear Tía Celia, Pauli was a kind of new woman, a pioneer who did not need men or approval. And she was the first to defend Pauli's right to silence about the identity of Rosa's father. (94)

Implied in the mother's change of heart about Pauli is a preexistent battleground where a young Latina's push for autonomy created a strained mother/daughter relationship, a conflict common across borders and literatures. Simone James Alexander observes that in Afro-Caribbean literature daughters may regard the mother as an adversary for imposing patriarchal rules reminiscent of the colonizer, the powerful mother-master over the powerless, colonized girl (45–47). Implied, too, in all the examples of Latina fiction previously mentioned, is the maternal figure that not only suffers "physically, emotionally, socially, [and] economically" at the hands of male kin, but who "must *be* suffered, or endured" by daughters who resist the patriarchal socialization that their mothers try to impose (McKnight 3). As observed here, many daughters depicted in Latina writing are turning the tables on their mothers by socializing or at least steering them to accept feminist ways of being. With different degrees of success, Latina daughters are using feminist convictions to win over their mothers as advocates for change in the lives of women in their families and communities.

CONCLUSION

This chapter has proposed that the politically charged term *coup*, typically related to the endeavors of men, applies to women's mothering feats, which frequently undermine the status quo and effect social change. In the case of the mothers of Plaza de Mayo, their subversive stance against the institutions of power in Argentina was radical within the dictatorial regime in which they operated. The mothers' public challenge that authorities answer to them about their disappeared children constituted a nonviolent coup. The women's agenda became the focus of national news, which eventually reverberated abroad and forced the Argentine government to acknowledge wrongdoing. Without a feminist label, mothers in distress mothered others like themselves and managed to build a network of women whose resilient campaign for human rights set an internationally recognized precedent.

As a grieving mother, Chilean Isabel Allende deals her own coup within the highly patriarchal literary establishment by inserting a mother's perspective as focus of her first nonfiction book, *Paula*. This bold narrative and feminist move needs recognition because, despite the number of popular women authors in Latin America, the dearth of mother-centered writing is a stark reality that needs to be redressed. With *Paula*, Allende, a best-selling and respected author worldwide, opened the way for other writers to specifically appropriate a mother's experience as worthy of inscription into the body of contemporary Latin American literature. In a similar vein, Mexican-American Cherríe Moraga incorporates her testimony as a lesbian mother into North American literary ranks and sets a precedent for other minority women. Her brave act to narrate the experience of motherhood from a lesbian perspective is unusual and daring, given the patriarchal nature of her Chicano birth family, the homophobic attitudes of society at large, and the reproductive prejudices of some in the queer community. If, as noted earlier, mother-centered writing is uncommon for any heterosexual, white, feminist, American woman, its production by a lesbian Chicana of color constitutes a revolutionary act, a literary coup and a challenge to the convictions of the hetero and homosexual communities.

Latinas writing fiction today commonly present daughters who appropriate a feminist and nurturing attitude toward their female elders, as they themselves strive for personal autonomy. The daily coups these young Latinas stage within family life introduce feminist ways of being that, while modeling options for other women, may culminate in the bold move to leave an oppressive home. The pursuit of educational goals presents a good, if not always unchallenged, reason to set tradition aside and relocate from the native community. In fiction, daughters are increasingly successful in bringing the mother around to appreciate life from their point of view. In winning their mothers over, daughters alleviate the strained relationship, recuperate or strengthen the mother/daughter bond so important in the Hispanic family, and gain a mother/comrade in their struggle for self-sufficiency. Although a Latina mother may not herself suddenly embrace or want liberation from tradition, acceptance and understanding of her daughter's life choices mean that the mother has been convinced to value new options for women. Given the influence of Latina mothers in the lives of their daughters, this is a significant step toward female autonomy in the Hispanic household and community. Intentionally or not, all these coups are rooted in the convictions of feminist mothering and promote different, but equally worthwhile, aspects of social change for diverse populations of Hispanic women.

NOTES

1. For mothers' initiatives during the dictatorship, see the section "Madres" in "Women and Democracy in Argentina" by María del Carmen Feijoó and Marcela María Alejandra Nari.

2. I use the terms *Latina* to refer to a writer born or raised in the United State with English as the dominant language, and *Latin American* to denote those born or raised in Mexico, Central, or South America who are native speakers of Spanish. My use of *Hispanic* is meant to denote inclusion of both groups (Latinas and Latin Americans) and serves as indicator that a common cultural heritage binds them in sisterhood.

3. Patriarchy is rooted in every aspect of Argentine culture as reflected in its dictators, the military class, and the indomitable *gaucho*, the cowboy of its vast plains or *pampa*. "Feminism was a foreign doctrine that threatened the core of Argentine's 'spiritual Catholicism,'" a belief that systematically had been ingrained

in the population since 1944 when the government "carried on a campaign for 'moral purity' involving the censorship even of radio soap operas and tango lyrics, and the banning of the sales of contraceptives and of newspaper advertisements for Uruguayan divorce lawyers" (Carlson 184–185). Carlson explains that in a political move to secure stronger support for his party, Juan Domingo Perón granted women the right to vote in 1947.

4. One example is the case of Luisa Bemberg, who, born into a wealthy family, followed the traditions imposed by her society. She married and birthed four children. Later she ended a ten-year marriage, fought to legally regain her maiden name, and, in her forties, launched a career, first in theater and later as filmmaker, which she financed herself because the industry showed little interest in the feminist issues and perspective of her productions. Among her most popular films are: *Miss Mary, Camila,* and *I, the Worst of All,* about the life of a seventeenth-century Mexican nun and intellectual, Sor Juana Inés de la Cruz.

5. In *Mujeres y feminismo en la Argentina,* Leonor Calvera records how UFA (La Unión Feminista Argentina) began and describes its drastic curtailment during the dictatorship (70). See also the section "The Feminists" in Feijoó and Nari's "Women and Democracy in Argentina," 115– 116.

6. The novel was originally published in Spanish in 1981 with the title *Conversación al sur.*

7. For a history of the Mothers of Plaza de Mayo narrated by one of its founders, Hebe de Bonafini, see the association's Web site: http://www.madres.org/.

8. As defined on http://www.wordiq.com/definition/Feminism.

9. See "Living the Legacy: The Women's Rights Movement 1848–1998" by Bonnie Eisenberg and Mary Ruthsdotter, the National Women's History Project, 1998. http://www.legacy98.org/move-hist.html.

10. That scale of female-organized, mother-centered public protest in the Southern Cone did not occur in the Caribbean despite equally repressive autocratic governments in the Dominican Republic and Cuba.

11. In Chile, the "arpilleristas" were mothers who met under the auspices of the Catholic Church to hand-stitch wall hangings or "arpilleras" (stemming from the Chilean word for burlap), that depicted and condemned police detentions during the authoritarian regime of General Augusto Pinochet (1973–1989). Chilean women in such groups shared a common experience from which they drew moral as well as economic support to alleviate the crisis that followed loss of a family member (Agosín viii, 11–12).

12. Phrase borrowed from Chilean writer Diamela Eltit, who has described marginal areas of social confinement: brothels, psychiatric hospitals, flop houses, jails, and so forth as "zones of 'pain." See page 73, note 3, of Nelly Richard's *Margins and Institutions: Art in Chile Since 1973.*

13. The Spanish seventh edition (Barcelona: Plaza & Janés, 1995) features a head shot of Paula that takes up the entire jacket cover.

14. For an analysis of the tradition-inspired Hispanic gender code of conduct and the characteristics to which Allende refers, see Evelyn P. Steven, "Marianismo: The Other Face of Machismo in Latina America," *Female and Male in Latin America*, ed. Ann Pescatello (University of Pittsburg Press, 1979) 89–101.

15. For an in-depth discussion of Allende's feminism in real life and in her fiction, see Linda Gould Levine's article, "Weaving Life into Fiction."

16. See Sandra Cisneros' story "Woman Hollering Creek" in the collection with the same title for an example of Chicanas (possibly lesbian, but definitely feminist) protecting an abused mother.

17. As politically engaged Mexican Americans began to identify with the struggles of the black civil rights movement in the 1960s, activists appropriated the term *Chicano* (male) and *Chicana* (female) to connect them with their indigenous ancestry. *Mexican—mexicano* in Spanish—originally referred to people who spoke Nahualt. The Aztecs, the largest of this group, were often called mexicanos, which phonetically was pronounced *mechicano* in Nahualt (Fisher 307; Forbes 18, emphasis added).

18. See the story of Mariana Romo-Carmona in Juanita Ramos's anthology *Compañeras: Latina Lesbians*, 185–193.

19. The preface and introduction to *Compañeras: Latina Lesbians* document the difficulty in compiling and publishing Latina voices given the personally and culturally imposed isolation Latina lesbians commonly live in: "So many times we don't know of any other women who feel about women the way we do. Our isolation is compounded by the fact that society, our families and the Church are constantly telling us that women who identify with other women in a sexual or loving manner are either sick, sinners or both (Ramos xiii).

20. See page 209 of Allende's interview with Jacqueline Cruz et al. in *Conversations with Isabel Allende*.

21. For Margarita's testimony about the rejection she experienced from the gay community, see the interview, "Lesbian Mothers: A Conversation with Cenen, Margarita and Carmen," conducted by Juanita Ramos in *Compañeras* (195–196, 207–208).

REFERENCES

Agosín, Marjorie. *Scraps of Life: Chilean Arpilleras—Chilean Women and the Pinochet Dictatorship*. Trenton, NJ: Red Sea Press, 1987.

Alexander, Simone A. James. *Mother Imagery in the Novels of Afro-Caribbean Women*. Columbia: University of Missouri Press, 2001.

Allende, Isabel. "I Remember Emotions, I Remember Moments." Interview with Virginia Invernizzi (1999). *Conversations with Isabel Allende.* Ed. and Trans. John Rodden. Austin: University of Texas Press, 1999. 439–461.

———. "Listen Paula." Interview with Alfred Starkmann (1995). *Conversations with Isabel Allende.* Ed. and Trans. John Rodden. Austin: University of Texas Press, 1999. 403–408.

———. "A Mother's Letter of Loss." Interview with Rosa Pinol (1995). *Conversations with Isabel Allende.* Ed. and Trans. John Rodden. Austin: University of Texas Press, 1999. 399–401.

———. *Paula.* Trans. Margaret Sayers Peden. New York: HarperCollins, 1995.

———. "A Snipper between Cultures." Interview with Jacqueline Cruz et al. *Conversations with Isabel Allende.* Ed. and Trans. John Rodden. Austin: University of Texas Press, 1999. 203–222.

———. "Writing to Exorcise the Demons." Interview with Farhat Iftekharuddin (1997). *Conversations with Isalbe Allende.* Ed. John Rodden. Austin: University of Texas Press, 1999. 351–363.

Alvarez, Julia. *How the García Girls Lost Their Accents.* New York: Plume, 1992.

Anzaldúa, Gloria. *Borderlands/La Frontera: The New Mestiza.* San Francisco: Aunt Lute, 1987.

Bruckner, Sarah. "Two Moms, Two Kids, and a Dog." *Mother Journeys: Feminists Write about Mothering.* Ed. Maureen T. Reddy, Martha Roth, and Amy Sheldon. Minneapolis: Spinsters Ink, 1994. 35–46.

Calvera, Leonor. *Mujeres y feminismo en la Argentina.* Buenos Aires: Grupo Editor Latinoamericano, 1990.

Carlson, Marifran. *¡Feminismo! The Woman's Movement in Argentina from Its Beginnings to Eva Perón.* Chicago: Academy Chicago, 1988.

Cisneros, Sandra. *Woman Hollering Creek and Other Stories.* New York: Vintage, 1992.

Davies, Carol Boyce. "Mother Right/Write Revisited: *Beloved* and *Dessa Rose* and the Construction of Motherhood in Black Women's Fiction." *Narrating Mothers: Theorizing Maternal Subjectivities.* Ed. Brenda O. Daly and Maureen T. Reddy. Knoxville: University of Tennessee Press, 1991. 44–57.

Feijoó, María del Carmen, and Marcela María Alejandra Nari. "Women and Democracy in Argentina." *The Women's Movement in Latin America: Participation and Democracy.* Ed. Jane S. Jaquette. Boulder: Westview, 1994. 109–129.

Fisher, Dexter, ed. *The Third Woman: Minority Women Writers of the United States.* Boston: Houghton Mifflin, 1980.

Forbes, Jack D. *Aztecs del Norte: The Chicanos of Aztlan.* Greenwich: Fawcett, 1973.

Garner, Shirley Nelson. "Constructing the Mother: Contemporary Psychoanalytic Theorists and Women Autobiographers." *Narrating Mothers: Theorizing*

Maternal Subjectivities. Ed. Brenda O. Daly and Maureen T. Reddy. Knoxville: University of Tennessee Press, 1991. 76–93.

Hirsch, Marianne. *The Mother/Daughter Plot: Narrative, Psychoanalysis, Feminism.* Bloomington: Indiana University Press, 1989.

King, John. "María Luisa Bemberg and Argentine Culture." *An Argentine Passion: María Luisa Bemberg and her Films.* Ed. John King, Sheila Whitaker, and Rosa Bosch. London: Verso, 2000.

Levine, Linda Gould. "Defying the Pillar of Salt: Isabel Allende's *Paula.*" *Latin American Literary Review* 30 (2002): 29–50.

———. "Weaving Life into Fiction." *Isabel Allende.* New York: Twayne, 2002. 1–17.

López, Josefina. *Simply María or The American Dream. Shattering the Myth: Plays by Hispanic Women.* Ed. Denise Chávez and Linda Feyder. Houston: Arte Público Press, 1992. 113–141.

McKnight, Natalie J. *Suffering Mothers in Mid-Victorian Novels.* New York: St. Martin's Press, 1997.

Mirandé, Alfredo, and Evangelina Enríquez. *La Chicana: The Mexican-American Woman.* Chicago: University of Chicago Press, 1981.

Moraga, Cherríe. *Shadow of a Man. Shattering the Myth: Plays by Hispanic Women.* Ed. Denise Chávez and Linda Feyder. Houston: Arte Público Press, 1992. 9–49.

———. *Waiting in the Wings: Portrait of a Queer Motherhood.* Ithaca: Firebrand, 1997.

Obejas, Achy. *Memory Mambo.* Pittsburgh: Cleiss, 1996.

Ortiz Cofer, Judith. *The Meaning of Consuelo.* New York: Farrar, Straus and Giroux, 2003.

———. *The Line of the Sun.* Athens: University of Georgia Press, 1989.

Ramos, Juanita. *Compañeras: Latina Lesbians.* New York: Routledge, 1994.

Reddy, Maureen T., Martha Roth, and Amy Sheldon. "Epilogue." *Mother Journeys: Feminists Write About Mothering.* Minneapolis: Spinsters Ink, 1994. 313–314.

Richard, Nelly. *Margins and Institutions: Art in Chile Since 1973.* Melbourne: Art & Text, 1986.

Romo-Carmona, Mariana. "Introduction." *Compañeras: Latina Lesbians.* Ed. Juanita Ramos. New York: Routledge, 1994. xx–xxix.

Stevens, Evelyn P. "Marianismo: The Other Face of Machismo in Latina America." *Female and Male in Latin America.* Ed. Ann Pescatello. Pittsburg: University of Pittsburg Press, 1979. 89–101.

Traba, Marta. *Mothers and Shadows.* Translated by Jo Labanyi. London: Readers International, 1986. Originally published as *Conversación al sur* (Mexico, D.F.: Siglo Veintiuno, 1981).

CHAPTER FOURTEEN

Maternal Activism

How Feminist Is It?

JANICE NATHANSON

WHEN CELENE KRAUSS published "Women and Toxic Waste and Protest: Race, Class and Gender as Resources of Resistance" in 1993, her voice was added to a growing number of feminists and social activists who saw motherhood as a starting point and resource for effecting social change. In her study, Krauss unveils how working-class women and women of color—all mothers—take on the issue of toxic waste at the grassroots level. In the process, they erode barriers between the private and public realms, they resist systemic racial and class discrimination, and they become "empowered citizens" (Ackelsberg 391), mobilizing change both within their communities and in their own agency. Deeply concerned about the health of their children and families, the impetus for activism among these women is motherhood. Their approach to toxic waste is not technical, but political. It is rooted in the feminist view that what has been personal, invisible, and unimportant is profoundly political. For these mothers, the personal involves the "levers which set in motion a political process, shaping the language and oppositional meanings that emerge, and providing resources for social change" (Krauss 249).

Just a few decades earlier, motherhood as a feminist issue was radically different. As women grappled with sexism, oppression, male dominance, and patriarchy, maternity was largely rejected. In *The Second Sex* (1989), Simone de Beauvoir attacked marriage and motherhood as the barrier to freedom and transcendence. In *The Feminine Mystique* (1963), Betty Friedan vilified work in the home as the cause of women's depression and addictions. As she put it, women "can find identity only in work that is of real value to society—work for which, usually, our society pays" (346). Shulamith Firestone called reproduction a "'bitter trap' for women" (qtd. in Scott 1058), and motherhood a "prime barrier to women's equality. . . . If women would resist the social and psychological pull toward maternity, we could enjoy some of the freedoms and achievements of men" (qtd. in Hirsch 355). Robin Morgan declared that "since the patriarchy commanded women to be mothers (the thesis), we had to rebel with our own polarity and declare motherhood a reactionary cabal (antithesis)" (qtd. in Hirsch 355). For the most part, feminists were protesting the private/public split and looking to end dominance by negating essentialist conceptions. Motherhood smacked painfully of the very source of women's oppression.

Yet a new reality is taking root. Increasingly, motherhood has become politicized, as legions of women in communities across the country, the continent, and the world are joining forces, as mothers, to create social change around the issues that affect them most: health, education, crime, housing, sanitation, safety, drunk driving, drugs, and kidnapping, to name just a few. Most often, mothers fight battles in their own communities, though at times with profound implications for inequities on a more global basis. And the phenomenon is not new. Christine Woyshner says that "the origins of political motherhood can be found after the American Revolution . . . when the Founding Fathers were faced with a central concern regarding the education of the citizenry. . . . One popular solution was the notion that it would become women's responsibility . . . to educate the nation's sons for the role of virtuous citizen. Since that time, the notion of mother as civic guardian has remained" (66). What is new, however, is that the struggle to generate change on behalf of families and communities is now a feminist focus. Nonetheless, feminism is rarely the motivation for maternal activism. In Nancy Naples's (6: 441–463) study on activist mothers from low-income neighborhoods, most women describe their activism simply as a means of improving the lives of their families and neighbors.

Does maternal activism, in fact, promote a feminist agenda? This chapter argues that it does on three counts. First, it exemplifies the very core of feminist ideology—that the personal is political. Second, it helps to negate essentialist notions of motherhood by transforming views of it from an "isolating or individualized experience . . . (to) . . . the inspiration for and foundation of visions of large-scale social change" (Orleck 3). And third, whether intended or not, it upsets traditional gender and power relations.

What is maternal activism anyway? One definition holds that it is "care for children beyond the nuclear family and the relationship between that care, motherhood and community action" (Naples, qtd. in Abrahams 770). Another claims it is the "means by which women have sought to regain control over their lives and the lives of their children" (Orleck 4). In African American culture, activist mothering speaks to an "othermother" tradition, where self, family, and communities boundaries are blurred in the struggle against racism (Collins, qtd. in Abrahams 770). In most cases, mothers mobilize because they perceive inequities or threats to the well-being of their families. And they do so in all parts of the world. In the Soviet Union, the Soldiers' Mothers Committee demonstrated and held hunger strikes to protest hazing practices inflicted on their sons and to call for military reform (Hrycak 68). In Argentina, Mothers of the Plaza de Mayo demanded that those who tortured and murdered their children in the Dirty War be prosecuted. Maternal activism crosses racial, ethnic, and socioeconomic groups, and is as prevalent among lower-class, racially diverse communities as among middle- and upper-class mothers, though the nature of the activism varies. Nor does maternal activism pertain only to radical forms of protest in response to crisis. It applies equally to everyday activities that embrace the needs of children beyond the nuclear family.

THE PERSONAL IS POLITICAL

No matter the issue addressed, the location or time of struggle, or the scope of effort, activist mothers are invoking one of feminism's most cherished ideologies—the "personal is political." The environmental justice movement, for example, is largely a product of mostly poor women and women of color petrified by the devastating effects of toxic waste dumping, pesticide runoff, and deforestation on their families. One of the most celebrated examples, Love Canal, is nothing short of a woman and a community transformed. Underlying housewife Lois Gibb's unanticipated foray into the deepest bowels of dirty politics was the personal horror of watching her children develop debilitating diseases that made no sense. In taking action, she made the personal political.

For activist mothers, the recognition that "personal troubles are politically constituted" (Naples 449) is central to their mobilization. Perhaps nowhere is the personal is political ideology more salient than in the recognition that while motherhood may be the common thread of women's struggle, diverse racial-ethnic backgrounds and class differences dictate what constitutes the personal, and inform interpretations of the problems and political strategies to be adopted in the context of individual social locations. Issues such as inadequate health care, unsafe housing, and discriminatory educational prac- tices, for example, are more likely to be threats to racially diverse, lower- income communities than to middle-class, white families. Mothers whose lives are marked by racism and poverty "learn to mother as activists fighting in their homes and communities against the debilitating and demoralizing effects of oppression" (Naples 457). Among black mothers, "community activism is driven by their shared, gendered experiences of slavery and has developed primarily out of their mothering practices . . . a transplantation of traditional African principles" (McDonald 776). In low-income communities, sharing of resources to ensure survival—such as welcoming strangers and those in need into their homes—is common among some racial-ethnic groups, and a practice brought into activist mothering. For Latinas, commu- nity work often begins with motherhood because in this culture, such work constitutes good mothering. As one study participant states, "The church and the school are the two most important things in (my children's') lives. . . . It's where they get all of their values, all of their ability to judge, and their strength. If I didn't support those two institutions . . . I don't know what kind of mother I'd be" (Abrahams 780). Further, repertoires of resistance are dic- tated by the nature of the challenge but also by the unique racial, class, and sexist oppression in a given community. Even on issues salient to all groups, differences emerge. Patsy Ruth Oliver, a black homemaker who rose in protest when toxics systematically sickened and killed residents of Carver Terrace, Texas, says that it was not the soil that distinguished her situation from Love Canal. "'If there's one thing I know,' she said, 'it's racism. I have a master's degree in Jim Crow'" (qtd. in Jetter 49). Like others whose fight is issue-specific but located in broader social inequities, Oliver faced not only sexism and class discrimination. "For the environmental movement was white, and she was a Black woman from the South. 'Sometimes I was all alone,' Oliver said. 'Sometimes I looked like a fly in a glass of buttermilk'" (qtd. in Jetter 50).

Krauss's research is an excellent depiction of this point. In exploring the experiences of white, black and native working-class women in their struggle against toxic waste, she begins from the point of view of the subject, and looks at social and cultural influences on diverse populations as a starting point for understanding distinct perspectives. "Blue collar women of differing backgrounds interpret their experiences of toxic waste problem within a con- text of their particular cultural histories. They start from different assump- tions and arrive at concepts of environmental justice that reflect broader experiences of class and race" (Krauss 249). For white working-class women, theirs is a story of an abiding belief in the existing political system, only to be disillusioned by its lack of response. "Their politicization is rooted in the deep sense of violation, betrayal and hurt they feel, when they find out their government will not protect their families" (Krauss 254). Their protest becomes a resisting of power inequities, a revised view of class exploitation, and a reinforcement of democratic principles. African American women, on the other hand, begin with a distrust in a system that has always betrayed them, and see toxic waste as environmental racism. Their primary goal is to change the discourse by addressing discrete issues in the context of racial discrimination. Their solution for environmental change is civil rights. The issue of toxic waste is a call to address racism as a whole. For Native American women, by contrast, environmental racism is compounded by a "genocidal analysis, rooted in the Native American cultural identification, the experience of colonialism, and the immanent endangerment of their culture" (Krauss 257). Here, too, women have little faith in the system. For them, toxic waste is a violation of their land and a negation of their cultural values.

In many instances of struggle, the personal begins with the most basic of perceived inequities, and ends by redefining the political landscape around much larger, systemic discrimination. Such was the case of Operation Life (OL). In 1969 Las Vegas, an underclass of black, uneducated women, led by hotel maid and mother of seven Ruby Duncan, asked simply that their children have shoes and clothing for school. The women used every means of protest possible: marches, rallies, sit-ins, threats, consultation, media, arrests, and class-action suits. What resulted was a twenty-year fight between welfare mothers and officials at every level of government that culminated in political and economic empowerment for poor mothers. By the late 1970s, Operation Life operated a medical clinic, day-care center, senior citizen housing, after-school program, teen recreation center, and job-training programs for women. It also brought millions of dollars in private and government funding to its projects. Most significant, OL reframed what popular rhetoric had labeled the welfare queen—"the 'irresponsible' welfare mother and her 'criminal' progeny" (Orleck 104) out to sap the system and sabotage the American dream. The results of the struggle were stunning. Many of the women involved ended their dependence on welfare. Ruby Duncan became a national figure, leading a delegation at the national Democratic Convention and advising government on welfare reform. Her ideology epitomizes the personal is political philosophy. "No one is more expert on the problems of women and children living in poverty than poor mothers themselves. . . . We can never hope to solve the problems of poverty . . . until we begin to listen to the solutions that poor mothers propose" (qtd. in Orleck 116).

MATERNAL ACTIVISM AND ESSENTIALISM

Despite the abiding feminist belief that issues relegated to the private domain must live in the public, the very fact that motherhood is an impetus for activism triggers cries of essentialism from many feminists. It is hardly surprising. For until the Second Wave of the feminist movement, the image of mothers had been firmly entrenched in public ideology as "apolitical, isolated with their children in a world of pure emotion, far removed from the welter of politics and social struggle" (Orleck 3). Underlying this view is that biology for women is destiny, an idea that dates back to the Victorian era's doctrine of separate spheres. Predicated on the notion of nature, this doctrine held that men and women are essentially different, and must therefore occupy different physical and psychological arenas. As an extension of her physical state, women's natural domain is the home, the cornerstone of civilized life, the oasis of calm, comfort, and solace for the battle-stricken man overwhelmed by the outside world of industry, politics, and cruel competition. In her maternal capacity, woman is pure and docile, capable but not overly intelligent, lovely to look at, but always modest, the caretaker of the family and the moral redeemer of man. According to John Ruskin, a preeminent critic of the time, man "is eminently the doer, the creator, the discoverer, the defender" (59), while "woman's intellect is not for invention or creation, but for sweet ordering, arrangement, and decision" (59). The doctrine not only confined woman to the home physically, but also imprisoned her psychologically, as "she existed only to bolster up the man" (Rowbotham 71). More than a century later, the sexual division of the sexes remains entrenched as society stays bent on glorifying the mind over the body, and on valorizing independence and competition over interdependence, nurturing, and an ethics of care.

Nonetheless, one of feminism's greatest contributions has been its focus on deessentializing women by undoing the notion that biology prescribes women's roles. In *The Second Sex*, Simone de Beauvoir famously declared that "one is not born, but rather becomes a woman" (VII). Friedan agreed. She challenged the deeply held assumption that women's femininity was located in the tidiest household, the tastiest meals, and the happiest marriage. She repudiated prevailing thought that "housewife and the mother (are) the universal models of womanhood" (Davis 22). Among other culprits, Friedan blamed Freud's adherence to "the strict determinism that characterized the scientific thinking of the Victorian era" (107), an anatomy is destiny ideology through which American sociology, anthropology, education, literature, advertising, and childrearing practices were articulated in the mid-twentieth century.

Does a 'motherist' politics reinforce essentialist views? Feminist cannot agree. On the one side are those who believe that "motherhood confer(s) upon them special insights and responsibilities to solve the problems plaguing their families and communities" (Orleck 4). This maternalist perspective emphasizes the giving and nurturing of life and is consistent with the platform of cultural feminists, who valorize women's inherent maternal and feminine qualities. The thinking goes that women are essentially good and men are "corrupt to the core. Men are the aggressive, evil oppressors and women are the exploited victims. No man can escape the taint of this original sin" (Elshtain 206). Some movements are born out of this view. In Women Strike for Peace (1960s) and Oxford Mothers for Nuclear Disarmament (1980s), for example, women "claimed that they are compelled to fight for peace because they are humanity's 'custodians of life'" (8). Sara Ruddick, author of *Maternal Thinking*, holds that maternal practice "influences women's disproportionate support for a 'politics of peace'" (qtd. in Naples 457). Lois Gibbs of Love Canal contends that "mothers have a particular role to play because mothers are the ones who are most passionate about the future of our children . . . they are the ones who think generation to generation" (qtd. in Jetter 43).

Critics decry many of these assumptions about maternity "for returning women to the destiny of anatomy" (Hirsch 361). Moreover, they see "maternal politics as symptom and cause of 'backlash' against women. In their eyes, women acting as mothers, however good their cause, and whatever increased skills and authority they gained from their actions, reinforced traditional stereotypes of femininity" (Ruddick 367).

Nonetheless, maternal activism does not promote essentialism. It challenges it. In the first place, it is difficult to conclude on close inspection that mothers consistently work for the common good, and focus on selfless, pacifistic goals. Mothers have been deeply involved in virtually every race-hate movement in twentieth-century America, from the Ku Klux Klan, to the neo-Nazi or Aryan movement, to Christian Identity—a group that "believes Anglo-Saxons are the lost tribe of Israel and that Jews, African-Americans and other people of color are inferiors sent to earth as a scourge of God" (Blee 248). Their role in the movement is integral to its operation. They speak, write, recruit, theorize, agitate, and demonstrate. Like most mother activists, they contend that their involvement is motivated by concern for their children's future. The difference, of course, is that they are protecting "a white future" (Blee 251). Mothers in these groups hardly represent an ethics of peace, caring, and nurturance, so often associated with women's biology. According to scholar Martha Ackelsberg, these movements "shatter the belief that women are somehow naturally open, nurturant and 'progressive'" (416).

Second, maternal activism helps to redefine traditional notions of women's personality. According to feminist psychologist Carol Gilligan, girls and women tend to see the world in terms of connection, interdependence, care, and in the context of a web of relationships. Boys and men, conversely, interpret their realities in terms of rights, responsibilities, fairness, and hierarchy. Moreover, Gilligan contends, women tend to fear success because it equals isolation. Women, she says, "construe danger to result from competitive success . . . a fear that in standing out or being set apart by success, they will be left alone" (Gilligan 42). Yet for Ruby Duncan and the mothers of Operation Life, caring was only the starting point. Their struggle was ultimately galvanized by a conception of rights, justice, and fairness, precisely the qualities Gilligan links to men. "The concept of welfare rights transformed these women's shame into a sense of entitlement. And the more they learned about state and federal politics, the greater that sense of entitlement became, enabling (them) . . . to channel deep anger over years of abuse and humiliation into political action" (Orleck 108). And, mother activists such as Duncan, Oliver, and Gibbs transitioned easily into the spotlight, heading organizations, consulting to governments, and attracting media attention. Patsy Ruth Oliver, for example, became an "international symbol for the environmental justice movement—chosen as part of the official U.S. delegation to the World Environmental Summit in Rio de Janeiro" (Orleck 25). Success hardly posed a problem for these women.

Third, maternal activism contributes to the reframing and valuing of motherhood by expanding its boundaries (from private to public), and by endowing it with qualities normally attributed to the public realm. Many traditional views of motherhood hold that 'good' mothers stay at home, mind the children, and keep out of politics. In some cultures, motherhood is at once glorified and devalued. In both Israeli and Palestinian society, for example, women are often idealized as "mothers of the nation" (Taylor 150), expected to fulfill their national duty by reproducing to ensure perpetuation of their respective nationhoods. At the same time, "they are relegated to the margins of their collectivities" (Sharoni 151) because in those societies the emphasis is on militarism and war. Yet Naples found that when mothers became activists, their "acts of resistance defied the dominant definition of motherhood as emphasizing work performed within the private sphere of the family" (449). In particular, maternal activism often becomes intertwined with politics. Julie Peteet's research on Palestinian women "challenges the dominant domestic image of mothers as the 'national icon' usually identified with a caring labor ethic and reproductive roles. As mothers of male martyrs . . . they have managed to transform the meaning of their traditional roles and endow them with political activism . . . by raising issues of gender equality and citizenship rights in the nascent Palestinian state"(Zureik 157). Even for Western middle-class mothers caught in the paid work/work-in-the-home quandary, participation in community on behalf of their children is "a way to assert the work of the devalued status of motherhood . . . and celebrate the importance of their work that women do enriching environments of their children" (Abrahams 781). In Padilla's study on activists in Peru, she found that even when activism is related to the domestic sphere, the "ramifications of the activities have an impact not only on the community as a whole, but also on the government and the local micro-economic system as women in their involvement deal with government agencies to solve problems of basic infrastructure and generate resources to satisfy their needs" (103). Thus, many women claim mother politics as a means of destroying patriarchal views of mothering, and they "strike out angrily at romantic images of family life that obscure real families and their very real problems" (Orleck 6).

UPSETTING GENDER AND POWER RELATIONS

For many mother activists, a feminist agenda is not always on the agenda. Many maternal activists do not see themselves as engaged in political action, but as caretakers of their families and communities. Even radical mothers and mother activists, says one scholar, "do not necessarily identify as feminists, or take feminism seriously" (Hirsch 353). Nonetheless, in the process of their activism, mothers take on nontraditional roles in which their action and agency provide a new sense of empowerment that often upsets traditional gender roles. And despite intentions to the contrary, feminist ideals are achieved. "Women's activism always challenges domestic as well as public power relations, because by the very act of taking a position in the public domain women violate their patriarchal assignment to domesticity" (Roy 115). In her ethnographic study of women who participate in organizations in Lima, Peru, Padilla claims that "women who are actively involved in popular organizations gain gender consciousness which, through activism, leads them to developing feminist gender identities" (93).

There are positive outcomes. Lois Gibbs describes herself prior to Love Canal as "a very shy, introverted person. I was afraid to talk. So it was really difficult for me to move out of that personality into a more aggressive, confrontational and articulate person" (qtd. in Jetter 31). Now Gibbs says she "can do anything" (qtd. in Jetter 41). In her study of feminist identity and rape crisis work, Naomi Abrahams found that activist "involvement in the

rape crisis centre created and reinforced a feminist definition of the meaning
of womanhood . . . (and activists) increasingly challenged sexism in their own
lives" (774). Among all classes of Anglo and Latina homemakers, community
involvement helped diminish their dependence on their husbands, as they
"created networks, resources, skills and interests that extended beyond the
nuclear family" (Abrahams 783). And the vast majority of the Peruvian
women studied by Padilla claimed that participation in grassroots organizations made them feel stronger, more confident, and more secure (99).

But the consequences of upsetting gender roles are real. Lois Gibbs says
that because men in her working-class community subscribed to a self-view
as "protectors and providers" (qtd. in Jetter 41), they had trouble watching
women take on that role. Suddenly, "men felt less like men" (qtd. in Jetter 41).
As chemical plants laid off men whose wives were involved in protest, marriages collapsed. While Gibbs acknowledges that women were liberated by
their activism, it came at a high price. "I became a different person but all of
these terrible things had to happen" (42). Similarly, though Palestinian resistance fighters are "valorized as female role models" (Hammami 164), some
cannot reintegrate into their communities.

Yet when activism arises out of motherhood without feminist underpinnings, it becomes questionable whether a feminist agenda is furthered. In
many cases, mothers employ accepted views of motherhood as a strategic
resource to further their political ends. And that's not new. "Throughout U.S.
history, women . . . have used Americans' collective sentiment and ideology
regarding mothers and motherhood in social reform. Essentially, this belief
holds that mothers are selfless, caring , and nurturing people" (Woyshner 66).
Women activists in 1960s Harlem used motherhood to fight for educational
equity "in both essentializing and strategic ways. In other words, they
described their motivations for political action as a natural extension of their
identities as mothers as well as understood that such claims increased their
credibility as political actors" (Naples 329). Community activists during glas-
nost used a "discourse of motherhood to elaborate a 'maternalist' collective
action frame to make new political demands. Soviet women thus turned
'maternalist' activism against the state" (Hrycak 70).

For those feminists opposed to maternal activism as a feminist idea, such
an approach reifies concerns that maternal activism only re-entrenches prevailing patriarchal views of maternity. They argue that the strategic use of
motherhood does not de-essentialize it—it just uses it to best advantage.
Others disagree. They contend that motherhood has always been politicized—often as a means of controlling women—through legislation, sexuality, reproductive rights, social conditioning, and objectification (Rowland and

Klein 271–303). Thus, while mother activists are using their motherhood status to justify action that would normally violate social norms, they are in fact taking advantage of the politics of motherhood, instead of simply being manipulated by it (Acklesberg 403). In the process, says Orleck, "burning through the mists of biological and emotional essentialism that shroud the reality of motherhood, women are reclaiming and reshaping the role that has so long been used to control them" (6).

The story of Mothers Reclaiming Our Children (Mothers ROC) supports this point. Founded in 1992 by poor, multiracial women (mostly the mothers of prisoners) to combat what they contend was the unjust rate at which the state of California was imprisoning their children, Mothers ROC has been enormously successful at engaging both the local and broader communities around issues of mutual interests. They have managed to get gangs to declare temporary truces and to come together in respect for slain sons and grieving mothers. As Gilmore puts it,

> The ineluctable salience of gender structures the means through which Mothers ROC critically deploys the ideological power of motherhood to challenge the legitimacy of the changing state. . . . The racial and gendered social division of labor requires mothers of prisoners to live lives of high visibility; ROCers turn that visibility to a politically charged presence, voice, and movement against injustice, such that their activism becomes the centerpiece of their reproductive—and socially productive—labor. The insistence on the rights of mothers to children, and children to mothers, is not a defense of 'traditional' domesticity as a separate sphere; rather it represents a political activation around raising awareness of the ways that the working-class 'domestic' is a site saturated by the racial state. (250)

CONCLUSION

In evaluating whether maternal activism promotes a feminist agenda, we need to consider two distinct issues. The first is how well maternal activism reflects and supports a feminist ideology and some forms of praxis. As this chapter has argued, the answer is quite well indeed. Maternal activism is a explicit example of the personal made political. It challenges the essentialization of motherhood. It often upsets gender roles, intended or not. And it can help bridge the gap between women in different racial-ethnic and socioeconomic groups. "No matter what the color of your skin, the toxic situation that we are in makes us kindreds. Because it is not disgrace to be a member of the human race—and toxics do not discriminate" (Oliver 61). The results are evident not only in the personal growth of the mothers, but often in the success of the social movements themselves.

The second issue is much more difficult to measure. How well does maternal activism lead to a feminist consciousness among participants in the struggle? And how important is that consciousness, given that feminist ideology and praxis are being advanced anyway? The answers to both questions lack consensus. While the very process of activism may produce even unconscious changes in women's politicization, some argue that "only an explicit feminist consciousness, an explicit commitment not just to children, but to women, can insure against (reactionary) appropriation and can inspire a more fundamental commitment to racial and fundamental social and ideological change" (Hirsch 364). Perhaps there is still another option. It might just be that the efforts of maternal activists today—whatever their motivations—are setting the stage for future generations. The women's movement of the 1970s, for instance, has had a huge impact on the consciousness and behaviors of women today, though they have had virtually no contact with the movement. It has reshaped attitudes, values, and expectations, providing girls and young women with opportunities unimaginable to their mothers and grandmothers. Perhaps maternal activism will do the same.

Maternal activism, as a practice, is as old as time. As a feminist focus, it is quite new. While the debate remains largely unresolved, one truth seems blindingly apparent.

> We need to politicize motherhood and to recognize the work that mothers do—we need to claim that work for feminism, to learn its strategies, so that we might convince mothers that as much as feminism needs motherhood, mothers also need feminism. (Hirsh 367)

REFERENCES

Abrahams, Naomi. "Negotiating Power, Identity, Family and Community: Women's Community Participation." *Gender and Society* 10 (1996): 768–796.

Ackelsberg, Martha. "(Re)Conceiving Politics? Women's Activism and Democracy in a Time of Retrenchment." *Feminist Studies* 27 (2001): 391–418.

Adamson, Nancy, Linda Briskin, and Margaret McPhail. *Feminist Organizing for Change*. Toronto: Oxford University Press, 1988.

Blee, Kathleen. "Mothers in Race-Hate Movements." *The Politics of Motherhood: Activist Voices from Left to Right*. Eds. Alexis Jetter, Annelise Orleck, and Diana Taylor. Hanover: University Press of New England, 1997. 247–256.

Davis, Angela. *Women, Race and Class*. New York: Vintage Books, 1981.

De Beauvoir, Simone. *The Second Sex*. Reprint. New York: Vintage Books, 1989.

Elshtain, Jean Bethke. *Public Man, Private Woman: Women in Social and Political Thought*. 2nd ed. Princeton: Princeton University Press, 1993.

Friedan, Betty. *The Feminine Mystique*. Reprint. New York: W. W. Norton, 1997.

Gilligan, Carol. *In a Different Voice: Psychological Theory and Women's Development*. Cambridge: Harvard University Press, 1982.

Gilmore, Ruth Wilson. "Pierce the Future for Hope: Mothers and Prisoners in the Post Keynesian California Landscape." *Global Lockdown: Race, Gender and the Prison-Industrial Complex*. Ed. Julia Sudbury. New York: Routledge, 2005. 231–253.

Hammami, Rema. "Palestinian Motherhood and Political Activism." *The Politics of Motherhood: Activist Voices from Left to Right*. Eds. Alexis Jetter, Annelise Orleck, and Diana Taylor. Hanover: University Press of New England, 1997. 161–168.

Hirsch, Marianne. "Feminism at the Maternal Divide." *The Politics of Motherhood: Activist Voices from Left to Right*. Eds. Alexis Jetter, Annelise Orleck, and Diana Taylor. Hanover: University Press of New England, 1997. 352–368.

Hrycak, Alexandra. "From Mothers' Rights to Equal Rights: Post Soviet-Union Grassroots Women's Associations." *Women's Activism and Globalization: Linking Local Struggles and Transnational Politics*. Eds. Nancy Naples and Manisha Desai. London: Routledge, 2002. 64–82.

Jetter, Alexis. "A Mother's Battle for Environmental Justice." *The Politics of Motherhood: Activist Voices from Left to Right*. Eds. Alexis Jetter, Annelise Orleck, and Diana Taylor. Hanover: University Press of New England, 1997. 44–52.

———. "What Is Your Wife Trying to Do—Shut Down the Chemical Industry? The Housewives of Love Canal." *The Politics of Motherhood: Activist Voices from Left to Right*. Eds. Alexis Jetter, Annelise Orleck, and Diana Taylor. Hanover: University Press of New England, 1997. 28–43.

Krauss, Celene. "Women and Toxic Waste and Protest: Race, Class and Gender as Resources of Resistance." *Qualitative Sociology* 16 (1993): 247–261.

McDonald, Katrina. "Black Activist Mothering: A Historical Intersection of Race, Gender, and Class." *Gender and Society* 11 (1997): 773–795.

Naples, Nancy. "Activist Mothering: Cross-Generational Continuity in the Community Work of Women from Low-Income Urban Neighborhoods." *Gender and Society* 6 (1992): 441–463.

————, Ed. "Women's Community Activism: Exploring the Dynamics of Politicization and Diversity." *Community Activism and Feminist Politics: Organizing Across Race, Class and Gender.* New York: Routledge, 1998. 327–349.

Orleck, Annelise. "Tradition Unbound: Radical Mothers in International Perspective." *The Politics of Motherhood: Activist Voices from Left to Right.* Eds. Alexis Jetter, Annelise Orleck, and Diana Taylor. Hanover: University Press of New England, 1997. 3–22.

Padilla, Beatriz. "Grassroots Participation and Feminist Gender Identities: A Case Study of Women from the Popular Sector in Metropolitan Lima, Peru." *Journal of International Women's Studies* 6 (2004): 92–112.

Rowbotham, Sheila. *Women, Resistance and Revolution: A History of Women and Revolution in the Modern World.* New York: Pantheon, 1972.

Rowland, Robyn, and Renate Klein. "Radical Feminism: Critique and Construct." *Feminist Knowledge.* Ed. Sneja Gunew. London: Routledge, 1990. 271–303.

Roy, Beth. "Goody Two-Shoes and the Hell-Raisers: Women's Activism, Women's Reputations in Little Rock." *No Middle Ground: Women and Radical Protest.* Ed. Kathleen Blee. New York: New York University Press, 1998. 96–132.

Ruddick, Sarah. "Rethinking 'Maternal' Politics." *The Politics of Motherhood: Activist Voices from Left to Right.* Eds. Alexis Jetter, Annelise Orleck, and Diana Taylor. Hanover: University Press of New England, 1997. 369–382.

Ruskin, John. *Of Queen's Gardens.* London: G. Allen, 1902.

Scott, Joan. "Gender: A Useful Category of Historical Analysis." *American Historical Review* 91 (1986): 1053–1075.

Sharoni, Simona. "Israeli Women Organizing for Peace." *The Politics of Motherhood: Activist Voices from Left to Right.* Eds. Alexis Jetter, Annelise Orleck, and Diana Taylor. Hanover: University Press of New England, 1997. 144–160.

Taylor, Diana. "Mothers and the State." *The Politics of Motherhood: Activist Voices from Left to Right.* Eds. Alexis Jetter, Annelise Orleck, and Diana Taylor. Hanover: University Press of New England, 1997. 141–143.

Woyshner, Christine. "Motherhood, Activism, and Social Reform. (American Thought)." *USA Today* (Magazine) 130.2682 (2002): 66(2).

Zureik, Elia. "Theoretical and Methodological Considerations for the Study of Palestinian Society." *Comparative Studies of South Asia, Africa and the Middle East* 23:1&2 (2003): 152–162.

CHAPTER FIFTEEN

Balancing Act

Discourses of Feminism, Motherhood, and Activism

PEGEEN REICHERT POWELL

WHEN MY SON first started attending daycare, he was fourteen months old. Almost every morning after dropping him off, and again on the way to pick him up, I would carefully count the hours and minutes he would be—awake—at daycare and the hours he would be awake at home with me. "Let's see, he woke up at 6:15, we left for day care at 8:45, I'm picking him up at 4:00, and he'll go to bed at 8. That's two and a half hours in the morning and four hours at night with me, a total of six and a half. He'll be at daycare seven hours, but with at least a two-hour nap, that's five hours he'll be awake." I'd reduce my son's daily life to a set of numbers and carefully put these numbers on either side of a mental scale.

As precise as my worst neuroses and as unrelenting as my worst moments of guilt, my mental scale was my active participation in the popular discourse of "balance" that surrounds most working mothers in North America. I chose to work with numeric values—sometimes painstakingly counting in ten-minute increments—but, for many women, the goods on the mental scale are much messier. This discourse—illustrated best in my mind by an old-fashioned set of scales, with two pans pivoting on a central point—belies the actual experience of many working mothers. The discourse keeps work and family (or alternately work and home or work and life) as two discrete enti-ties. The goal is to achieve a state in which neither sphere interferes with the other and both are satisfied and satisfying. As I write, I don't need to look far to come up with images in my daily life that seem to challenge that discourse: the breast pump on top of the stack of articles I need to read for my research or my daughter's picture on the desktop of my computer, spotted by icons for drafts of student papers. Although the discourse is about striking a balance between work and family, these images suggest that in reality these realms are quite literally layered, that they almost always share both time and space.

The problem is not just that this discourse doesn't capture lived experience. Most politically charged discourses like this one don't. Rather, it's what this discourse *does* that I'm concerned about. Citing Ann E. Kaplan, Gillian Ranson argues that "master discourses" like the discourse of "the full-time mother," and I would add the discourse of "balance," "organize not only how we think but what we do—our daily practices" (58). In this chapter, I rely on critical discourse analysis (CDA) as a methodology that helps explain the relationship between language practices (such as the use of the metaphor "balance" in popular media) and the social, political, and ideological implications of these practices; in other words, CDA can help explain what the discourse of balance can do for and to mothers.

CRITICAL DISCOURSE ANALYSIS AND THE DISCOURSE OF "BALANCE"

Although it has evolved from language-based disciplines, CDA is a deliberately interdisciplinary methodology (Fairclough 226); thus, it is appropriate for research on mothering, which benefits from the perspective of a variety of fields, such as history, sociology, literature, psychology, political science, and so on. Moreover, CDA is a deliberately politicized methodology. As Norman Fairclough and Ruth Wodak explain, "What is distinctive about CDA [as a methodology] is both that it intervenes on the side of dominated and oppressed groups and against dominating groups, and that it openly declares the emancipatory interests that motivate it" (259). Thus, CDA is particularly useful for research on *feminist* mothering because the methodological approaches of CDA are designed to identify ways that language contributes to oppression, and ultimately, how we might intervene in that oppression.

In CDA, sentence-level details (like whether "balance" is used more frequently as a noun or verb, for example) and the ideological implications of these details (like how women might internalize the sense that they are failures if they don't achieve balance) are theoretically and methodologically connected through the concept of discourse. Fairclough, a key figure in the growing body of CDA scholarship, situates himself, on the one hand, between linguistic and sociolinguistic approaches to discourse analysis and, on the other hand, the social, theoretical approaches such as those of Michel Foucault. In so doing, Fairclough argues for a view of discourse as "a mode of political and ideological practice":

> Discourse as a political practice establishes, sustains, and changes power relations, and the collective entities (classes, blocks, communities, groups) between which power relations obtain. Discourse as an ideological practice constitutes, naturalizes, sustains and changes significations of the world from diverse positions in power relations. (*Discourse* 67)

Fairclough asserts that discourse constitutes social structure in both conservative and innovative ways; that is, discourse is not merely the function of those in power to reproduce their power but also is the function of those who challenge and change the nature of that power. While discourse constitutes social structure in multiple ways, Fairclough further emphasizes the dialectical relationship between discourse and society (*Discourse* 65). Current elements of the social structure—gender, race, class, identities based on place, the type of government, for example—profoundly shape the ways discourses function.

What CDA adds to the Foucauldian view of discourse is the conviction that a focus on language is necessary for the study of discourse. According to Fairclough, discourse is always manifested in actual language use, specific spoken or written texts: "If being an instance of social (political, ideological, etc.) practice is one dimension of a discursive event, being a text is another" (71). In this chapter, therefore, when I refer to the discourse of balance, I am signifying a configuration of textual and social practices. I am talking about the ways that the language, arguments, images, and history that surround "balance" function politically and ideologically. The discourse of balance works through advice columns to "help" women meet their responsibilities both inside and outside the home, through statistics from human resources touting a business's flextime opportunities, through research reports about the negative effects on children when mothers aren't at home with them enough. In all these examples, people do things through the discourse of balance— they might encourage mothers to forgo promotions in favor of more time at home, or they might recruit women to work for a company. To study the discourse of balance is to explicate how discourse might contribute to these effects. Still, the discourse of balance, as I use the word *discourse*, is always manifested in particular texts that the critical discourse analyst can study— articles, a business prospectus, reports.

The texts that I study here all come from the *New York Times Magazine*. Specifically, I study an article written by Lisa Belkin entitled "The Opt-Out Revolution," published in the magazine on October 26, 2003; letters to the editor written in response to Belkin's article; and ten months of Belkin's biweekly column entitled "Life's Work," five months before the article was published and five months after. Belkin's column came to my attention mainly because of the brouhaha surrounding the publication of "The Opt-Out Revolution," an article about professional, upper-middle class women who "opt-out" of their high-powered careers to focus on raising children. Belkin asks whether these women are betraying the work of early feminism or reinventing it, whether this is a backlash of feminism in general or a new kind of feminist mothering. The article seems to argue for the more optimistic view that these women are at the forefront of a feminist "revolution."

According to the *Times*, the article "drew record-breaking mail" ("Introduction"). It also spawned conversations on listservs, as well as articles and editorials in other on-line and print media.[1] Much of this response was criticism. Among the most common critiques are that Belkin bases her observations and arguments on a very small group of Ivy-League graduates, excluding a large majority of working mothers who can't afford to "opt-out"; that neither Belkin nor her interviewees discuss the institutional prejudices and policies (such as inadequate leave or childcare) that prevent women from simultaneously succeeding in their careers and thriving in their families; and that the article doesn't address the inequities in many dual-career households, where women still do the majority of housework and childcare, despite exerting as much effort as spouses on jobs outside the home. Regardless of one's perspective on the article, there is no doubt that it has been widely read and discussed.

The same can be said for Belkin's column. According to the *New York Times* Web site, at the time Belkin's article was published, the Sunday paper (which includes the magazine, in which Belkin's column is published) had a circulation of 1,677,003, and over half of these readers live outside of the New York area. Seventy-one percent of the readers of the magazine are regular readers (defined as reading three or four out of the last four issues) ("Advertising"). My corpus includes twenty-three installments of her column, spanning the period of June 8, 2003, to March 28, 2004. The byline of her column states that it is about "the intersection of jobs and personal lives" and, thus, much of what she writes about falls within the discourse of balance, as it is commonly understood.

The discourse of balance encompasses more than just the word *balance* itself—it includes a lot of the policies, language, and arguments that people use to navigate the terrain of work and family life. An increasingly common construction, for example, is "work/life," used to signify private businesses' attempts to create family-friendly policies. But even this construction presupposes the metaphor of balance; aurally and visually, work/life seems to enact a kind of balance, with the same number of syllables and letters pivoting on the fulcrum of the slash. Much of the discourse, in fact, presupposes the metaphor of "balance," the actual use of that word, and thus in my analysis, I largely focus on how this metaphor works. Metaphors, according to Fairclough, "structure the way we think and the way we act, and our systems of knowledge and belief in a pervasive and fundamental way" (194). Understanding the metaphor of balance can help us understand the discourse writ large.

OFF BALANCE: A METAPHOR AND ITS IMPLICATIONS

When studying metaphor, one can identify the component parts of the figure: the tenor is the idea being expressed or the subject of comparison, the vehicle is the image by which the idea is conveyed, and the associative realm is the area of human experience from which the vehicle is drawn. In the case of balance, part of the slippery nature of this particular metaphor is that while there is one tenor, there are two vehicles, from two different associative realms. In common conversation, most instances of "balance" connote what a person does or the state a person achieves when managing her responsibilities both at work and at home; this is the tenor of the metaphor. As I say earlier, the vehicle that I believe best captures this experience is the old-fashioned set of scales—a balance—with two pans, one for work and one for home (or family), pivoting on a central point. An associative realm for this vehicle is science, an historically masculine realm, a realm of measures, data, precision. When this is the vehicle at work in this metaphor, it is unclear where the human agent is—is the person the device itself, thus inhuman, or is the person removed from the image entirely, yet still responsible for putting elements of work and home onto the scale?[2] There is another vehicle, which is all human agent, and that is the actual act of balancing, like on a tightrope or beam. The associative realm of this vehicle is physical activity, like gymnastics (typically a feminine realm) or circus performances, a realm much more fraught with human limitations.

The difficulty this metaphor poses, then, for the objects of it—most frequently working mothers—is that when we remove the human agent from the metaphor, thus removing from her all control of the action, we are in the realm that demands the most precision. And when we imagine the more active version of this metaphor, the one in which the human herself is performing the action, we also allow for the possibility that the person might fall down every now and then. It might be somewhat tempting to say simply that we should just use the metaphor and picture someone walking a tightrope; at least the person is in control of the action, and may develop some skill at not falling down. However, the nature of metaphor is such that we can't dictate how it will be understood; in fact, all of these meanings are bundled up in it. What's worth noting is what arguments are made, what meanings are suggested, in actual usage, and this is what initially motivated my analysis of Belkin's column, her article, and the letters written in response to the article.

In the entire corpus, twenty-three biweekly columns and "The Opt-Out Revolution" by Belkin and twelve letters, there are twenty instances of some form of the word "balance." Some examples of how the word gets used:

> Back in 2001, Elizabeth Holder and Xan Parker, two thirty-something filmmakers, decided to find out how superstressed, supersuccessful women managed to *balance* their lives (Belkin, "Wall Street Stories")

> 50 Years of *Balancing* Acts and Guilt Trips (Belkin, "50 Years")

> If not, then their ability to *balance* life and work will be no different than their mothers', after all (Belkin, "Opt-Out")

> Sanity, *balance* and a new definition of success, it seems, just might be contagious (Belkin, "Opt-Out")

> But the issue of *balancing* work and personal life remains a major concern, partly because of child-bearing issues (Woods)

This is a discourse primarily about individuals' (and typically working mothers') daily activities and experiences. Therefore, it's important to understand how this metaphor constructs individual human's participation. And, given the slippery nature of this metaphor, it's worth recognizing in particular whether humans have some agentive control over the action of balance.

When I talk about "participation" here, I'm alluding to a particular type of linguistic analysis, originating with M. A. K. Halliday. Halliday explains that

> Language has to interpret the whole of our experience, reducing the indefinitely varied phenomena of the world around us, and also of the

world inside us, the processes of our own consciousness, to a manageable number of classes of phenomena: types of processes, events and actions, classes of objects, people and institutions, and the like. (qtd. in Stillar 22)

Critical discourse analysts study what kinds of processes—action, mental, event, or relational—are coded in the grammar of a sentence, and what kinds of participants are involved (participants can be animate as well as inanimate objects, and can be classified as the agent, patient, experiencer, goal, possessor, instrument, among other roles). (See Fairclough 179–182; Stillar 22–32.)

For example, in the simple sentence, "Elizabeth balances work and family obligations," Elizabeth is the agent of an action process, balance. It is a directed action, and the patient(s) of the action (more popularly understood as the object of a transitive verb) are "work and family obligations." In fact, this example seems to capture the action that is presupposed throughout the discourse of balance. A simple commonsense understanding of the discourse of balance, in columns like Belkin's, in human resource brochures about flex-time policies, or in conversations among friends, seems to turn on working mothers' ability to perform the action of balance.

And yet, in all the instances of the word *balance* in my corpus, there are none in which, grammatically, a person is an agent of the action of balance. In fact, in all the clauses in which the word *balance* appears, there are only three that contain action processes. Sixteen of the clauses contain mental, relational, or event processes, and one (the title previously quoted) does not contain a verb phrase. The effect of the grammatical realization of the metaphor of balance is that, overwhelmingly, in this discourse sample, human action is not a factor.

Moreover, overwhelmingly, balance tends to appear as a nominalization or in verb forms that grammatically act as nouns. A nominalization typically omits the agent of an action and, in Fairclough's words, "turns processes and activities into states and objects, and concretes into abstracts" (182). There may be various motivations for doing this. It may be that the participants of the processes are unknown; for example, in a headline that reads "Police investigate shootings," it may be that police or the media don't know who did the shooting or the identity of the victims. But one effect of turning actions into states, as nominalizations do, is that human agents figure less prominently in the scene. Balance gets nominalized thirteen of twenty times in my corpus in phrases like "work–family balance" or "a generation seeking balance" or "sanity, balance and a new definition of success" ("Careers Settle," "For Some," and "Opt-Out," respectively). In these cases, balance is not something a working mother can do, but a state or object to be achieved.

Thus, at the core of the discourse of balance is a contradiction: although the discourse, ostensibly, is about getting control over one's life, at the sentence level, the individuals involved have no control. This fact is all the more disturbing considering the violence that infuses this discourse. Belkin says, for example, "My editors describe this column as being about the intersection of life and work. I have long described it as being about the *collisions* (maddening, though hardly life-threatening) that happen at all those intersections" ("Pursuing Balance"; emphasis added). And throughout the column in the months that I analyze, she uses words like "demands," "conflicts," and "scrimmage," to describe the relationship between work and personal lives.

Feminist mothers, I argue, should be suspicious of a discourse that surrounds women with violence, and even more so if women are stripped of agency in this discourse. As I argue below, we should seek alternatives to this discourse, alternatives that empower both home-based mothers and mothers who work for pay outside the home to change the conditions in which they work so that they can do the work they choose for adequate pay and simultaneously perform their roles as mothers in the ways they believe are best for them and their children.[3]

OFF BALANCE AND SEEKING ALTERNATIVES

According to Fairclough, critical discourse analysts should look for "cruces" or "moments of crisis" in a discourse, "where there is evidence that things are going wrong: a misunderstanding . . . exceptional disfluencies . . . sudden shifts of style" (230). It might be said that in the discourse sample of Belkin's biweekly column over the ten months I analyze, "The Opt-Out Revolution" constitutes such a moment of crisis. In addition to the genre-shift from serial column to feature article, considering the metaphor of balance, this article seems to mark a shift in her style. Belkin uses the word *balance* eighteen times in this time period, including her article. Of those eighteen, eleven instances of balance come after the article was published, and six occur in the article itself. She only uses the word *balance* once in the five months preceding "The Opt-Out Revolution." I don't claim to know the reasons, the effects, or even necessarily the implications of this shift in her vocabulary, but I believe it does suggest that this article marks a turning point, in this discourse sample at least. More important, though, if we are to consider "The Opt-Out Revolution" a moment of crisis, is the response it received, especially among the original readers in the *New York Times Magazine*.

I study twelve letters that appeared in the magazine in the month following the publication of "The Opt-Out Revolution." In these letters, *balance*
appears only twice (as opposed to the six times it appears in the article itself,
plus the two times in her column in the month following "Opt-Out"). One of
the instances of balance in the letters is from a writer very supportive of
Belkin; Cathleen McGuire writes of the women in the article, "By seeking
more balance in their lives, their impact on society may well prove women to
be the ultimate change agents" (McGuire). In contrast to this endorsement of
the discourse of balance, however, the majority of letter writers position
themselves within a more recognizably feminist discourse.

For example, Stephanie McCurry writes,

> The personal is political. Remember that? Feminism was never just
> about reaching parity in the workplace; it was also about remaking love
> and marriage so that we could reach parity at home. If there is, as Belkin
> says, something revolutionary in the decision by privileged women to
> opt out of paid work, it looks anything but revolutionary from the per-
> spective of the family. . . . Combining professional work and mother-
> hood over the long haul—now that's something new. We never thought
> we could remake work without remaking the family. Those of us who
> still choose work remain committed to that project. (McCurry)

Noteworthy here is the insistence on a collective effort to change systemic
problems. Whereas the discourse of balance tends to center on the individual,
McCurry begins with the statement "the personal is political," and speaks in
first-person plural throughout, invoking a shared "project" at the end. Moreover, she recognizes that change is not just the responsibility of an individual
woman, but instead the goal is to "remake work" and "remak[e] the family."
Others echo her references to a collective movement. Andrea Banks writes,
"If women are going to talk about motherhood as a movement, then it should
involve ways to be a mother without losing the career you worked so hard for"
and Ellen Willis claims, "From the perspective of this early feminist, the
point of the movement was never 'standing at the helm in the macho realms
of business and government and law.' It was, among other things, about transforming those realms" (Banks; Willis).

Still others seem to oppose the individualistic discourse of balance with
questions or statements about the larger structural patterns of inequities that
should concern feminist mothers. Harriett Woods states, "The problem is
this: women's status has changed but not the institutions and power structures

in which they must function. . . . It's time to change the system," and Karen Blinder Akerhielm asks about her own decision to stay home with her children, "Is it really a 'choice' to stay at home or rather a lack of options from which to choose?" These letter writers, in very short responses to the article, demonstrate the importance of identifying systemic conditions that contribute to what often feel like very personal problems.

And in stark contrast to the tendency of the discourse of balance to construct a static, abstract condition in which women *do* very little, some of the letter writers identify very specific actions that need to be taken. Andrea Banks asks, "What about more leave time, husbands' taking on equal responsibility for child rearing or federal funding for child care?" (Banks) And Barbara Stark says of the women interviewed in Belkin's article, "They have not demanded any state support for working parents nor, despite the hopeful last paragraphs, have they won any real concessions from the private sector" (Stark).

What the letterwriters like Stark and the others tend to do is resist the discourse of balance that is pervasive in "The Opt-Out Revolution," and instead focus our attention on the larger forces at work on their lives and the material conditions that need to change for working mothers to succeed in their careers, families, personal lives, politics, and so on. Perhaps it is this shift in focus demanded by the criticism of "The Opt-Out Revolution" that compels Belkin to emphasize "balance," to repeat the metaphor over and over in her column in the months following the article.

I don't mean to attribute to Belkin any malice or deliberate complicity in the oppression of women. After all, this discourse is used frequently by and for working mothers, and Belkin herself is a working mother. What is the seductive appeal of the discourse of balance, then? Methodologically and theoretically, one can't separate this discourse from the social and ideological context in which it operates. According to Sharon Hays's persuasive argument in *The Cultural Contradictions of Motherhood*, this social and ideological context is marked by a fundamental opposition between the ideology of intensive mothering that currently dominates childrearing advice in the United States and the "competitive, self-interested, efficiency-minded, and materialistically oriented logic" of the marketplace (9). Hays argues that the struggle of working mothers is that they are positioned between these two opposing logics and must constantly choose between them.

I argue that the discourse of balance actually makes it a nonchoice. This discourse, with the spheres of "work" and "family" neatly separated but mutually dependent, attempts to accommodate both ideologies within one easy framework. The discourse holds out hope that choices needn't be made, as long as balance is struck. The instances of the balance metaphor in the discourse sample I analyzed are consistently paired with metaphors of pursuit: "attempting to balance," "pursuing balance," "search for a work–life balance," "seeking balance," "looking for more balance" ("Sick Child," "Pursuing Balance," "Sharing a Life," "For Some," and "Opt-Out," respectively). The discourse resolves the contradictions of motherhood that Hays details, not by offering real solutions, but the promise of a state in which the contradictions aren't as keenly felt.

The insidiousness of this discourse, however, is that despite that promise, as is seen in my grammatical analysis, women do not have any real control over how to fulfill it. Counting minutes I was away from my son while he was at daycare gave me a way to describe my situation, but no way to respond proactively to it. A second reason to be wary of this discourse is that balance is a static condition, frequently realized in texts as nominalizations. In order to maintain balance, a woman needs to remain still, not disturbing the status quo; yet it is the status quo that creates the contradictions that induce a woman to seek balance in the first place. Third, the pursuit of balance, though performed by countless women, is nevertheless a profoundly individualized condition, and thus the fault of individuals when balance is not achieved. As I sat counting in my car alone, the discourse I was participating in gave me no way to see beyond my own relationship with my child. Engaged in a uniquely private activity, I was unable to recognize the social and political circumstances that might have led me to these tabulations in the first place. In other words, the cultural contradictions of motherhood become the contradictions privately felt by individual women when the discourse of balance is invoked. Not only does this intensify the guilt and despair of working mothers, but it distracts us from addressing the real systemic inequities and injustices that pervade both workplaces and homes. And, finally, this discourse allows for only two spheres—work and family—excluding the public spaces where activism, and thus change, happens.

What the authors of the letters in response to "The Opt-Out Revolution" suggest is that there are alternative discourses from which to draw. Discourses of feminism and collective action give women the option of agency, and shift the emphasis away from individual failure to shared goals. Such a shift is crucial if we are going to change the conditions that lead working parents to seek solace in the discourse of balance in the first place. Interrupting the discourse of balance—interrogating it in conversations with others and reading critically when we see it in print—is an important element of critical discourse analysis, and an important element of changing social relationships like those that keep working mothers trapped in a net of guilt. Nevertheless, Fairclough cautions against overemphasizing the role of discourse in constituting the social. He says,

> It is important that the relationship between discourse and social structure should be seen dialectically if we are to avoid the pitfalls of overemphasizing on the one hand the social determination of discourse, and on the other hand the construction of the social in discourse. The former turns discourse into a mere reflection of a deeper social reality, the latter idealistically represents discourse as the source of the social. (65)

Thus, not only should the critical discourse analyst avoid unqualified arguments about how the discourse of balance simply reflects patriarchy, but she must also avoid implications that merely discouraging this discourse will improve the lives of working mothers everywhere. Therefore, I conclude by briefly describing an activist organization I helped found, which strives to improve the material conditions of people who simultaneously care for families and work outside the home for pay. As this narrative suggests, though, activism about mothering is not a straightforward feminist enterprise.

OFF BALANCE AND INTO ACTION

Fed up with the exhaustion of being a working mother with a very young child, along with the isolation of counting minutes in my car alone, I sought out other women who might be having similar experiencs. In the spring of 2002, a couple of colleagues and I posted fliers up on Duke University's campus, where we worked, inviting people to an informal meeting where they could "come share [their] experiences, concerns, and questions about the legal, social, and political climate for mothers and prospective mothers at Duke" (flier). What became clear very quickly after talking with the thirty or so women who showed up at the first meeting was that they were not interested in a "support group" or a social club. Rather, they came with serious concerns about the policies and climate at Duke that made it very difficult for them to be simultaneously good mothers and good employees. They were interested in a group that would advocate for change, an activist organization that would press the administration to provide paid maternity and paternity leave; to ensure that employees had access to quality, affordable childcare; to designate areas on campus where nursing mothers could pump; to institute flextime policies to accommodate child and elder care; and in general, to

improve the climate on campus for people who must attend to family responsibilities while meeting their responsibilities at work. Motivated by these
goals, Parents@Duke was born, and we eventually boasted an active steering
committee and a listserv of over one hundred people.

It's worth noting that an activist organization like Parents@Duke does
not have a place in the metaphor of balance. Our group resisted the too-easy
separation of work and family because we all participated explicitly as simultaneous parents and workers. And to do the labor of the group, we had to
steal time from both work and family. Moreover, a group organized for collective action defies the isolated immobility of the discourse of balance. Finally,
the discourse of balance excludes those political, public spaces—like meetings
of Parents@Duke or the Parents@Duke listserv—where women might act to
change oppressive conditions under which they live.

While my previous experience with collective action helped me think
strategically about how to build a supportive base, how to establish alliances
with other groups on campus, and how to position ourselves in relation to the
administration, to the extent that "feminism" connotes a particular kind of
political ideology, I struggled to determine how "feminist" our group is. For
example, when I began the group with my two colleagues, I pushed for the
name "Mothers at Duke" because the acronym, MAD, suggested that working mothers were either angry or crazy or both. But early on in the organization's life, others suggested quite strongly that we change the name to
"Parents at Duke" in order to include men in both our agenda and our support base. Not surprising, though, Parents@Duke, as we came to be known,
was run almost entirely by women. Who provided the labor for this group
was, to me, a feminist issue, but to others this wasn't a political issue at all,
simply a matter of who showed up for meetings.

What united the group was the focus on changing the institution to
better accommodate working parents, but, for many members, this is a personal, not a political matter (and many use the discourse of "balance" to discuss their motivations for participating). Both evidence and consequence of
the difficulty of seeing mothering as a political issue was the constant
turnover in the Parents@Duke steering committee. We held recruitment
meetings twice a year because we found that people don't recognize the
importance of issues like paid leave and childcare until they are about to
become parents. And once they did become parents, the difficulty of the transition into life as a working mother frequently meant they no longer had time
or energy to devote to the organization. What was missing for many Par-
ents@Duke members was an understanding of how the issues that matter
most to mothers fit into a larger framework of feminist politics. Without this

larger framework, it's easy to understand how people's participation might drop off once they returned from their leave and secured a slot in a daycare center for their new baby.

Although my own feminist politics motivated me to continue my work with Parents@Duke, I'm not sure that we would have had as widespread participation in the group if we were a self-identified feminist group. Most members easily identified as parents or supporters of parents' rights, but those who didn't also identify as feminists might have been reluctant to declare affiliation with Parents@Duke if we talked about our work as a feminist project, and we could have lost the important support base. As a feminist, at times this distressed me. But as a feminist mother, I recognized the strategic value of opening up the politics of mothering to a wide range of political perspectives. If balance is a static condition in which mothers are denied agency, then one of the best ways to disrupt this discourse and the social conditions that sustain it, is to encourage action and activism among all mothers.

NOTES

1. A search on Google for "opt-out revolution" turns up well over three hundred hits.

2. It might be worth exploring the implications of the fact that justice—often figured as a blindfolded woman who actually becomes the scale—relies on the same metaphorical construct.

3. I get the term *home-based* from Gillian Ranson, and I believe it reflects better than some alternatives the fact that mothers who do not work outside the home for pay are nevertheless engaged in work that frequently takes them outside the home, for their children's activities, for volunteer work, and so on.

REFERENCES

"Advertising in *The New York Times*." *The New York Times on the Web*. 2004. Accessed 17 May 2004 www.nytadvertising.com.

Akerhielm, Karen Blinder. Letter. *New York Times* 9 November 2003, late ed., sec. 6:14.

Banks, Andrea. Letter. *New York Times* 16 November 2003, late ed., sec. 6:18.

Belkin, Lisa. "50 Years of Balancing Acts and Guilt Trips." *New York Times* 7 December 2003, late ed., sec. 10:1.

———. "Careers Settle Within a Thriving Home." *New York Times* 4 January 2004, late ed., sec. 10:1.

———. "For Some, a Job Puts a Life in Perspective." *New York Times* 28 September 2003, late ed., sec. 10:1.

———. "The Opt-Out Revolution." *New York Times Magazine* 26 October 2003: 42+.

———. "Pursuing Balance, Day by Day by Day." *New York Times* 21 December 2003, late ed., sec. 10:1.

———. "Sharing a Life, a Family and a Workweek." *New York Times* 9 November 2003, late ed., sec. 10:1.

———. "A Sick Child Tips the Balance for Parents." *New York Times* 29 February 2004, late ed., sec. 10:1.

———. "Wall Street Stories Take a New Turn." *New York Times* 14 Mar 2004, late ed., sec. 10:1.

Fairclough, Norman. *Discourse and Social Change.* Cambridge: Polity Press, 1992.

Fairclough, Norman, and Ruth Wodak. "Critical Discourse Analysis." *Discourse as Social Interaction.* Ed. Teun van Dijk. London: Sage, 1997. 258–284.

Hays, Sharon. *The Cultural Contradictions of Motherhood.* New Haven: Yale University Press, 1996.

"Introduction." *New York Times* 9 November 2003, late ed., sec. 6:4.

McCurry, Stephanie. Letter. *New York Times* 9 November 2003, late ed., sec. 6:16.

McGuire, Cathleen. Letter. *New York Times* 16 November 2003, late ed., sec. 6:18.

Ranson, Gillian. "Paid Work, Family Work and the Discourse of the 'Full-Time Mother'." *Journal of the Association for Research on Mothering* 1.1 (1999): 57–66.

Stark, Barbara. Letter. *New York Times* 9 November 2003, late ed., sec. 6:14.

Stillar, Glenn. *Analyzing Everyday Texts: Discourse, Rhetoric, and Social Perspectives.* Thousand Oaks: Sage, 1998.

Willis, Ellen. Letter. *New York Times* 9 November 2003, late ed., sec. 6:14.

Woods, Harriett. Letter. *New York Times* 9 November 2003, late ed., sec. 6:14.

Contributors

Aimee E. Berger holds a Ph.D. in English from the University of North Texas, a Master of Fine Arts in Creative Writing and Graduate Certificate of Women's Studies from the University of South Carolina, and a B.A. in English from the University of Dallas. She is currently an Instructor of English at Texas Christian University, and an associate faculty in the UNT Women's Studies program, teaching upper-level courses in feminist theories. Berger is a member and former cochair of the NWSA Feminist Mothering Task Force, and advocate, in the classroom and beyond it, for greater recognition of mothers' work.

Kristin G. Esterberg is a professor of sociology at University of Massachusetts, Lowell, where her work focuses on gender and sexuality, social identities, and qualitative methods for social research. Her books include *Lesbian and Bisexual Identities: Constructing Communities, Constructing Selves*, and *Qualitative Methods in Social Research*. Esterberg has published numerous books and articles on gay, lesbian, and bisexual identities and social movements; lesbian parenting; and qualitative research methods.

Fiona Joy Green is Chair of the Women's and Gender Studies Department at the University of Winnipeg. She has published research on feminist mothering in the journals *Socialist Studies* and *Journal of the Association for Research on Mothering*, and in the books *Mother Outlaws* and *Motherhood to Mothering*. Green's more recent work addresses the representation of mothering in reality TV in the journal *Storytelling* and the forthcoming book *Mediated Moms: Mothering and Popular Culture*.

Shirley A. Hill is a Professor of Sociology at the University of Kansas. Her research and teaching interests include families, medical sociology, qualitative methods, and social inequality. Among her publications are *Black Intimacies: A Gender Perspective on Families and Relationships*, *African American Children:*

Socialization and Development in Families, and a coedited volume (with Mar-
lese Durr), *Race, Work, and Family in the Lives of African Americans*.

Amber E. Kinser has spent the last sixteen years weaving her own feminist
mothering knowledge and experience into her professional activities of speak-
ing, teaching, and writing. She is editor of *Mothering in the Third Wave* by
Demeter Press. Kinser holds a Ph.D. from Purdue University and is Associate
Professor of Communication Studies and Director of Women's Studies at
East Tennessee State University.

Colleen Mack-Canty is the Director of the Master of Public Administration
Program at the University of Idaho. She holds a Ph.D. in political science,
with an emphasis in feminist theory, from the University of Oregon. Her
research and publishing are in the areas of Third Wave feminism, parenting,
and ecofeminism. Her publications include articles in the *NWSA Journal* and
The Journal of Family Issues.

Shelley Martin was killed in an automobile accident in May of 2007, shortly
before she was to have received her Ph.D. from the University of Louisiana at
Lafayette. Her degree was awarded posthumously in May of 2007. She was a
native of Victoria, British Columbia, Canada. Prior to coming to the Univer-
sity of Louisiana at Lafayette to pursue her doctorate, she completed a Bach-
elor's Degree in English at the University of Victoria in Victoria and a
Master's Degree in Writing and Publishing at Emerson College in Boston.
Her dissertation topic was *Femininity and Feminism at the Fin de Siècle: The
Single Woman Narrative in the Work of Helen Fielding, Candace Bushnell, Sophie
Kinsella, and Jennifer Weiner*.

Kecia Driver McBride is an Associate Professor and newly elected Chair of
the Department of English at Ball State University in Muncie, Indiana,
where her research and teaching center on narrative theory, American fiction
after 1865, cinema studies, and gender theory. McBride's recent publications
include a book on the visual media and the humanities, and articles on Susan
Glaspell, Ann Petry, and Edith Wharton. She is also the mother of five children, ranging in age from two to sixteen.

Janice Nathanson holds a Ph.D. in communications and culture from York
University, a Masters of Science in communication from Boston University,
and a B.A. in French literature from York University. Her area of research and

study is social change communications and framing theory, with a particular focus on social movements and public education campaigns.

Gisela Norat is Associate Professor and Chair of Spanish at Agnes Scott College. Norat teaches courses in Latin American and Caribbean civilizations and culture. She is author of *Marginalities: Diamela Eltit and the Subversion of Mainstream Literature in Chile.*

Andrea O'Reilly, Ph.D., is Associate Professor in the School of Women's Studies at York University. She is co-editor/editor of more than ten books on motherhood, including *Mother Outlaws: Theories and Practices of Empowered Mothering,* and *Maternal Theory: The Essential Readings.* O'Reilly is author of *Toni Morrison and Motherhood: A Politics of the Heart* and *Rocking the Cradle: Thoughts on Motherhood, Feminism, and the Possibility of Empowered Mothering.* O'Reilly is founder and director of The Association for Research on Mothering (ARM), founder and editor-in-chief of the *Journal of the Association for Research on Mothering,* and founder and editor of Demeter Press, the first feminist press on motherhood. Her current research project is "Being a Mother in the Academe." O'Reilly has presented her research at more than fifty conferences in over a dozen countries and was a keynote speaker at the National Women's Studies Conference in 2006, and she has been interviewed widely on the topic of motherhood. Andrea and her common-law spouse of twenty-five years are the parents of a twenty-three year old son and two daughters, ages eighteen and twenty-one.

Pegeen Reichert Powell received her Ph.D. in English from Miami University, Oxford, Ohio. Her research interests include writing pedagogy, critical discourse analysis, and feminist mothering studies. She has published articles in composition studies journals and edited collections. Since her children were born, she has turned her interests in critical discourse analysis to the discourses surrounding parenting. Powell was named Maverick Mom of the Year in 2004 by *Working Mother* magazine for her activism surrounding parenting issues at Duke University. Powell is on the faculty at Columbia College Chicago.

Michele Pridmore-Brown has been a research scholar at Berkeley since 2005. She writes for both the scholarly and the popular press. Her publications include a prize-winning essay in PMLA on Virginia Woolf's response to the rise of fascism, and articles in *The Times Literary Supplement, The Nation,* and

Salon.com on topics ranging from Henry Adams to stem cell research to postmodern families.

Judith Stadtman Tucker is a writer, activist, and the founder and editor of the award-winning website, The Mothers Movement Online (www.mothers-movement.org). Tucker is recognized as a leading expert on the formation and activities of the North American mothers' movement.

Sarah Trimble is a doctoral student in the Department of English and Cultural Studies at McMaster University. Her current research involves a redirection of the work of Hannah Arendt as an intervention in contemporary biopolitical discourses. Related research interests include apocalyptic science fiction, monster narratives, and other grim and fantastic (re)visions of the world.

Sue Marie Wright, Ph.D., serves as Director for the Children's Studies Program at Eastern Washington University. She holds a position as Professor in the Department of Sociology and Justice Studies, teaching courses on children, gender, and family. Wright's published articles include "Bridging Third-Wave Feminism and Family Pluralism" and "Educated Mothers as a Tool for Social Change: Possibilities and Constraints."

Index